THE KINGDOM OF GOD
AND THE SON OF MAN

LUTTERWORTH LIBRARY, Vol. IX

THE
KINGDOM OF GOD
AND THE
SON OF MAN

A Study in the History of Religion

By

RUDOLPH OTTO

TRANSLATED FROM THE
REVISED GERMAN EDITION

BY

FLOYD V. FILSON

AND

BERTRAM LEE WOOLF

London

THE LUTTERWORTH PRESS

THE UNITED SOCIETY FOR CHRISTIAN LITERATURE

4 BOUVERIE STREET, E.C.4

Made in Great Britain

UNWIN BROTHERS LIMITED, LONDON AND WOKING

CONTENTS

5

PART IV—DETAILED CONSIDERATION OF THE
MESSAGE THAT THE KINGDOM IS AT HAND

BOOK TWO

THE KINGDOM OF GOD AND THE SON OF MAN

6

CONTENTS

BOOK THREE

CHRIST'S LAST SUPPER AS THE CONSECRATION OF THE DISCIPLES FOR ENTRANCE INTO THE KINGDOM OF GOD

BOOK FOUR

THE KINGDOM OF GOD AND THE CHARISMA

BOOK FIVE

APPENDICES

NOTE TO THE ENGLISH EDITION

FOR the purposes of the present translation, Dr. Otto specially revised his work *Reichgottes und Menschensohn*, and, by deleting various passages, altering and adding others, he produced what is really a new edition. He also revised and approved the first draft of the translation as made by Prof. Filson, but his lamented death early in 1937 prevented his seeing the final form, for which Dr. Lee Woolf has assumed sole responsibility. The translators and publishers hope, however, that they have been able to give English readers a worthy rendering of this impressive book, and a fitting memorial to the ardent and profoundly Christian spirit of its author. An index has been added to the English edition.

BOOK ONE

THE KINGDOM OF GOD
IN CHRIST'S PREACHING

PART I

THE ANTECEDENTS OF JESUS' PREACHING
OF THE KINGDOM

CHAPTER I

INTRODUCTION

JESUS was distinctive and unique, but without prejudice to his distinctive and unique character we may say that Jesus belonged to a general class. Of this class a few dim records have survived. He was an itinerant preacher, and indeed one of a class typical of Galilee. Persons of this type must have been familiar. Even the rabbis speak of the 'ober g^{e}lila'ah (Galilean itinerants).

> A wandering Galilaean Rab and preacher was a common sight and specially known by the title of "Galilaean itinerant.' . . . Like every other Rab or preacher he had a following of regular and casual disciples. — J. Klausner, *Jesus of Nazareth*, London, 1929, p. 253 ff.

In particular he was an itinerant preacher of eschatology; indeed, this was, perhaps, the more usual case. If we may trust the testimony of Celsus (in Origen, *Contra Celsum*, vii. 9), preachers of this sort were to be found in Syria, and we must remember that Syria was adjacent to Palestine, and surrounded it. The frontiers were open, and, geographically, one country passed into the other. Celsus speaks of prophets who appeared with the message:

> I am God, or the servant of God, or a divine spirit. But I am coming, for the world is already in the throes of destruction. And you will soon see me coming with the power of heaven (= God?).

Even if the terminology of these prophets has possibly been adapted by Celsus to Christian terminology for polemical reasons, yet, unless his assertions are sheer inventions for controversial purposes, his words would prove that the class of eschatological itinerant preachers still existed in his time in the region near Galilee.

Jesus' message of the kingdom did not fall from Heaven as a completely new thing, but had long been prepared for. In particular, Jesus' preaching of the kingdom is manifestly connected with (and yet, as we shall see, in definite contrast to) an earlier historical phenomenon, i.e. the later Jewish eschatology and apocalyptic. These constitute an extraordinary feature in the history of religion, and Jesus' preaching both reflects and transforms them. From the standpoint of the historical criticism of religion, his message must be described as one of their important forms.

2. But just for this reason, Jesus' message was not purely Jewish. Jesus was a Jew and was descended from Jews. But the late Jewish apocalyptic was not purely Jewish, if one understands by that term something which derived and developed from purely Israelite traditions. Rather, being a late Jewish form, it was inherited from ancient Judaism, but with an intrusive element which came not from that source but from the Chaldean and Iranian east. Indeed, at first, it had a remoter origin, viz. in ancient Aryan sources, and these arose prior to the separation of Aryans into Iranians and Indians. The intrusive element was the great Aryan eschatology of Iran, vitalized by Chaldean features, in particular, as manifested in the doctrinal term, 'the kingdom.' Before 'the kingdom' was a definite technical term in Israel, it was used in this sense among Aryan priests and theologians.

As far as Israel was concerned, there is no doubt that the occasion when eastern influences of this sort made themselves felt was the captivity in Babylonia (and Media) a region where Persian and Chaldean ideas mingled. In detail, the eschatological systems such as were put together in the apocalyptic book of Enoch, and on which the eschatology of Jesus and his circle was largely dependent and modelled, 'point to North Palestine' (C. Beer) as their place of origin. Galilee was a land through which pilgrims journeyed on their way from the eastern Jewish diaspora in Babylonia. At the same time, Galilee was closely connected with Syria by highways and foreign residents, and by a Jewish diaspora which had spread out from Galilee as far as Tyre, Sidon, Damascus, and through Syria generally. Now if Celsus is to be trusted, even Syria had been stirred by eschatological preaching (and this, again, can scarcely be explained otherwise than by eastern influences). But in that case we must suppose not only that eastern eschatology penetrated into Galilee, through its contact with eastern Judaism, but that Jewish eschatology and apocalyptic perhaps formed part of a movement which in a more general way had stirred the Aramaic and Syrian world.

In any case, late Jewish eschatology was not purely. Jewish. Likewise the strict differentiation usually made between Palestinian, Oriental, and Hellenistic is open to question. Even Jesus' eschatology of the kingdom of God was not purely Palestinian. The apocalyptic teaching which has come to us from him had long contained elements which did not originate in Palestine. And to make 'Palestinian' a test of whether a certain word was or was not actually spoken by Jesus is a mistake from the start, because 'Palestinian' is itself an uncertain norm. Not even 'Gnostic' is a reliable canon of spuriousness. For as Gressmann correctly says (*Zeitschrift für Kirchengeschichte*, 1922, p. 179):

> Gnosis is of the very spirit of apocalyptic teaching. And even as early as Enoch's apocalypticism, on which Jesus was dependent, we find definite gnostic traits and terms. . . . Official Judaism turned away from Hellenistic religion and became a rigid legal religion, which found its final form in the Talmud. Another stream, which one can designate unofficial Judaism, led in a straight line to Jesus.

3. As a Galilean, Jesus belonged to unofficial Judaism, which was certainly not typically Jewish. W. Bauer has

thrown light upon this fact.[1] He shows Jesus in his specifically Galilean character. Of course, after the fall of the Israelite northern kingdom, Galilee was not a land of Gentiles in the sense that it had been emptied of its Israelite population (any more than was Samaria), and it is hardly true that the ancient Yahweh cult had completely vanished here.[2] Nevertheless, it was not really 'Judaized' until scarcely more than a hundred years before Christ. It had to a great extent the character of the diaspora, and was relatively untouched by the strict doctrinal and scholastic training of Judea and Jerusalem. Presumably for that very reason it was more open to the influence of religious movements such as apocalyptic, which by its nature was out of line with official or typical Judaism.

At any rate, Jesus' preaching of the kingdom contains elements which are certainly not of Palestinian origin, but point definitely to connections with the Aryan and Iranian east, and some of which are stressed by him in a manner not the case even in Enoch's apocalyptic.

4. To this must be added a further observation: The ancient Israelite population was by no means taken into captivity in its entirety. Rather, the majority of the people remained where they were, as was also the case in Samaria. They were the 'lost sheep of the house of Israel.' It is, therefore, arbitrary to assume that at a later date the Church invented the idea that an obēr Galilijjah, a Galilean itinerant, extended his wanderings into these districts. The gospel records about the matter are on the contrary quite in keeping with the facts. When Jesus turned in this direction, he was not going 'on the highways of the Gentiles' but into the districts of the lost sheep of the house of Israel, districts which had long been penetrated by a veritable Jewish dispersion. Jesus' answer

[1] Cp. his essay, dedicated to Jülicher, *Jesus, der Galiläer*.
[2] The ancient Israelite northern kingdom extended, as the district of the tribes of Naphtali and Asher, to the Leontes, i.e. northward beyond the district of Tyre and of Caesarea Philippi.

to the Canaanite woman, Mt. xv. 22 ff., fits these circumstances. He was near to Tyre, yet he replied:

> I am sent only to the lost sheep of Israel,

whom he was seeking there also. Naturally, his vocation as the 'latent Son of Man' directed him only to Israel. But through the conversion of Israel even the nations were some day to attain salvation. Thus it is intelligible that when Jesus was won over by the specially powerful faith of such non-Israelites as this woman and the centurion of Capernaum, he occasionally exercised his charismatic healing power even on non-Israelites, although he felt it should normally be restricted to the limits of his special mission. In their faith, he glimpsed a higher mandate. And he was helped to this attitude by the fact that he was a *Galilean* itinerant preacher and miraculous healer. W. Bauer has set these relationships once for all in the right light; on p. 27 of his essay he says:

> Galileans grew up outside the jurisdiction of scribalism and Pharisaism, in considerable freedom from the Law and without the torturing anxiety that the proximity of the Gentiles would contaminate them. Jesus spent his childhood in Nazareth, scarcely five miles distant from the half-Gentile Sepphoris. One who at that time took up preaching in the open air on the sea of Gennesaret or elsewhere in Galilee was not in a position to exclude Gentile hearers. . . . [P. 29]: The Galilean Jesus represented Judaism in a form inclined to a universal outlook, or, if one prefers, in a form syncretistically weakened. He certainly felt himself to be a son of the theocracy and was conscious of being sent to his fellow-countrymen, but he did this somewhat in the way in which Paul conceived his apostolate to the Gentiles.

And it is for the same reason that Jesus as a Galilean itinerant had, as Lk. ix. 52 reports,[1] no scruples about undertaking a journey through the Samaritan district.

---

[1] This statement, again, has been regarded as a creation of the later church, on the grounds that the events of vv. 57 ff. could not

That Jesus as a Galilean belonged to a land which was Judaized only at a late period, and which was always open to foreign influences; that in Capernaum and Bethsaida he necessarily preached and worked among a mixed public; that he travelled in regions which were not really Jewish; that he could also have planned to journey through Samaria; that at times he exercised his charismatic healing power on non-Jews; that as he travelled between Samaria and Galilee (in a border district with presumably a mixed population), he used his healing power without asking whether the patients were Jews, and even healed a Samaritan (who, being the only grateful one, was praised); that he could put forward a Samaritan as an example of neighbourly love—these traits combine to form the harmonious picture of a man who was not a Jew in the orthodox and one-sided sense. At the same time they correspond to the fact with which we shall become familiar, that his preaching was dependent upon apoca-

have happened in Samaria, and that Luke assures us in xvii. 11 that Jesus travelled 'through the midst of Samaria.' In reality, Luke reports that Jesus wanted to journey through Samaria, but encountered resistance in a village near the Galilean border. Of necessity he then turned away and took the familiar alternative road to Jerusalem through the wady Galud (the very road that I have travelled in the reverse direction). Thus he journeyed literally 'between Samaria and Galilee,' went past Beth-Shan, crossed the Jordan, and reached Jericho via Perea.

Regarding the phrase dia meson in Lk. xvii. 11 in the sense 'between,' my deceased friend Jakobsohn (all honour to his memory) once wrote me:

> The best parallel to Lk. xvii. 11 is Xenophon, Anab. 1.4.4, where the River Carsus flows between two walls, which form the pulai tēs Kilikias kai tēs Syrias, the borders between the two lands: 'dia mesou de rei toutōn potamos Karsos.' The phrase dia mesou is to be understood in the sense in which, in classical usage, dia stands with the genitive in place names. The accusative in this connection is found only in Homer and in the poetry which is often dependent on him; but it was preserved in the Ionian dialect and crops up again in Hellenistic prose from the time of the early emperors. Accordingly, it is established that dia meson = 'between' = metaxu.

lyptic, especially the apocalyptic of the books of Enoch. These, too, are Jewish. They are, however, neither orthodox nor typical Jewish books, but combine ideas from the east with Jewish ideas. Whence they originate and of what sort they are, we shall discuss in the following section.

CHAPTER II

THE ARYAN LINE OF DEVELOPMENT
THE KINGDOM OF ASURA

IT is now generally accepted that the eschatology of late Jewish apocalyptic with its particular associations goes far beyond the Messianism of ancient Israel; that it developed under the interaction of, and by direct borrowings from, Iranian eschatology; and, in consequence, that Jesus' message of the Kingdom was affected by such influences. Its source is to be found in the religion of the great Aryan prophet Zoroaster of Bactria, a later form of it is enshrined in the Avesta. What I here desire to point out first of all is that the ultimate source of the idea of the Kingdom lies still farther back in the prehistoric period of Aryan religion, viz. in the Asura religion. The latter arose before the separation of Iranians and Indians, whose oldest sacred documents exist interspersed in the Veda of India.

In my books: *Gottheit und Gottheiten der Arier*,[1] pp. 92 ff., and *Gefühl des Ueberweltlichen*,[2] chapter vi, 'King Varuna, The Evolution of a God,' pp. 125 ff., on the basis of the Veda, I sketched the great Aryan godhead, Varuna. On pp. 116 ff. and 307 ff. in GÜ I have translated a number of ancient Vedic hymns which show in detail the evolution and nature of this god. I shall now give a brief summary of the matters which are of importance for our present purpose.

1. The mythological and primitive category of 'sickness-senders and sickness-averters' rise, by means of seer-like vision, to the figure of the great Asura as the deity

---

[1] *Deity and Deities of the Aryans*. Published in 1932 in *Aus der Welt der Religion*, a series on the Science of Religion, volume vi, published by Töpelmann, Giessen; hereafter cited as GA.

[2] *The Consciousness of Supramundane Reality*. Published by C. H. Beck, Munich, 1932; cited as GÜ.

of certain Aryan tribes. These tribes were at the same time
cult fellowships of a certain kind, and we call them
Asurians after Asura, the name of their tribal deities.
Their traditions, their rites, their hymns, were taken up
into the later pantheon of the Indian deities and into the
great syncretistic hymn-book of the Veda. Here their
asuras stand side by side with their rivals, Indra, Rudra,
Vishnu, and others. In this association, the asuras lost their
original form, in the end being forced to yield place to
their rivals. They became subordinate figures in the later
Indian pantheon; deposed from their high place, they
were eclipsed. The songs which I gathered together under
the collective name of Vasishta hymns (GÜ, 306 ff.),
are among those which testify to their former importance.
Bhaga, Amša, Aryaman, Varuna, Mitra, and others are
asuras. One arrangement gathers them up in a cycle of
six or of seven. In nature they are alike, and originally
the names mentioned were probably nothing but words
current in different tribes for essentially similar numina.
Tribal relationship, perhaps political alliance of tribes
and the inner agreement of the differently named but
essentially similar numina of the asuras, unite them in
the cycle of the 'seven ādityas.'

(a) The most prominent figure among them, and the
best drawn, is Varuna. A clearly perceptible tendency
towards monotheism conjoins the seven firmly together.
The heptad becomes a unity in Varuna, so that one can
speak (GÜ, 120) of the heptad of Varuna, and Varuna
says of himself:

> I possess all asuryam,

i.e. the entire asurian being, i.e. all deity and lordship. He
is *the* asura *par excellence*, the Asura.

(b) Asu-ra means he who possesses asu. Asu is vital
power, the secret power which causes man and beast and
gods and every living thing to move and live, to be
healthy and sound, and in general to exist. It is numinous
force and power. Thus asura becomes a name for gods and

for God. Thus also, starting from the meaning of what is numinously powerful, asura becomes 'Lord,' and, therefore, this word, when secularized, may later designate lords in general, even earthly lords and princes. In itself, however, the term means numina and numinous beings as lords, divine lords; the divine Lord and Lord God.

(*c*) A chief characteristic of Lord Varuna is his wisdom. This is not human wisdom but secret divine wisdom. Thus he is called kavi (he who possesses the magic wisdom of the seer) and kavitama (he who possesses such wisdom in the highest degree), and medhi-ra (possessor of wisdom, etymologically the same as the Iranian mazdā), pracetas (wise). When later Zoroaster's great God is called Ahura or Mazdā, combined, as Ahura Mazdā, or Ormuzd, all this had been foreshadowed long before in the ancient Aryan figure of Asura. Indeed, in the late Vedic tradition, the name Varuna is beginning to give place occasionally to the designation Pracetas, 'the wise,' which here, in the case of Mazdā, is becoming almost a proper name.

(*d*) His most solemn title of majesty, however, is, as in the case of Yahweh, 'the king,' rājā. This title clings to none of the other gods of the Veda as it does to him. Hymns are sung to this king, which are but little inferior in royal splendour to the 'royal psalms,' xlvii, xciii, xcvi, xcvii, xcix, in our Psalter. He formerly won this royal splendour for himself, when he 'led the attack and ascended to heaven' (GÜ, 121). Now he sits enthroned above and, from his palace 'under the waters (of heaven),' rules heaven, earth, and the underworld. In addition, when making his ascent, he subdued all hostile demonic power and sorcery by his 'foot of flame,' i.e. by his fire, the holy fire, of hearth and altar, the consecrated symbol of all worshippers of Asura (down to the Zoroastrians, who worship the fire of Ormuzd). Having captured heaven, he became divas asura, the Lord of heaven (a baal shāmaim).

(*e*) It is noteworthy that we also meet with similar traits in the descriptions of Yahweh as king. Gressmann notes them on p. 295 of his *Ursprung der Israelitisch-jüdischen*

Eschatologie. Even Yahweh is described as once having become a king. We still have the echo of this in the praises of Ps. xciii, xcvii, xcix, etc. In his case, too, ascending the throne signifies that he has assumed world rule. Indeed, there is still an echo in Ps. xlvii. 5 which testifies of Yahweh's 'going up.' Gressmann asks whence such traits can originate and seeks for historical borrowings. But the circumstance that similar traits are found far in the east, where there can be no talk of borrowings, seems to me to prove that such traits should not raise the question of borrowings. These elements belong to the logic of numinous emotion in general, and may, therefore, have originated independently of one another in different places and times.

(*f*) Varuna's kingship differs from the rule of other gods, not only in quantity but, above all, in quality. He is king not only as all-powerful, but because he alone of all the gods rules by his ṛita, by holy ordinance, by right and by that which is right, by the law. By the ṛita, by holy divine ordinance, he establishes heaven and earth and all else in its place; he appoints fixed paths for the sun and stars; he orders the year and the seasons. Still more important than this cosmic ṛita is that by which he establishes, arranges, and guards the moral order among men. Here he watches with searching eyes over justice, custom, holy rites, and moral law. Nothing which a man does or thinks is hidden from his eye, and the glorious psalm cxxxix. 'O Lord, thou hast searched and known me,' was similarly sung by ancient Aryan Asurians (GA, p. 135). Moreover, this king was already served by a religion developing a moral conscience, and men prayed to him for his pardon and guidance:

> Thus will I serve him, the jealous God,
> As a servant his lord,
> To the fool, he, the faithful, gives insight,
> The one who (through affliction of sin) has
>   become wise he will lead to salvation,
> He, the most wise. (GÜ, 119.)

23

(g) Therefore, this god is called pūta-daksha: the 'pure-minded.' This purity can scarcely be translated otherwise than by 'holiness,' though this term is not quite accurate; at bottom it distinguishes the ancient Aryan divine type from the remaining Vedic figures. Connected with it, and not for the first time, is the strict exclusiveness of Zoroaster's religion towards rival gods and cults; we find it even among the ancient Asurians (GÜ, 119). Here the 'anyakas,' the worshippers of other gods, are cursed with stern maledictions. That is not mere preference for the tribal god which they happen to possess. It expresses the feeling that one actually has a god qualitatively different from the others.

(h) As king, who orders the divine ṛita, he is likewise the judge. He pursues the sinner with his fearful wrath. He strikes him with evils and binds him with cords. He seizes him as a hunter his game. He sees everything as though he were close at hand. His never-tiring spies throng everywhere between heaven and earth. With a thousand eyes they survey the whole earth:

> What is between heaven and earth and what is above,
> Everything Varuna, the king, sees clearly.
> The very blinking of men's eyes he numbers.
> He who moves, he who stands, he who hides himself,
> He who slips away or secretly steals into hiding,
> That which two, sitting together, secretly debate,
> That is known by Varuna, the king, as third. (GÜ, p. 201.)

(i) This king has his kingdom, his kshatram. That a king should have a kingdom is self-evident. But the point of importance here is that the kingdom does not first acquire a special emphasis in Zoroaster, but has already done so in the ancient Asura. It becomes a definite term and plays its own rôle. Rig-Veda vii. 87 (GÜ, 306) describes how he extends his kingdom over the entire world:

> A king over this entire world of existence,
> He leads his kingdom to victory against all opposition.

24

It is the kshatra varshishta, the most glorious kingdom (Zoroaster calls it the chshathra vahishta). It is jyotishmat kshatram, the shining kingdom. It is anāpyam, i.e. the kingdom attainable by no other than himself. It is avihṛitam, i.e. the kingdom which cannot be wrested from him. It is adorned, lofty, glorious. Occasionally it is even called a yājata (Iranian yazata), 'worthy of sacrifices,' and thus it is on the very verge of being hypostasized. It is called 'spiritual, truthful, and directed towards its goal.' And the prayer is offered:

> O, that we
> In your far extended kingdom
> Which protects many, may be made one.

(k) Kshatra has for its primary meaning not kingdom as a province under sovereign control, in the sense of ruling a country, people, state, or area, but sovereignty in the sense of being a lord, prince, or king. He who possesses kshatra is thereby designated as falling under the concept 'lord.' It is the essence of lordship. At the same time it signifies the dignity, the splendour, the glory of the one who possesses it, the majesty of the king. With this is also connected another connotation: kshatra is likewise dynamis, it is power and might, coercive ruling power, and especially victorious power, which conquers enemies and oppositions, which is capable of mighty working, and which, especially as divine power, can regulate, fashion, and create. The parallel and also subordinate meaning of kshatra, as the power of the Lord, is immediately associated with that of the dignity of the ruler.

(l) But a ruler also implies something ruled, an object to which he is superior in dignity and which yields to his effective power, a realm over which the kshatra extends and which it embraces because it is power; a sphere where the lordship is exercised and the dignity of the lord recognized, where his sovereign will is followed, and his sovereign might is operative. This meaning is clearly associated with the word in the verse last quoted, for one can only be united in something when it is conceived or implied as a comprehensive sphere.

In English the word empire, or kingdom, may best express it. The 'Roman Empire of the German nation' signifies the 'imperium.' Imperium is firstly supreme authority with effective power of command and coercion, but it likewise possesses and contains the associated ideas of the Roman people, state, province. We keep it in mind, nevertheless, that the conception of province or sphere is not the meaning of the primitive root, but an added connotation: a connotation, however, which necessarily belongs to the complete conception embraced by the term. Where a kshatra, a malkūth, a basileia, is meant, where it is to come or to be realized or is real, there also an empire or kingdom in the sense of a province is necessarily implied.

2. The ancient Asura religion succumbed in India. It gained the victory on Iranian soil among the related Aryan people. It did so through Zoroaster. He was the greatest of all Asurians.

(a) His god had not borne a proper name for a long time past. Here the process was completed which began in India, and the title 'the wise' began to take the place of a proper name. Zoroaster's god was now called 'Mazdā,' the Wise; or simply Asura (Ahura), which had long meant God or the Lord. Both designations are joined: Ahura Mazdā = God, the Wise. And naturally there is only one Ahura, only one Lord and God.

(b) At the same time the differences in the religion of Zoroaster as compared with the earlier stage are significant. They do not consist mainly in Zoroaster's peculiar theology of 'hypostases,' for this had already begun explicitly in the Vedic Asura; nor in the replacement of the seven ancient adityas by the strange theological hypostases which Zoroaster ranges with the Lord, for this too was already being brought to pass in India (GÜ, 156). Even in Rig-Veda x. 92, the strange, hypostatic theological abstractions of 'The Triumphant Justice,'

'The Great Adoration,' 'The Glorious Piety,' begin to enter into the old sevenfold scheme.

The essential differences are rather: (α) the incomparably profound idea of God's warfare against God's enemy, and (β) the beginning of eschatology.

(α) Even Varuna at one time ascended victoriously to heaven, in warfare against ungodly abomination. But that idea was far from having the profound meaning of the struggle of Ormuzd against Ahriman, of the contest of the divine light with the demonic darkness of ungodliness. This, however, is the meaning of the doctrine of the conflict between the 'holy spirit' as implied[1] by the name of Ormuzd, and the 'evil spirit.'[2]

---

[1] Spenta mainyu, the 'holy spirit,' often fused with Ormuzd himself in later times, but not in the very beginning. (Cf. Hermann Lommel, *Die Religion Zarathustras*, 1930, p. 18.) Here *both* spirits, the holy spirit as well as the evil spirit, stand not beside the Lord but subordinate to him. In close connection with the holy spirit stands the hypostasis of vohu mano, 'good thinking' (Lommel, p. 36).

[2] Opposed to Spenta mainyu stands Angra mainyu, from which Ahriman and Ariman evolve. In GÜ, 67 ff. and 85, I pointed out the relation between Ahriman and the chthonian dragon, the Ahi Budhnya of the Veda. Ahi Budhnya is a being like Pluto. In Mithraic portrayal, Ahriman is represented as Pluto and Hades. Plutarch called Areimanius Hades, and says of him that he 'is destroyed at the end.' The ancient Ahi budhnya in the Veda has not quite reached the stage of the devil. He is a sinister demonic figure, a numen of terror, but not in the first place either an adversary of the gods or a principle of evil. He only becomes this in the Asurian religion of Iran. Here first arises the important conception of a being who is by nature opposed to God, not only in the sense of a demonic abomination generally, but in the sense of an adversary of the holy spirit of the deity with which he is in fundamental conflict, and indeed in conflict from the beginning. This idea did not arise upon the soil of Israel, but came down from Aryan times.

As the early Ahi budhnya, Ahriman must himself have been at one time draconic. The warfare with the demonic abomination in the form of a serpent-dragon is likewise a primordial Aryan conception, and therefore several early mythical ideas of a warfare intermingle with that against Angra mainyu. Thus the ancient Vedic serpent Dahaka appears as Azhi in Iran as a parallel being to Angra mainyu. Indeed, at times, Dahaka becomes the chief figure, in so far as it

The struggle of the good against a terrible, single, opposing evil, of truth against falsehood, of light against darkness, thus enters into the cosmic process in general; although this is the least important point. It becomes religion; it becomes the meaning of man's existence and of his conduct of life. Man's duty now is to take part in this strife, to oppose God's enemy with an absolute decisiveness that determines life, to wage war against him on the side of the good spirit of the Lord, and so to become an ally in the great warfare of the very gods.

(β) Furthermore, in the Indian Asura, one cannot yet speak of a real eschatology. Whether the preparation for, and development of real eschatology began in Iran before Zoroaster, we do not know. But for him eschatology

swallows the Angra mainyu and with him in its body carries on the final struggle until it is itself destroyed. Or it plays a rôle beside him in the struggle, is conquered or chained for a long time by the divine hero and ally Keresāspa or by Thraetaona āthvya = Fretūn. Thus in the Veda, Indra simply routed the Vṛitra, i.e. 'the enemy.' Long before Indra, an 'ancient god' Trita āptya, who became a satellite of Indra, had routed an ancient serpent monster with three heads and seven tails: but afterwards he lost status and faded to a demi-god or hero. Cf. GÜ, 69. It is this very Trita āptya that became the Iranian Thraetaona āthvya (inasmuch as the adjective āptya, when no longer understood, was assimilated by popular etymology to a patronymic form). His ancient three-headed opponent now received the name of the serpent azhi dahaka.

All these lines converge in the eschatological picture of the final victory of the Lord over the enemy of God. They are added together, they are interwoven, they mingle, and, in the mythological tradition, now one, now the other emerges again separately and more clearly. In the Christian 'Book of Revelation' we see in the apocalyptic monster a figure which is remarkably like the most ancient of these conceptions, viz. the monster which Trita once routed.

The original genesis of the myths of a primordial war was discussed by me in greater detail in GÜ. Here I would merely add that Gunkel's thesis as to the reversal of beginning and end is confirmed. What in very ancient times was a myth of an aboriginal strife and victory on a mighty scale is turned into a myth of the final epoch. 'The ancient dragon,' whom Trita had already routed in the primordial era, returns only to be routed by the Lord and His warriors at the end of the world.

is of the essence of the message. At the end, the great final battle is fought against God's enemy, and he is decisively defeated; then comes the resurrection of the dead, the final judgment, and lastly the 'wondrous new creation' of the world.

(c) And with all this we must include the chshathra (= kshatra) of the Lord.

Chshathra too signifies royal *dignity*. It connotes royal splendour, the glory, the doxa, which streams forth in the brightness of the hvarna.[1] Furthermore, chshathra is also strength, dynamis, royal power as victorious over God's foe. The three synonyms which we are accustomed to use in the familiar conclusion of our Lord's Prayer: 'For thine is the kingdom (basileia) and the power (dynamis) and the glory (doxa),' would also suit the chshathra of Zoroaster. But as the actual lordship established by combat and final victory, it likewise connotes the final condition of the world and mankind, though still to be attained, the condition of a community obedient to the Lord in purity, righteousness, and truth, in a miraculously created world. It carries this added connotation. Lommel says (p. 55):

> As such a condition, or as a world in which such a condition exists, Asura's lordship is the Kingdom of God. As such it is the eschatological blessing of salvation and is therefore called *varya*.

(d) This means two things.

(1) Varya is a gerundive from the root var, choose, synonymous with the root vi-ci, decide. A varyam is that which one should choose, for which one should decide. It is that which 'places us in the situation that calls for an act of will,' and this of an essential and complete kind. The decision is so fundamental that it actually constitutes man's being and attitude of mind inasmuch as it is conceived— in a way similar to Kant's act of will in a state of transcen-

---

[1] Such doxa is found even in the ancient Asura, as Varuna's tvishi (GÜ, 321).

dental freedom—as a free, primordial act prior to the earthly life of man. It is not determination by a nature which is dualistically divided into good and evil, but because it is a var and applies to a varyam, it is a choice made freely and by one's own decision.

(2) On the other hand the root var also means 'wish.' Therefore, varya is not only that which claims our decision, but also that which as a great and unique good awakens our desire and longing. The chshathra is at the same time the sanctifying good of the final age, which is desired, longed for, and striven for on account of its salvation. Thus Zoroaster confesses:

> I will be an open enemy to the heterodox, but to the orthodox a support, that according to my desire I may receive the reversion of the kingdom.

(e) From a purely etymological point of view, the primary meaning of chshathra in Persian also is that of the dignity, power, and function of lordship. But even in ancient Persian the idea of kingdom was added, and this in the narrower sense of a governed district. A sphere of sovereign power, with an approach to the idea of a commonwealth organized by sovereign authority, with magistrates and subjects.

> The word . . . signifies the area under sovereignty, the kingdom ruled, as well as governmental power, sovereign might, and regal dignity. Among these, the concrete meaning kingdom is the rarer and evidently emerged from the more abstract meaning [of lordship]. [But] it is found in Old Persian, when Darius says in the inscription of Suez: 'Ahuramazdā, who made Darius king, who gave him the great kingdom, which has excellent horses and men.' In the later Avesta it is apparently a designation . . . of the district or estate of a free lord of the manor (Lommel).

The final kingdom of Ahura is conceived as an imperial sphere, when it is spoken of as the house of Ahura, e.g.:

He has promised us that, through truth and sound thought, we shall have in his kingdom health and immortality, in his house everlasting strength (Lommel, p. 56).

At the same time, through the emergence of the above-mentioned connotation of dynamis, power, and strength, the connotation of 'a power' may be contained in it.

This is the case in Y. xxxiv. 15: 'Through thy sovereignty, O Lord, make existence really marvellous according to thy will' (Lommel, p. 56).

(*f*) Lommel rightly points to the fact that the conception of the chshathra thus approaches the idea given us to-day by the term 'Kingdom of Heaven.' The expression kingdom of heaven naturally signifies too that God will rule in it, that there His dignity, power, and glory will radiate, that His will shall be done. But in our use of the expression we place more emphasis on the *kingdom* of heaven, i.e. the higher, transcendent, holy, and blessed world in contrast to this world; the other-worldly and supramundane existence which awaits us as the wholly future state; heaven, the heavenly Jerusalem, Paradise, or whatever mythical images we may choose as ideograms for this wholly other existence and this wholly other realm of being. Here the conception appropriate to the original root no longer applies; rather we have to do with a complex of different connotations. Kingdom, now, is not royal dignity, royal sovereignty; it is not a district or realm, nor a people or a community, but all these together and intermingled. God's might and holiness and glory, His throne and governing power, His angels and their ordinances, the redeemed holy ones by His throne, the fellowship of the righteous, the triumphant church, the new heaven and earth, the transfigured life and the heavenly salvation, the life of eternity and 'God all in all'—these belong together here as a unified whole. And this kingdom is to 'come' some day and we are to 'enter' it. (Yet, somehow, it is already present in a mysterious way as foretaste and expectation; in faith and regeneration we are, properly speaking, already in it.) All this is meant, and for all this a Christian prays, when he prays: Thy kingdom come.

The chshathra approximates to such an idea of the kingdom of heaven. Lommel says (p. 56):

> The chshathra appears in perfection, like a kingdom of heaven, when it is called the sunny kingdom; here the conception is similar to that of Y. xxxi. 7, where Ahura fills the spaces of Paradise with light.

Such expressions are, of course, far removed from perfection, but there is undoubtedly present the idea of a redemptive whole, in which the primitive root of chshathra has long since lost the narrowness of the first concept, and has been enlarged to embrace various connotations and to signify the final state of a transfigured paradise and divine world.

(g) Even in the Veda, as we saw above, central conceptions of faith such as righteousness, reverence, piety, achieve a characteristically hypostatic form. This tendency reaches its goal in the seven hypostatic beings, which surround Ahura as his 'immortal holy ones,' the yazatas, the spirits of the Lord. (We saw that in one passage in the Veda, the same feature occurred with the kshatram, which even there is called a yazata.) For Zoroaster, the chshathra has definitely become one of these hypostatically conceived yazata beings. Chshathra is one of the seven great genii or angels near Ahura. It is probably true to say that the royal power of the god is represented in personal form as such a genius. As genius, it is not conceived, generally speaking, in a specially eschatological manner, although eschatological associations cling even to this hypostasized form of the chshathra.

> In the designation 'Chshathra varya,' which is also customary at a later time for the genius Chshathra, it is the eschatological meaning of the concept chshathra which is manifestly preserved (Lommel, p. 57).

Clearly so in Yasna xxx. 8 ff. (according to Darmesteter's translation):

> And on the day when vengeance comes upon sinners, O Mazdā, thou wilt give Chshathra with Vohu Mano to those who according to thy instruction . . .

Or Yasna xl. 5 ff.:

> . . . at the final revolution of the world . . . when thou wilt come with Chshathra and with Vohu Mano . . .

(*h*) Zoroaster also anticipates as near at hand the End with the Judgment and the 'wondrous new creation' of the world. He thinks that he himself will live to experience it. Here, too, the eschatological perspective only became widespread among the later community of the Mazdayasnians. And further, here too the proclamation of the Judgment and the 'placing in the situation which calls for decision' is not the whole of the message: it is a necessary element of a message which as a whole purports to be a message of salvation.

(*i*) For the End is the 'wondrous new creation' of the world. We would say, the transfiguration of the world. The future state is for the most part only described as an improved continuation of the accustomed and familiar existence of the world. But one distinctly feels that something deeper is really in question, viz. the opposing of a completed and wholly other, a really supernatural existence, to the present one. The future place is at first conceived as this earth itself, freed of evil and disorder. But as Söderblom says in *La vie future d'après le Mazdéisme*, p. 269:

> Already in our Avesta heaven is represented as the place to which pious men aspire. There is no longer any difference between heaven and earth. The earth extends to the sphere of the stars. And the Lord is coming on the earth.

These are attempts to symbolize something incomprehensible.

CHAPTER III

THE ISRAELITE AND JEWISH LINE OF DEVELOPMENT. THE MALKŪTH YAHWEH

THIS has been traced so often that, for our present purpose, it is only necessary to give an account of the connotations of the term kingdom, and the extensions and changes of its meaning, and to do this as precisely as possible.

1. Yahweh is King, Yahweh became King—that, particularly in the above-mentioned royal psalms, is an expression of praise, which occurs exactly like a formal creed. It confesses Him as the highest, as most mighty and most glorious, and as unique in regard to exaltation, glory, and might. Instead of calling someone king, we can also say that the kingship = malkūth or mamlākah belongs to him. No special or technical meaning is thereby expressed. It is only a tautology. Hence, the malkūth which, in this sense, belongs to Yahweh is synonymous with the dignity, function, and coercive power of lordship in general, as for example in Num. xxiv. 7. The various connotations which the word includes stand side by side in 1 Chron. xxix. 11 ff.:

> Thine is the greatness and the power and the glory and the praise and the majesty. For everything which is in heaven and upon earth is thine. Thine is the kingship. Thou art ruler over all. In thy hand are power and might.

Obviously all else that is mentioned belongs to the kingship by way of connotation, even the sphere of sovereignty, which here is heaven and earth. They are the kingdom to which his kingship relates, and the latter cannot be conceived without the former. The primitive meaning of the root is immediately extended to cover this wider meaning.

In the same book of Chronicles the malkūth then acquires the narrower and special meaning of Yahweh's kingship and kingdom, as far as this is the kingdom of Israel. 1 Chron. xvii. 14:

> I will place them (viz. David and his descendants) over my malkūth for ever.

Here malkūth is naturally not God's own existence as king—including His royal power. Even here, one can still translate the word as my kingship, but only in the enlarged meaning in which kingship itself no longer signifies only being king together with the royal dignity or function, but actually at the same time a royal realm which is given in fee to a representative in order that in this realm he may exercise the kingship as the agent of the giver. To the malkūth of Yahweh in this sense belong Israel and Israel's land and people, its servants and warriors; and nothing of this signifies His kingly position and His sovereignty, but their object and sphere. This malkūth is not conceived along eschatological lines.

2. The conception of the king acquires a certain eschatological meaning in the context of the early prophetic expectations of the End. Although Yahweh is naturally always king, it is said that He will become so. Thus in Is. xxiv. 23:

> For Yahweh will be king on Mount Zion and in Jerusalem.

Cf. Is. xxxiii. 22; Zeph. ii. 15; Zech. xiv. 16. Here Yahweh is king, especially as king of a future time. But it is striking that in such expressions the term malkūth falls into the background. *Malkūth* is manifestly not properly and emphatically an eschatological term. Nothing is said of a basileia theou in a technical sense. Therefore the very definitely eschatological term basileia, in the definite form that we find even in Christ's preaching, has hardly sprung from the bare idea that Yahweh will one day be king.

35

3. Von Rad rightly remarks in the *Theologisches Wörterbuch zum Neuen Testament*, p. 569:

> The sharp apocalyptic division between present and future age, first occurring in Daniel, brings with it for the first time a much sharper delineation (i.e. the technical character) of the kingdom of God.

Daniel's world of thought, however, points to Persia. I should be inclined to assume that it was through eastern influence that 'the kingdom' first became a truly eschatological term.

4. In the sense in which we to-day speak of the kingdom of heaven, i.e. as the world above, the expression kingdom of God first appears in the Wisdom of Solomon, x. 10:

> He led the righteous (Jacob), who had to flee before the wrath of his brother Esau, and showed to him the kingdom of God.

This passage refers to Jacob's vision of the ladder reaching to heaven, the ascending and descending messengers of Yahweh, and the opened heaven. The Kingdom of God is accordingly meant here, in the specific sense of the world above, the kingdom of heaven. And that world above, in contrast to the earthly one, is now the kingdom of God in the technical sense. In this passage it is not conceived eschatologically, but as something purely transcendent and other-worldly. It is the blessed and reserved beyond, from which the angels come and where the angels dwell, and where God, His throne, and His kingdom are to be found. It is the world above in complete antithesis to this world, and it has nothing more to do with the malkūth of Yahweh as kingdom of Israel, nor with the dynasty of David and the Davidic-messianic king. It is precisely the kingdom of heaven. At the same time we must note that the original meaning of the old root malkūth has here been long overshadowed, indeed forgotten. For naturally Jacob does not see the royal sovereignty, the function of God's rule, but the world in which He rules, the world above, especially as the world of angels. It is idle to ask whether in so doing he saw a kingdom, and whether the kingdom had the meaning of the thing ruled or of the sphere of rule. The old root serves in this case only as a pedestal for the idea of a transcendent, glorious, divine, and miraculous world into which the elect person is permitted to look.

5. The apocalyptist wanders through this other world in his fantasies and dreams, measures its length and breadth, tells of the groups and activities of the angels who live there, rises from one heaven to another, and returns from them to earth. The simple man of religion knows nothing of such secrets. But he knows about the kingdom of God above, about a blessed heavenly world with God. When he learns that the kingdom of God is coming, then he knows not only that the time is near when God's royal claim will be fulfilled, and judgment will be at hand, but also that the kingdom of heaven will descend from above, that the world will undergo a marvellous transformation. Such expectations are put into a concrete form in the later ideas of a Jerusalem that comes down from heaven; they form the inevitable connotations surrounding all preaching of the coming of the kingdom of God, and of every prayer for it.

6. That includes rather than excludes the fact that old associations remain alive and give birth to new expressions. One of them is to take upon one's self the yoke of the kingdom of God or of heaven. The original meaning of malkūth was royal dignity, royal sovereignty. As such, one can take upon one's self the malkūth when one bows to it in obedience and recognizes God's command in will and action. This is another distinctive and new meaning for the realization of the malkūth of Yahweh. It takes place now; not by defeat of enemies, nor by the exercise of coercive royal power, but where men confess the royal authority by obedience to it, and in as far as they carry out the king's will. Lord and servant are reciprocal terms.

37

Sovereignty may become effective where coercive power subjugates. But it may also become effective where men voluntarily subordinate themselves and, by their obedience, permit the other to become lord. This idea of a malkūth established by taking the law of God upon one's self was familiar to the rabbis. We also find a reminiscence of it occasionally in words of Jesus. But it would be turning everything upside down if one were to think that from such conceptions the idea of the kingdom of God and of its coming—an idea rich in associations—was to be interpreted essentially by Christ's usage, or that the later petition for the manifestation of the kingdom of God meant this. Even when Jewish prayers of a later date ask for the revelation of this kingdom, they are not to be understood primarily as desiring that as soon as possible all men might take upon themselves the Torah, but that the marvellous entity called the kingdom of heaven might finally appear. And of course that is the case in the Christian Lord's Prayer.

7. The Lord's Prayer teaches men to pray:

> Thy Kingdom come.
> Thy will be done in earth as it is in heaven.

These two petitions are mutually explanatory, but they are not simply synonymous. The earth in the second of these petitions is conceived as that which is earthly in contrast to that which is supramundane and heavenly. Upon it shall be found what is already found in heaven. That can only take place when that which is heavenly comes, i.e. if the kingdom descends from heaven. Where it comes, to that place comes also what is connected with it and what has long been realized in it, viz. that the will of God is fulfilled. The relation of the petitions is not an identity of meaning, nor a mere tautology, but a relation of foundation: the coming of the marvellous entity, the kingdom of God, makes it possible for that to take place upon earth which is not yet taking place, and cannot take place without that coming. Least of all can it take place by decisions on the side of men. They do not establish it by some sort of voluntary resolves, when they take upon themselves the sovereignty of God. It does not come by human decision, but, as Luther says, it 'comes of itself.' When it comes, then also the will of God is done by it and in it. As pure miracle coming from heaven, it transforms what is earthly and transforms it so that now the will of God is done also among men.

8. The characteristic elements of apocalyptic show themselves in these two petitions of the Lord's Prayer. It is only against this background, and not by modernistic toning down, that one can grasp its concrete and strictly unique meaning. The features calling for discussion are the following:

(a) The new motives which are active in the eschatology of late Jewish apocalyptic are far from being absolutely and radically alien to ancient Israelite religious feeling, for in that case we should have to do with a syncretism in the sense of mechanical addition, and the eschatology of late Judaism would then be simply and solely an alien phenomenon, which is not the case. Rather they work upon germinal ideas found even in ancient Israel. Jacob at that early period sees Yahweh enthroned high above the earth; He lives in heaven. There is His throne, His divine court and His messengers, who descend thence and ascend thither. Even the prophets of ancient Israel, when they portray the day of Yahweh and the time of salvation and peace which then begins, think of it as a definitive final condition and also attribute to it heavenly traits of a miraculous character. But the thing lacking in ancient Israel, and first beginning to develop with apocalyptic, was a dualistic sense of a world of God, which is by no means this world, but which, as the real world of God, is ever more strictly distinguished from, and gradually opposed to, it. Even if spatially conceived, particularly as localized in heaven and in the skies, even if now conceived with heightened earthly images, nevertheless we can feel, and know really for the first time, the

39

clearer consciousness of a transcendent, unworldly supra-mundane existence, an existence which befits God and divine things. There is a world, a sphere of existence, which in the narrower sense is the sphere of God and where in the narrower sense also the will of God is real and where it is done. Holy men like Elijah, Enoch, Esra, and others, can be transported into it, view it, and preach about it. Yet it is above, and quite distinct from, the mundane sphere. Such a removal and estrangement of God from the world has been regarded as dualistic and rightly so. This dualism has been criticized as a breach in, and disturbance of, the ancient naïve connection between God and the world, but wrongly so. For it is only through some such a dualistic opposition between the entire present world and the 'wholly other,' divine world that religion comes into its own. This dualism is essential to higher religion, and without it the latter cannot exist. It is characteristically and most appropriately described by the words of Enoch concerning the angels who left their home and descended to earth: they left 'the high, eternal, and holy heaven.' These words reveal an eschatology which has far outgrown all ancient Israelitish naïve folk eschatology. They contain at the same time a quite peculiar dogmatic theology and also something of the great developments and explanations of numinous apperception in the sphere of religious history. Heaven is on high. That was at first a concept due to an external and spatial standpoint. But this mere spatial view becomes the framework of an idea of value; the mere elevation becomes majesty and eminence—this too at first is only a spatial predicate; we no longer think at all of its spatial origin but only of a dignity and majesty which stoop down, win the heart, and constrain to veneration, almost to adoration. Heaven is eternal. At first this implies a temporal standpoint. Everything *in* the heavens changes and varies: the meteoric phenomena, the position of the heavenly bodies and their courses, the years, months, and days which are determined by the change of position of the heavenly bodies. But the sky remains immovable, without change, unchanging, ever unchanging, eternal. Thus dawns the idea of an existence which, compared with a temporal and changing existence, is a wholly other existence, removed from change and time, resting in itself, not only always—which would be mere extension of time —but eternal, removed from the category of time itself. Heaven is holy. The feeling of loftiness and eternity awakens numinous apperception, and with it a sense of value, which not only ontologically but also axiologically places its bearer in contrast to the wholly other, which in turn is utterly incomparable with all that otherwise claims to have value, meaning, and worth. Thus heaven, and existence in heaven, and the kingdom of heaven take on a sharp, dualistic opposition to everything which is not heaven, which is not above, and which does not come from above as the wholly other. It is the completely marvellous, and also that in which alone there can be righteousness and holiness. One must keep that in mind in listening to preaching about the Father in heaven, the heavenly Father, the kingdom of heaven, and 'in earth as it is in heaven' (cp. *The Idea of the Holy*, p. 85 f.).

(*b*) At the same time, however, we grow aware of a change of feeling regarding this earthly world. It does not become entirely separated from God; it remains under His omnipotence. But administrative angelic powers step between Him and the world as intermediaries. They are not evil demons but powerful angels of God. They are, as it were, satraps of the great king. Similarly the world is God's, but it is no longer God's world in the real sense.

9. This removal of the world from the direct sphere of divine control has been traced back to the political conditions in late Judaism. There are no proofs. Rather it seems to me that the operative factor was an idea necessary to religion, and necessarily pressing its way more definitely into consciousness, viz. the idea of the transcendence of the divine over all that is of this world. It is the idea of the wholly other, the supramundane, which was

41

first worked out in a mythical form in the contrasts between, and in the spatial superposition of, two spheres, that of earth and that of heaven.

10. Whether this had already come to pass under eastern influences may be questioned. But such influences cannot be questioned when the idea emerges that real *demonic* powers occupy an intermediate position, and when Iranian ideas of a real divine warfare begin to become operative. Traces of this are plain in the apocalyptic writings still extant, but scarcely one of them shows these traces in so decided and emphatic a way as does the preaching of Jesus himself. Here we encounter the very terminology of the eastern idea of this warfare, which as such was foreign to ancient Israel. We hear of the two kingdoms opposed to one another in war, of the victory of the already dawning Kingdom of God over the kingdom and house of Satan, and of the fall of God's defeated enemy from the heavenly heights. We then find this dualism brought into its sharpest form, sharper even than the east knew it, when the demonic powers are actually designated by Paul as the rulers of the world and Satan himself as the prince of this world.

11. It is in connection with such influences from the east that we must understand the two following facts:

First, we begin with the ancient accusing angel, known even to Israel. He was one of the sons of God, who as such belonged to the court of Yahweh Himself, and as such was neither a fallen angel nor the power of darkness. From him the actual devil developed, i.e. he took over in every respect the form of the Aryan Ahriman, the ancient Angramainyu of Zoroaster.

Secondly, we must note the immense power which the conception of the demonic won over men's minds in that period. Persons possessed by evil spirits had long been known, at all times and in almost all parts of the world. But not all ages were beset by demons. Demonism is a phenomenon which moves in waves through history; it increases and subsides; and it may even appear as suddenly as an epidemic. Our gospel narratives show that in Jesus' time a particularly strong wave of demonism had overflowed the world of Palestine. It does not admit of doubt that this wave was connected with the appearance of the above-mentioned ideas. At the same time its presence is important in interpreting a message—the message, indeed, of a typical exorcist—which ran:

The kingdom of God has come.

Such a message, when seen in these connections and brought by such a person, is something altogether different from a call to recognize a claim and make a decision. Since it was a message to a generation in which Satan's kingdom was powerful, and since it was the message of an exorcist, it was in its essential nature and in every respect a message of salvation, an 'euangelion.' For it said: Satan's kingdom is at an end, *et tristitia cum eo abducetur*, for God's kingdom has come.

12. All interpretations of a term are necessarily false if they start from the mere root of the term, but leave out of account the associations, enrichments, and shifts of meaning which the root has received in the course of its history. All interpretations of the term basileia in Jesus' mouth must be inadequate, if they fail to recognize that Jesus' conception of the kingdom—let it in other respects mean for him what it may—includes in the most substantial and realistic manner the conception of a *dynamis* before which the basileia of Satan must yield. Moreover, it must necessarily be false to think we can take Jesus' words as a thought complex complete in itself and separate from his personality. In understanding the meaning of the words, the character of the speaker is simply not a matter of indifference, and if his significance as a person is not comprehensible, the prime meaning of his words remains obscure; it becomes a subject of arbitrary interpretations made not from the standpoint of that person, but according to the fancy of the interpreter. To grasp what Jesus meant by the basileia it is necessary to know more concerning

43

his character than that he drove out devils and performed miracles. To enter into an understanding of the sayings about the kingdom it is of immediate importance for us to know that they were spoken by one who did not belong to the category of a John but to that of a charismatic evangelist, and in particular an exorcist, who knew that the basileia theou was operative in himself as a dynamis against Satan and his basileia, and who as such was in every respect a redeemer.

13. In late Jewish apocalyptic, the Iranian and the Israelitish expectations regarding the end meet and fuse. This fact may be best illustrated by examples drawn from the apocalypse of Enoch. But since this book is especially important for us in a later connection, I shall postpone its treatment in order to avoid a piecemeal discussion.

BOOK ONE

THE KINGDOM OF GOD
IN CHRIST'S PREACHING

PART II

THE KINGDOM OF GOD AS PREACHED
BY JESUS

CHAPTER IV

CHARACTERISTICS OF JESUS' PREACHING
OF THE KINGDOM

1. SUPPOSE someone came to-day and stirred the world
with words such as these: 'O men, the kingdom of heaven
is coming. It is at the door. It may break in at any
moment.' Perhaps we should consider him a fool (that
happened to the first preacher of these words), but we
should understand what he meant. We should not be
aided in our understanding by an analysis of the concept
of the kingdom. We would not say in our hearts: 'Kingdom' signifies a more or less political organism, a community organized according to laws of a polis or civitas.
Least of all should we think that the person concerned
understood thereby—somewhat in Ritschl's sense—a community bound together by the idea of the kingship of God,
and developing according as its members fulfilled their
moral calling and lived in mutual love. Nor would it be
more helpful to consider the fact that kingdom originally
signified lordship. Rather we should hear a long-familiar
word, which would awaken a series of associated ideas.

This is what had long been the case in the time of
Jesus. Everyone knew all that would come when the
kingdom of heaven came. The new and arresting feature
was that it was coming, perhaps even to-morrow; indeed,
that it had come, and hence that there was the most
urgent reason for considering how one might enter it and
be saved. Jesus did not speculate nor teach anything
special and peculiar about its content, because he himself
was not an apocalyptist, and he brought no apocalyptic
speculations, no new disclosures concerning the world
of transcendental supramundane matters. Fully as his
preaching rested upon the late Jewish eschatology, itself
borne forward by a swelling apocalyptic, yet it did not

47

move in the direction of continuing the apocalyptic-fantasy.[1] He was, however, a consistent eschatologist, and therefore his preaching of the kingdom necessarily included the following fundamental features:

(*a*) First, an element contrasted with the here and now, and essentially a matter of feeling rather than of description by means of specific terms. 'Supernatural' or 'supramundane' is too weak an expression for this contrast between the coming order and the present. We use these words to indicate the entirely marvellous, the 'wholly other' character of that which is expected. The images which Jesus uses for it, the naïve presuppositions which he makes regarding it, even the suggestion that we shall be 'as the angels,' or that heaven and earth shall pass away, do not express it fully. Later sayings declare:

It is not yet made manifest what we shall be,

[1] On this point, in *Leben und Wirken Jesu nach historisch-kritischer Auffassung*, Göttingen, 1901, p. 43—a little book now long out of date—I said: 'If we compare the preaching of Jesus with the surviving fantasies and eschatological speculations of his time, we see how far removed he is from it all. In comparison all his eschatological views are astoundingly meagre, chaste, and simple. At that time men used to write entire books of fantastic speculations on the final epoch. Scarcely any of such elements can be found in all Jesus' teaching. Even these hardly agree among themselves. Thus he speaks in one passage of eating and drinking in the kingdom of God, i.e. a continuation of earthly conditions; but in another passage he definitely excludes this: "They will be as the angels in heaven." He does not speculate on the When and How of the kingdom's inbreaking, as was done elsewhere. He does not know time nor hour at which the kingdom is to appear. He says practically nothing concerning content and conditions of the new kingdom. Nothing of all this has any independent interest for him.' These words are still valid in my opinion. But at the same time I must add that I then much underestimated the great spiritual content of late Jewish apocalyptic, and that I was not clear at that time as to the central significance of eschatology—in distinction from apocalyptic—for Christ's message and for the meaning of his person, nor as to the essential connection of that eschatology with the basic element of Biblical religion, viz. 'the holy.' This only came home when the idea of 'the holy' itself became clearer in my mind.

and:

> Eye hath not seen, nor ear heard, neither have entered
> into the heart of man, the things which God hath prepared
> for them that love him.

Here we find for the first time more adequate expressions
of the eschatological order. They point—necessarily by
pure negations and contrasts—to a world and the condition and content of a world which as a wholly other
form of existence do away with and surpass everything
humanly conceivable, and thereby all earthly existence
and circumstance. As categories of existence they correspond to the categories of value: 'to be justified,' 'to be
sanctified'; and both are embraced in the symbolic terms:
'to be reborn, to be renewed, spiritual existence, the
resurrection state.' The inner logic which binds the
elements of existence with the elements of value is this,
that holiness and righteousness are not possible in the
present, earthly, fleshly, worldly existence, or in an
existence and situation of an earthly kind. Rather, they
require the wondrous new creation, the transformation,
the transfiguration as the ontological presupposition of
their possibility. Only this logic, springing from the idea
of holiness itself, really supports genuinely religious
eschatology and eschatological metaphysics. The idea,
however, of such an eschatological order, i.e. the idea that
righteousness, as a state of sanctification, and that blessedness are not possible in an earthly form of existence but
only in the wholly other form of existence which God will
give; that they are not possible in this age but only in a
new age; that they are not possible in the world but only
in heaven, and in a kingdom of heaven—this idea is the
hidden mainspring in the formation of eschatological, as
distinct from merely Messianic, conceptions. Beneath the
surface, as it were, this idea is at work in the process of
the development of eschatology. It is active in a mild form
as soon as the conception of a final Davidic kingdom which
is to be established at the End, and which will be also a

kingdom of righteousness and of obedience to Yahweh's will, begins to take on fantastic miraculous traits. It is active when the kingdom of God is removed from the sphere of this world into heaven. It is active in the ideas of a new heaven and a new earth, in the conceptions that we shall be as the angels, and that at the end of all other final events the eternal heaven and the eternal earth will be created (Enoch xli. 16 ff.; Apoc. of Bar. xxxii. 6; 4 Ezra vii. 75). It is active in the words of Jesus that heaven and earth shall pass away, in the conception of a life 'in the resurrection' which is not a mere vivification of dead bodies but a 'lifting up' to a spiritual and supramundane existence. It is expressed most purely in those antithetic conceptions cited above from Paul. Necessarily it is expressed here purely via negationis et remotionis, since its positive content cannot be expressed, but, for beings who are themselves still in and of the world, can only be given in feelings beyond words. It is not born of earlier mythical forms where it received a purer expression, nor has it 'developed by heterogenesis' (Wundt) out of them; rather it has brought them forth and guided their rise. With Jesus it is veiled in the simplest of apocalyptic conceptions such as those of the great Messianic banquet, the existence as angels, the sitting upon thrones and the judging of Israel. But that the coming of the kingdom does not mean a mere correction of previous existence but the end of all previous and present forms; that the kingdom as a treasure and a costly pearl, that the vision of God which he promises to those who are pure in heart are wholly other goods than earthly goods or values; that they are, indeed, goods of a kingdom of heaven—that has surely been grasped by everyone who has grasped them from the viewpoint of the one leading idea of all Biblical material, i.e. the idea of the holy. The holy is an utterly supramundane value, and requires for its realization a supramundane existence. One can only be holy in heaven.

(b) It follows that the preaching of the kingdom is also and of necessity consistently eschatological, and this, of

JESUS' PREACHING OF THE KINGDOM

course, means that it includes insistently the temporal
opposition between now and then. It is quite the fashion
to-day, in a certain school of exegetes, to go to the limit
in eschatology. As if it were quite obvious, this school also
asserts that the eschatological order is outside the sphere
of time, and that it merely signifies being placed in a
situation which calls for decision. Thereby, the circumstance is masked that such an exegesis is at bottom out
of harmony with the spirit of genuine ancient eschatology,
and is attempting to save the appearance of it by allegori-
zing. Some add that God meets us, and man has an after-
life, but it is not noticed that if these vague words are to
have any meaning at all, they belong to the sphere of time.
Such modernisms are further cemented together by the
aid of borrowings from a fashionable 'existence' philo-
sophy; in this way points of view and ways of thinking
are imported into the preaching of Jesus, with which the
preaching had nothing to do, and which falsify it. For
it is not my existence which Christ's call to repentance
places in question but my righteousness before God; and
it is not assurance of my existence which his message
places in prospect but salvation. To reduce the question of
salvation to a question of existence, however, or to bring
it into the same category, is surely the most fatal of false
philosophies and secularizations that can attack fundamentally religious conceptions. Of course I must exist, if
I want to attain salvation and righteousness in the
kingdom of God. But I also exist if I go to hell; and if I
am anxious about my existence I shall go there, perhaps,
with the greatest certainty. I must exist if I strive to
fulfil a great task or a high desire; in certain circumstances
both quests may result in my surrendering of my existence.
It is not interests of existence that direct me in that case,
but interests of value and cause, which as such are completely different matters. Blessed are those, not who
hunger and thirst after existence, but who hunger and
thirst after righteousness, even if body and soul thereby
perish.

2. The eschatological order 'comes.' It comes, according to the original conception, as something which breaks in upon the final generation universally. At the same time, and with carefree inconsistency, Christ's preaching also contains the idea of the individual's entrance into the final order after death. Immediately after death, Lazarus goes to Abraham's bosom and the rich man to hell. But in both cases its coming is a change of condition; it is the entry of something really coming at a subsequent time. Because the eschatological order comes, and may come at any moment, it arouses men. It does not claim a decision—the categorical imperative does that—but calls to repentance; it summons men to abandon a way by which they would miss it. It is not a mere allegory for a 'radical claim' but the real goal to which man is to come and which is to come to him. Moreover, its coming does not mean that the divine demand has become concrete, and certainly the latter is not eschatological in itself. For that demand exists ever and the same, and the basis of its validity and of its claim is not in the coming of the kingdom but in itself, i.e. in God's holiness. The command to love God above all things and one's neighbour as one's self is not valid because the kingdom is coming, but by its very nature it puts us into a position where we feel we need repentance, and its demand cannot be made more concrete in any way by the circumstance of eschatology. Since it is in itself a holy and divine command, it is absolute. That which is absolute, however, permits of no heightening. The coming of the kingdom is not the claim and does not make it, for this was made by the ancient primordial saying which determines every Biblical utterance, viz.:

Ye shall be holy, for I am holy.

In its character of a demand, this cannot be filled out by any eschatology. Rather, the coming of the kingdom arouses men. It awakes the sleeper from his sleep, that he may watch. It arouses the confident from his confidence. It shows to the blind the abyss before which he stands, and in which he will lose not indeed his existence but rather his salvation. And all this not allegorically, but because salvation or damnation really comes, because it will have an actual, temporally real, advent and parousia, and because man actually and in an actual future will have salvation or damnation.

Thus consistent or, better, genuine eschatology includes two things: (a) There is the idea of the wondrous new creation, i.e. the kingdom of heaven as a new and different sphere and form for a sanctified, and therefore necessarily no longer earthly, existence. In this idea lies the contrast between that which is Yonder and that which is Here; (b) There is also the idea of its real coming, in which lies the contrast between the Future and the Present. Without these elements (a) and (b), talk about eschatology is a vain attempt to adapt ancient religious conceptual and experiential material to a poverty-stricken modernistic standpoint. But with both elements the coming of the kingdom is rousing, shattering, awakening. It leads men to realize a call to repentance in the one unchangeable divine requirement of holiness (which, as such, is valid of itself alone and is derivable from no eschatology as a 'consequence'). It leads them also to realize the idea of transcendent and future *salvation*, and to strive after it.

3. Since the expression kingdom of God does not cover a strictly unified conception, but rather a complex of connotations, one must not ask how the kingdom of God is to be defined, but to what objective the whole of this term is directed. Naturally, there is always the thought that some day the time will come when God will really be king, and His character as king will be openly and fully maintained. Nevertheless, it would imply too narrow a meaning if the word basileia were to be translated 'royal sovereignty,' instead of 'kingdom,' lest the word kingdom introduce the too modern conception of an organized community, a polis or politeuma, or even the idea of a fellowship achieved by human action.

(a) One should rather say: realm of royal sovereignty.

For even if it is quite undefined, yet quite in the fore-ground stands the idea of a divine realm which embraces, includes in itself, and contains, many people and many things; it is the idea of a world, and indeed of a world which is first of all in heaven. Further, when it is said that the kingdom comes, the idea is always present to some extent that it comes down from above. It would, perhaps, be going too far if one were to say frankly: 'a new world, which descends from above,' but undoubtedly the idea lies along this line.

Because it is such a realm, one can enter into the king-dom; the phrase would have no meaning in regard to a basileia which was nothing other than the function, or the dignity, or the sovereign claim, of the divine king. It can be opened or closed up like a fortress which has gates. Men can be hindered from entering its gates. One can be in it. One can recline at table in it with Abraham, Isaac, and Jacob. It is like a net which can encircle, enclose, bring together many kinds of fish. It is like a tree in whose branches the birds of the heaven can nest. It may begin in a small way and become larger and spread out; i.e. by growth it can enlarge its extent, its sphere. It stands opposed to the kingdom and the house of Satan, and thus it is like a kingdom and a house. One can inherit it, as one can inherit land. It is analogous to the promised land, and is, indeed, its transcendental form.

(b) Germane to this realm as its equipage is the equipage of the heavenly world (just because it is the heavenly world itself), viz. the heavenly Son of Man, his throne, the Holy Spirit, the angels of God, the persons of old who have been exalted to the presence of God, Abraham, the bosom of Abraham, angelic existence, the heavenly banquet, and the children of the kingdom, i.e. its people and inhabitants. There are ranks and differences; there are small and great in the kingdom of heaven. In it are God and His throne. In it one sees God. And all this comes and descends when and because the kingdom comes.

(c) Connected with the idea of an inbreaking realm

54

of heavenly sovereignty is the idea of a *dynamis*, i.e. a supernatural, wonderful, coercive, and operative power from above. We have seen that the idea of the kingship and of the royal sovereignty was necessarily associated with that of a ruling, victorious, subjugating, compelling, miraculous authority. It appears most decidedly in Jesus' idea of the basileia and in his own activity, viz. in his charismatic activity. (If we desired to connect it with the idea of the wonderful realm, we should have to compare the latter to a 'field of force,' which spreads out and embraces an area by the fact that it works in and encompasses that area with its forces. The basileia stands opposed to the realm of Satan's sovereignty, to his kingdom and house, not only as a new and different realm that takes the place of the Satanic realm, but also as a coercive authority through which the stronger subdues the strong. It is dynamis, and therefore the dynameis, the exousiai, the mighty works of Christ are very closely related with his message of the kingdom. This association between the kingdom and the power includes his healing, and especially his exorcizing work, as he himself expressly implies when he sees therein the coming of the kingdom or the working of the Holy Spirit. But his message is equally included, for it is itself exousia; so also is his own person, for it is that of the unrevealed Son of Man, i.e. part of the kingdom which is already in process of dawning. All these elements are closely related, each part supporting and requiring the rest.

(*d*) From the other side, the word kingdom covers the idea of the new *ideal* for the existence and conduct of men, the ideal of the 'righteousness which is better than that of the Pharisees.' The preaching of the kingdom is the proclamation of a new obedience towards God and His will, of being perfect as your Father is perfect. On this side the 'kingdom' and 'his righteousness' are almost synonyms. Such preaching of the kingdom does not correspond to an incidental decision 'just now,' but to a fundamental, radical conversion in repentance. It presses for a decision which goes to the depths of the soul, to the very disposition, and thus to our deepest inner self. Thereby it sets up the goal of a radical change of mind, which as such is beyond all capacity of the will. It therefore announces that the kingdom is not within human power but must grow of itself, or that it is unexpectedly found, like treasure in a field, and it reaches its consummation in the words: He who does not receive the kingdom as a child shall not enter it. Children do not decide and do not toil; they receive naïvely, without reflection or premeditation, and, as R. Bultmann aptly says, they accept the gift.

(e) Because the connotation of the wholly other and the supramundane belongs to the word kingdom, the modernistic idea of a crisis—Jesus knew nothing of crises—does not belong to it, but rather the idea of a supernatural breaking off of the entire world process. As such it is accompanied by the Last Judgment; the preaching of judgment is part of the preaching of the kingdom, and is sharpened by a sense of the immediate nearness of the judgment. Yet the kingdom is not the judgment but the consolation of Israel, the blessed final time of consummation, for which the 'quiet in the land' waited. Hence, in addition to the idea of the absolute ideal in a new righteousness, the terms 'kingdom' and 'coming of the kingdom' imply the idea of an absolute domain of salvation, indefinable and undefined as are all domains of salvation. Its highest content is that he who is pure in heart will see God, and what that signifies is again not defined. Enough to know it as the only treasure and the costly pearl. He who stumbles upon it without knowledge and volition, without expecting it, and, indeed, contrary to his expectations; he to whom it opens when the kingdom is preached, and who can feel it through its mythical images, its vague contours, and its different connotations, needs no further claim. For him it is the chshathra varya, the desired, longed-for, sought-after kingdom, which sets will and effort in motion, not through claims but through its desirability. He willingly sells all that he has and buys the one supreme thing.

Divine dignity and glory; sovereign claim and the requirement that the will of the Lord be effective; realm of sovereignty and heavenly realm; heavenly world coming into this world; miraculous power and coercion of the devil; healing and performance of miracle; charismatic preaching and seeking of the lost; consciousness of mission as the secret Son of Man; divine judgment and sternest call to repentance; new righteousness with strongest tension of will, and yet praise of a childlike attitude which no will can create and no man can confer on himself; transcendental domain of salvation, which does not harass the will by threatening but draws it by attraction; purely a coming and future reality, and precisely as such on the point of breaking in, indeed, already in the process of breaking in; mysterious, imperceptible, but visible to 'blessed' eyes; an operative and penetrating power—all that is meant and included when the kingdom of God is preached.

4. This entire complex conception is certainly not identical with the popular eschatology and the Davidic Messianism of ancient Israel and its prophets. Moreover, it is not the logical development of ideas immanent in the latter. Yet the former does not simply abrogate, but absorb the latter. The ideas of a kingdom of heaven, in essence transcendentally conceived, which as such had for a long time been much more nearly related to the antithesis between the righteous and the sinful than to that between Israel and non-Israel, are mingled in a naïve and undefined manner with the traits of the earthly renewal of Israel (the implication is also that the transcendent Son of Man of the kingdom of heaven will also be the 'basileus tōn Ioudaiōn'). As a consequence such preaching was taken up, on the one hand, by the circles which were affected by apocalyptic tendencies, and especially by such as hungered and thirsted for righteous-

57

ness and for the vision of God; it necessarily operated, on the other hand, to arouse and excite such as waited chiefly for the breakdown of the ungodly world power of Rome, and for the establishment of the kingdom of David.

Furthermore, when one came who roused the masses with the message: 'The kingdom has come' (by which he must have also understood that the end of every world empire, including the Roman Empire, had come); who let men know that in his own work the dynameis of the kingdom were already actually breaking in; and who finally confessed, in response to judicial inquiry, that he himself claimed to be the ruler of this empire; such a one had to be nailed to the cross by the Roman magistrates. Conversely, he was nailed to the cross because he was really such a claimant and was not made one later by the theology of the Church. For Pilate would, perhaps, regard as a fool and drive back to his Galilean mountains any mere itinerant rabbi who came only claiming immediate decisions, but he would not nail him to the cross.

CHAPTER V

CONCERNING THE ESCHATOLOGICAL TYPE AND ITS ESSENTIAL IRRATIONALITY

JOHANNES WEISS and Albert Schweitzer have taught us that the person and message of Christ are to be understood in a strict eschatological sense. Schweitzer prefers to speak of the 'consistent eschatology' of Jesus. At the same time he speaks of his 'marvellous ethic.' In so doing he seems to me not to notice that when these two expressions are brought together, there would be an inconsistency if one did not pay regard to the peculiar irrationality which essentially inheres in a genuine eschatology. For without this irrationality an ethic, just in as far as it is marvellous, and even as an 'interim-ethic,' would be inherently inconsistent with teaching that the end is at hand.

1. Jesus preached: The time is fulfilled. The end is at hand. The kingdom has come near. It is quite near. So near that one is tempted to translate: It is present. At least, one can already trace the atmospheric pressure of that which is ready to break in with mysterious dynamis. From its futurity it already extends its operation into the present. It is perceptibly near.

Now other sayings of Jesus, indeed his entire attitude, seem to be strangely contrasted with this fundamental conviction or, more correctly, with this quite real and acute feeling of immediate nearness. He worked more than two years, which in any case is a considerable period, and it was manifestly interposed between what was to come and what was immediately present. On the one hand, he spoke in the strongest terms of the kingdom's immediate nearness, indeed, of its actual arrival, and yet, like the ancient prophets (whose type is repeated in this respect), he uttered prophecies which of necessity pointed to a certain interval of time. The Son of Man will come, will appear. When? It will certainly be soon, very soon. Nevertheless, even the Son knows nothing concerning the hour. Only the Father knows that. Perhaps He still delays. In any case, the hour of the Son of Man is not immediately now nor to-morrow.

The following individual features call for consideration here:

(a) In keeping with the apocalyptic doctrine, Jesus reckons with the Messianic woes which are to precede the final catastrophe, the mighty convulsions in the world of men and nations; he reckons with peirasmoi, sufferings, oppressions, and trials for believers. He reckons, accordingly, on an undefined length of time. He prophesies: this generation will not pass away, until everything comes to pass. Thus he reckons on a not inconsiderable interval of time. With reference to the temple he prophesies:

> Days are coming in which not one stone will be left upon the other.

Hence he reckoned on wars waged by the Roman Empire, on a crisis in the political situation of his people, that is, on the passage of a considerable time. He prophesied his death, and therewith a considerable time in which his followers, left alone, must prove true in the coming afflictions. He said:

> There are some among those who stand here who will not taste of death until they see the kingdom of God come with power.

He prophesied specially to Peter—as Harnack seems to me to have proved—that he would see the kingdom of God come in his life-time. All this proves that he looked to a certain remoteness of time. But above all he presented the will of God and its fulfilment in a message, whose content was neutral with respect to the question whether the Kingdom was coming at an earlier or a later time. We must make this point clearer.

What would be the purely logical and only possible

consequence of the bare idea: the end is at hand? Evidently nothing more than: therefore make haste; repent, that you may escape judgment. An act of remorse, quickly brought about, is all that could be required in these circumstances, a petition for forgiveness, possibly a swift and complete surrender to the mercy of the judge. Whatever went beyond that would be inconsistent eschatology. The eschatology would be particularly inconsistent if it developed a marvellous ethic, for in consistent eschatology there would simply be no time for this. Whether what Christ set forth as the ideal attitude towards God and man could be called an ethic of Jesus would still require proof. In any case, his preaching of a 'righteousness which is better than that of the Pharisees' was full of content and drew manifold examples from practical life and concrete situations; it presupposed life and time and duration. His preaching did not correspond with the circumstance of a 'last brief hour,' in which, before the inbreaking end, there was only just time for quick conversion, but with lasting relationships and attitudes. It required the loving forgiveness which was repeated again and again; love towards one's neighbour as a lasting attitude of the disposition. Hence it presupposed a variety of enduring and changing circumstances of life. It required humble service, of a kind that could not be discharged in a fleeting final hour; watchfulness against temptation by eye or hand; trustful confidence towards the heavenly father; abandonment of anxiety, indifference towards the treasures of this world, a child-like disposition, and faithful service in God's vineyard. Of course, the strongest of eschatological tensions was active throughout, and no element was neutral towards the eschatological order itself; nevertheless, the whole matter would be meaningless if Christ's eschatology were consistent in the sense that all his words or deeds were nought but consequences following from the idea of the immediate nearness of the eschatological order.

This is expressed most clearly in one of Jesus' boldest

and most genuine sayings. The verses, contained in Jn. ii. 19, bear an almost involuntary witness to his genuine quality, and are acceptable to us only by allegory. It was so bold that the retrograde movement of thought among his followers, beginning immediately after his death, could no longer contain it. He said:

> I will destroy this temple made with hands, and in three days build another, which is not made with hands (Mk. xiv. 58).

The saying anticipates a time in which there will arise from the work of Christ a temple not made with hands, i.e. a service of God in opposition to that with which Israel was acquainted, and which the law had sanctified —one is almost compelled to say a new religion instead of the old. This opposition is not that between God's kingdom and the present mundane period, and the saying does not speak of the inbreaking of the eschatological order. Rather, the latter conception now recedes, and the reference is to something in the mundane period itself, opposed to dissolving, and surpassing what has gone before. And it is indeed a something which will have a future, a stability, and duration, as against what had been wiped away, and was of a provisional and transitory character.

2. Thus we encounter a peculiar double-sidedness, which must appear paradoxical. On the one hand the liveliest feeling of the immediate inbreaking of the supra-mundane future; on the other hand a message which is completely undisturbed by the former fact in its relation to time, the world, and life, which reckons on duration, on continuance in time and in temporal and world affairs, and is related thereto. This it is which we call the irrationality of the genuine and typically eschatological attitude. That this irrationality is of the essence, and is typical of a special attitude, is proved by the circumstance that it is not accidentally found only in Jesus, but recurs in typical form, and may break forth with the same characteristics at different times and in different places.

Zoroaster, indeed, belongs to the same category. His preaching was strongly eschatological, and indeed not only in the sense that he believed in an eschatological order to which men had to take up an attitude, but also in the very sense of the immediate nearness and the immanent inbreaking of the eschatological order. And yet Zoroaster was also an energetic and active reformer, desiring to intervene in and shape the life of the Iranian tribes. He too desired to build up and achieve something that ought to abide, and therefore ought to go forward in that form. He actually built up an ethic, marvellous in its way, which carried in itself the germ of its own form of culture, and that not only for the individual but for different races, peoples, and periods.

It was the same with Muhammed. He was explicitly a prophet of the day of Allah as immediately threatening, and he preached a most definite claim and decision (these terms fit no one better than him). But without considering when the eschatological order would come, as founder of a religion, as unifier of Arabia, as organizer and moulder, he was not hindered by the nearness of the day of Allah from accepting time and world process as every man does and undertaking a work which had meaning only in a temporal duration.

This irrational quality is repeated in every place where genuine eschatological feeling exists. It is no less characteristic of Francis and Luther. It is rationalized away if we rob it of one of its antithetic elements by explaining that the eschatological order does not belong to the sphere of time. Its irrational quality is obscured when we speak of a consistent eschatology, and yet include a marvellous ethic in spite of the inner contradiction between the two elements. It is, of course, an inconsistency to the natural *ratio*. But to religious feeling, an inner logic demands that they should be side by side, and to this feeling the only consistent eschatology is the one which contains in itself both elements indissolubly connected.

THE KINGDOM OF GOD
IN CHRIST'S PREACHING

PART III

THE ORIGINAL ELEMENT IN JESUS' PREACH-
ING OF THE KINGDOM AS COMPARED
WITH THE MESSAGE AND PERSON OF
JOHN THE BAPTIST

CHAPTER VI

THESES

1. In order to estimate an historical phenomenon rightly, one must attempt to see it in its historical connections; and if it is new or presents a new element, it is still more important to see what particular contrasts it offers to its predecessors. For our purpose, the most important predecessors are those with which the phenomenon in question has stood in closest connection. The movement initiated by Jesus was most closely connected with John's call to repentance. Jesus' person and message stand out in clearest relief when compared and contrasted with the person and message of John, from whose 'school' he separated himself, and then towards whom he consciously placed himself in antithesis.

Both John and Jesus were borne along by the eschatological movement of their time. Nevertheless, Jesus stands in clear contrast to John, who was a preacher of repentance; inwardly he was essentially different, our primary assertion being that Jesus was a charismatic evangelist who was also an exorcist.

2. I hope to describe him elsewhere more in detail, and at the same time to show that the term charismatic evangelist is only the framework within which the uniqueness of Jesus must be more closely defined. For the moment we shall only deal with the elements in the eschatological message itself which were of special significance in separating the disciple from his master and making him greater than his master. To do this I should like to set forth and prove two theses:

1. Instead of a message of the menacing Day of Yahweh, such as John proclaimed, Jesus came with the message of the kingdom of God; this was something new and different.

2. Instead of the magical dynamis of an eschatological sacrament of water, Jesus proclaimed the spiritual dynamis of the eschatological order as manifested in the 'day is at hand' of the kingdom. And this was a fundamental feature of his teaching, although obscured by the later tradition.

CHAPTER VII

THE KINGDOM OF HEAVEN REPLACES
THE DAY OF YAHWEH

1. ONLY in Mt. iii. 2 do we find it said that John spoke
of a coming kingdom of heaven. Neither Mark nor Luke
put forward, or knew anything of, this saying on John's
part. Nor does Acts xiii. 25 say anything about it. Even
intrinsically Mt. iii. 2 gives the impression of an editorial
interpolation (and not a skilful one) for the purpose of
providing a basis for the subsequent prophecy. John's
preaching does not begin in the proper sense until v. 7,
after he himself has first been depicted. If an account of
the coming kingdom of God had been present originally
in the early records about John, it would have been
impossible to suppress it later, for that account is just
what would have shown him to be Christ's forerunner and
pathmaker. It follows that the statement was interpolated
editorially in Mt. iii. 2. John did not preach of the coming
kingdom of heaven, but of the coming judgment of wrath.[1]

2. The profound difference between John and Jesus
is immediately perceptible when one places their key
words side by side. On the one hand,

> The judgment of wrath is coming;

[1] In Lk. xvi. 16 it is expressly said:

> The law and the prophets were until John: from that time
> the gospel of the kingdom of God is preached.

The plain sense is that even John had not brought any message
of the kingdom of God, and that this was the characteristic difference
between Jesus' message and John's. Luke here reproduces an early
logion of Christ's, and in a more polished form than it originally
possessed. The original form is preserved in Mt. xi.13, where, as we
shall see later, the idea is expressed more forcefully. But even in Lk.
the point is preserved: the difference between John and the new
epoch is that, in his case, there was as yet neither a kingdom of God
nor any preaching of the kingdom of God.

THE KINGDOM OF GOD IN CHRIST'S PREACHING

and on the other,

> The kingdom of heaven is at hand.

The latter was different; it was a new message, a man with the second message could not remain in the following of the first; it was a message by which the first man could not avoid being offended, and, in fact, he was offended.

In an illuminating historical reconstruction on the bases of clues that still survive, Maurice Goguel,[1] has shown that Jesus worked at first as an actual disciple of John, and followed his methods, and that, later, difficulties arose and there was a breach. That could not fail to occur, because Jesus no longer came forward as a preacher of repentance but as an evangelist, with a gospel for his message. The appropriate and characteristic substance of this message—true in content, even if it be but the narrator's summary statement—is given in the verse Mk. i. 14. ﬧ 15.

> He preached the gospel of God (viz.): 'The time is fulfilled and the kingdom of God is at hand.'

3. The text of Jesus' preaching did not abrogate that of John, for the record at once goes on to say that Jesus preached:

> Repent and believe in the gospel.

But Jesus' text takes up the meaning of John's into a much more comprehensive whole, richer in associations, in which John's is only a part. The earnestness of the call to repentance is not mitigated, nor is the demand less urgent; on the contrary, the demand is more definitely radical with Jesus than with John. But the very formula, 'The *kingdom* has come,' must have awakened in that era an emotional reaction totally different from John's message. For to people of that age it did not announce primarily that a threat, but a promise was to be fulfilled. In spite of the full earnestness of the repentance with which it was

---

[1] *Au seuil de l'Évangile: Jean Baptiste* and *La Vie de Jésus*.

bound up, it did not cast men down, but set them on their feet. The term did not arise from the message of the wrathful day of Yahweh as preached by the old prophets of doom, but from the apocalyptic expectation of salvation; and it included the latter connotation. It did not primarily threaten the offspring of vipers, but was directed to the lost ones of Israel, and to the kind of persons who waited for the consolation of Israel, from whom Jesus himself came. Just because it was a message of the kingdom, a later saying harmonized with it, viz.:

> Lift up your heads, for your redemption is near.

As a message of the kingdom instead of the coming judgment of wrath, it was a message of one who obviously contrasted himself with the comminatory John, when he said:

> Come to me, all ye that are weary and heavy laden.
> I will refresh you.

4. He continued with the words:

> My yoke is easy and my burden is light.

This saying appears astounding when one compares what is said in the Sermon on the Mount, for surely a heavier yoke was never imposed than the Sermon's radical demands. Yet the saying is true. For the hardest thing becomes easy when it is part and parcel of a message that redemption is at hand, and of a preaching the quintessence of which is a gospel of salvation. Such a message makes possible what is impossible to a man of a fearful conscience, frightened but not comforted. Indeed, because it grows of itself, it produces something which at bottom is beyond the range of any decision of the will, however earnest.

CHAPTER VIII

THE KINGDOM OF GOD AT HAND AS A REDEMPTIVE REALM OF SALVATION AND AS DYNAMIS

1. THE first point we had to make in comparing and contrasting Christ with John was that Jesus brought the saving gospel of the coming kingdom, instead of a message of the day of Yahweh. In so doing he made use of ideas belonging to the sphere of apocalyptic. But he ranged far beyond them by an idea which was entirely unique and peculiar to him, that the kingdom—supramundane, future, and belonging to a new era—penetrated from the future into the present, from its place in the beyond into this order, and was operative redemptively as a divine dynamis, as an inbreaking realm of salvation. This factor also served to remove him to the opposite extreme from John.

From the days of Ritschl it has been disputed whether the kingdom of God is transcendent or immanent, whether it is purely future or has long been present. Weiss and A. Schweitzer opposed the rationalistic speculations of Ritschl, but with the result, it seems to me, that the new enthusiasm for logical eschatology obscures the truth just as much as, if not more than, Ritschl. For whether future or present, whether transcendent or immanent—the chief thing is that the kingdom of heaven is a pure *mirum*, pure miracle. Mystērion is Christ's term.[1] Not everyone sees this mystērion. But he who does see—'blessed are his eyes.' To open men's eyes to this mystērion is the real objective of the finest parables of the kingdom of heaven.

[1] In Hebrew sod; in Aramaic radsa. Cp. Dan. ii. 28: 'There is a God in heaven that revealeth secrets, and he hath made known . . . what shall be in the latter days.' Cp. R. Otto, *The Idea of the Holy*, p. 85.

Without this purpose they have none at all, and he who has not grasped that fact may well ask—as has happened in all seriousness—what they really teach, and whether Jesus is here holding a mere monologue.

2. Ordinary things can only be either future or already present. Purely future things cannot sally forth from their future and be operative here and now. Marvels can be both and do both. That is the very reason that they are marvels—mystēria. Thus with Jesus the conception of a purely and strictly future thing passes over into that of something working even now, 'in your midst.' His words on this subject are the simplest, clearest, and most unmistakable. Logical eschatologists lament over the tortuous exegesis to which such words of Jesus have been exposed, but themselves proceed to torture them further with all sorts of quibbles, and invert their obvious, forthright meaning.

In an earlier book[1] I dealt with Jesus' conception of the kingdom as at hand and operating in advance. I also dealt with the consequences for our understanding of the relation of Christ's message to later conceptions of the activity of the Spirit and to the enthusiastic and spiritual character of the subsequent church of Jesus' followers. It is obvious that this character was inchoate in those experiences of the eschatological order which was already in operation and already breaking in.[2] I shall now proceed to discuss this conception further.

[1] R. Otto, *Leben und Wirken Jesu*, fourth edition, 1903. Out of print. (Still available in English translation made from third edition by H. J. Whitby and published by the Open Court Publishing Co., 1908.—TRANSLATOR.)

[2] R. Otto, *West-Oestliche Mystik*, 1926, second edition, 1929, p. 181: 'The kingdom of God is, on the one hand, the wholly transcendent, primarily future thing to which the community of the new covenant looked forward in hopeful expectation. But, on the other side, even in the gospels we read, "The kingdom of God is among you." In other words, the transcendent kingdom is already throwing its mysterious shadows ahead; it is there working secretly and quietly as a secret power in the germinating faith of the first community; it renews and transforms, and gives "peace and joy in the Holy Spirit." '

3. Among recent exegetes this view has been aptly expressed by B. W. Bacon in *The Story of Jesus and the Beginnings of the Church*, New York, 1929, page 212. He is dealing particularly with the parables in Mk. iv, and says:

> All four comparisons have a common object, to confirm the glad tidings of the coming kingdom as a power of God already at work. . . . Note, then, how in this group of parables of the kingdom the chief lesson is the present, inward working of God's Spirit, unseen by dull or hostile eyes, a kingdom of God which is already in the midst, silent, omnipotent, overtaking unawares those whose spiritual eyes are closed . . . (as the prophet says:) 'Not by might nor by power, but by my Spirit, saith the Lord of Hosts.'

To these words of Bacon it must be objected that they are too explicit. He speaks expressly of pneuma, of Spirit, and of spiritual power and operation—a terminology which Jesus only rarely uses, and is neither highly evolved nor definite in his case. These expressions are familiar to us, although they only became definite at a later date. Bacon's argument goes too far in unfolding the meaning of something which at first was left quite unexplained, in no way reduced to fixed, almost dogmatic concepts, but was something only just giving hints of itself, something only just brought to consciousness, but not yet made a matter of theory. Apart from this, however, he is right. As I have said elsewhere, what later became *explicit* in the spirit-centred life, was first given implicitly here, in the experience of the basileia as dynamis, in the experience of the eschatological order as effective and powerful in its anticipative formula 'the day is at hand.' Bacon goes on to say correctly on page 213:

> Such an idea of the kingdom as an omnipotent power already silently at work is not that of current Jewish conceptions [nor is it that of John, we add]. . . . Jesus' doctrine of the kingdom was new, distinctive, different. But it was not obscure . . . it did not even contradict

the old. It only glorified and transfigured it with the touch of One who could see God at work.

4. In order to take full measure of the differences between the Baptist's own message and that of Jesus about the kingdom in general, and about the kingdom as already operative and miraculously present, we should have to take Jesus' and John's messages as a whole and compare them in their entirety. In order to grasp rightly the meaning of their messages, we should have to sketch the contrasts between the two persons, since the significance of the message depends on that of the person who carries the message; person and message form a unity, and they must be comprehended in their oneness. To discharge such a task fully goes beyond the scope of this work; it will be attempted, I hope, at some other time. What follows is a mere outline.

THE CONTRAST BETWEEN THE PERSON AND MESSAGE OF JESUS AND THE PERSON AND MESSAGE OF JOHN

1. JOHN'S CATEGORY

THE records about the Baptist in our gospels and in Josephus are brief but characteristic. Their few traits combine and supplement one another to give a figure belonging to a definite category which is comprehensible in religious history.[1] The following elements combine into a clear typological unity:

1. The rigorous preacher of repentance, recognizably portrayed, who kindles a movement of repentance which grips the people. Like other and later movements of repentance, it spread out far and wide, among high and low, like a mighty epidemic, and this forms the quite immediate background for the subsequent movement belonging to Jesus.

2. In closest typological connection with (1) John is portrayed as a strict ascetic in dress, attitude, manner of life, and as living in a remote place withdrawn from society. By this very fact—as also in the case of later ascetics who preached repentance—he drew the multitude to his preaching.

3. Again in close typological connection therewith: his 'circle of observers.' He and his adherents are called Nazoraioi, observers, similarly perhaps to contemporaneous or earlier movements of ascetic repentance, as is proved by the figure of Banus, whom Josephus depicted

---

[1] Banus, the master of Josephus, already belonged to this category. He too lived in the wilderness, was strangely clothed (in a garment of leaves), ate only wild fruits and bathed often, day and night, in cold water, as penitents and baptists were accustomed to do.

and whose disciple he himself was. 'Observers' are men who follow certain ascetic practices as rules of life, conceived to be necessary for the way of salvation. In the Johannine circle the particular observance known to us was fasting. Special fasts were recognized by Jewish ritual and against such fasting Jesus expressed no opposition. But here the fasting became a characteristic practice, an observance, and it was felt to be striking when Jesus (who for that reason was reproached as the glutton and winebibber) and his circle, although they too were named Nazoraioi, did not observe the custom.

4. Again, in close connection therewith, belongs a characteristic of the ascetic and repentant cast of mind: the attitude of a gloomy, fearful disposition, to which Jesus opposed the bridegroom's joy of his circle.

5. Finally, the sacrament of water baptism operating magically and ritualistically to wash away sinful matter. Ascetic and magical soteriological practices belong closely together. To understand the relation between Jesus and John it is significant that for both salvation was attained by way of the forgiveness of sins. For the *contrast* between them it is significant that such forgiveness of sins took place with Jesus in the way indicated by his parables of the Prodigal Son and of the Pharisee and Publican; and that Jesus did not baptize, while with John the forgiveness of sins took place through a magical and sacramental rite of washing, which was intended to give assurance in the face of the coming judgment of wrath.

II. JESUS' CATEGORY

It seems to be almost a religio-historical law that ascetic movements of repentance produce their opposites out of themselves. The bright, serene figure of Gautama Buddha was born out of the gloomy, ascetic, penitent school of ancient India. From the rigorously ascetic, penitent school of the first Sufis arose the figure of Rabia with the message of blessed divine love. From the repentant observances, ascetic practices, and fear-bound feelings of late medieval monasticism came Martin Luther with the message of comfort of conscience, certitude of salvation, confident faith and trust. From John's school of repentants was born Jesus' message of the kingdom that brings salvation.

Jesus interpreted John as his forerunner; the later tradition interpreted him as the preparer of the way. Both had historical justification. The eschatological preaching of John, the mighty convulsion of consciences produced by him, his stern call to repentance, were the historically necessary prelude to the appearance of Christ and to the possibility of his activity. As M. Goguel has shown, Jesus himself worked at first, before his appearance in Galilee, as a disciple and fellow-worker of John, and at first he too practised baptism. But it came to a parting of the ways. John 'took offence' at him. Jesus transferred his work to Galilee. Although he paid loyal and grateful tribute to his old master and forerunner as the greatest among those born of women, nevertheless it was with the cleanest of cuts that he divided John from himself, and from the time of fulfilment which was breaking in with himself. Even John belonged to the past, which had come to an end:

> The law and prophets were until John. But from the days of John the kingdom of heaven operates by violence, and men of violence capture it.

The 'children of the kingdom' came later, and John does not belong to them, for

> The least in the kingdom of heaven is greater than he.

What was the next move?

1. The most striking difference externally was that Jesus abandoned baptism. That was no accidental detail, but connected with the new factor which Jesus brought;

78

Jesus characterized it most sharply as something new, precisely in comparison with John. It was connected with the new way of salvation, which John did not know.

John had preached: Repent and receive the eschatological sacrament. Jesus preached: Repent and believe the besorah (= 'good news'). Even if these words in Mk. i. 15 are a summing up by the narrator, nevertheless they show, in a way as characteristic as it is brief, Jesus' antithesis to John's activity (which Mark portrayed just before, and to which he now set Jesus' activity in clear contrast). It was no longer a magical sacrament, but a message, and indeed 'good news,' which mediated the salvation of the eschatological order; and it was not the reception of a sacrament, but the voluntary opening of oneself in faith, the believing acceptance of a gospel message.

2. Hence also the time of observances was past. In future, neither fastings nor other ascetic practices were the way of God, not the strange habits and peculiar life of dwellers in the desert, but a child's disposition, watchfulness, overcoming of temptation, service to one's neighbour in the world, humble repentance, trust, and love towards God.

The mood of gloomy, ascetic fear before God's day of wrath was also past. Jesus' preaching also required the earnestness of repentance, and he could terrify at times with the One who was able to destroy body and soul in hell. But the attitude which he brought about and desired was not the fear characteristic of ascetic penitents. Paul said later:

> We did not receive a spirit of slavery but a childlike spirit, by which we cry: Abba, dear Father.

This word of Paul's could have been the text of Christ's 'good news' in contrast to John's. He gave confident, assured security in God to an age in which God was far removed, and in particular to a generation which had been seized by John's threatening preaching. The bridegroom's joy instead of the fear felt by John's disciples was to distinguish Jesus' disciples from John's.

3. All this stands in closest unity with Jesus' message of the kingdom, and, indeed, the kingdom which was actively breaking in upon the world.

The contrast between Jesus and John in this respect is characteristically illuminated by a trait preserved almost by accident in Acts xix. 1 ff. This passage mentions disciples of John, and notes a noteworthy difference between them and the Christians. The disciples of John know nothing of the Holy Spirit. But this is the very difference which most profoundly separates Jesus from John. For what is the Spirit according to genuine ancient Christian conception? It is the supramundane gift of the new age, the divine dynamis. It is also arrabōn, i.e. pledge, and aparchē, i.e. first dawning of the supramundane future salvation itself. It is the eschatological order itself as dynamis, in its anticipatory first dawning, and it is impossible to find another or a better definition of what Jesus meant by the basileia, which had been 'powerfully active from the days of John the Baptist.' It was the eschatological order itself, working as dynamis, as already at hand. This dynamis was at work in Jesus himself, conquering Satan's kingdom, depriving him of his booty. He himself was a part of the inbreaking and saving sphere of power, and thus was himself the saving eschatological redeemer. By this 'eschatological awareness of power,'[1] which was identical with the awareness of the kingdom which was now exercising its power, Jesus was in the sharpest and most characteristic contrast with John. John brought his water sacrament, which with its magical dynamis was to provide a charm against the menace of the eschatological order, but in Christ's person and message the eschatological order itself came, its energy was operative, and it drew men into its saving realm of power. The distinction between the two was aptly

[1] R. Bultmann's phrase.

expressed in words which were probably not formulated until a later time:

> I baptize you with water, but he will baptize you with the Holy Spirit,

although Christ neither baptized nor spoke at length about the Spirit. Instead of the water sacrament giving salvation against the future order, there was now the future order which itself gave salvation.

CHAPTER X

THE LITERARY TREATMENT OF JESUS' PRO-NOUNCEMENTS ON THE INBREAKING KINGDOM

1. BEFORE our present gospels existed, and in addition (to one or several) symposia which consisted chiefly of sayings of Jesus and to which the name Q has been given, there was an ancient anonymous writing which undoubtedly also contained sayings of Jesus from the outset but which was mainly a narrative presenting Christ and his activity, preaching, suffering, and death as the eschatological redeemer. The writing arose from oral missionary preaching about him. Its original character, outline, and content are indicated even yet in Acts x. 37–43. It is known as St. (= Stammschrift, parent document). St. is the common basis of our first three gospels, the synoptic gospels, and is the outline into which the three authors, whom we call Matthew, Mark, and Luke, inserted traditional material deriving from other sources. It is not identical with any of the three present gospels, but it gleams through all three. Doubtless it had already undergone enrichments, additions, transpositions of materials, and editorial fashioning before Matthew, Mark, and Luke took it over, revised, enlarged, and altered it. And it was certainly not an officially edited book existing in identical copies, but a kind of manual for preaching, reading aloud, and edification. Possibly each individual copy received supplements, or suffered omissions, alleged or real corrections, and transpositions. Even the shortest of the canonical gospels, viz. our Mark, is not altogether identical with St. Undoubtedly Luke and Matthew have occasionally preserved its materials better than Mark, and Luke actually goes back to an earlier and considerably shorter form of St. than Mark. But in Mark its origi-

nal build is least disturbed by the insertion of other material.

That Luke as a finished work is later than Mark or Matthew may be regarded as certain. That he nevertheless used a form of St. older than the one used by Mark and Matthew may be regarded as definitely established by the penetrating investigations of W. Bussmann, *Synoptische Studien*, Halle, 1925.

I am surprised that even Bussmann says, in a note on page 2, 'the first collections of narratives and discourse fragments were not gospels but units (= isolated sections) which were only later gradually joined together.' That is impossible if the narratives really owed their origin to missionary labours. For the missionaries did not carry abroad single unconnected fragments, but, as Acts viii. 12 reports, and as cannot have been otherwise, they went out to 'carry the good news of the kingdom of God and of the name of Christ.' In other words, they preached the kingdom of God and a saving eschatological redeemer, through whose name, i.e. in the name of whom, one obtained the kingdom and its salvation. (As had already been said in the Book of Enoch: 'In his name are they saved.') The name of this person was not a 'thought complex'[1] and not single logia or sayings; rather it was the essence of this person as one who brought salvation. No matter how vaguely defined was the significance of this person for the eschatological salvation, it was the central element of the preaching. The preaching of this name, i.e. the telling about this saving person, and not first of all the reciting of separate groups of sayings, was the business of the eschatological missionaries who preached about that kingdom of God. For them, attaining this kingdom was conjoined with a believing relation to the person of the redeemer. The preaching of this name was, of course, not a life of Jesus, and not a character study of an interesting Nazarene named Jesus bar Josef, but an account of the wondrous man who had appeared and with whom the eschatological salvation was conjoined. Such a preaching was necessarily and actually a complete unity. Its unity, however, was not expressed in

[1] R. Bultmann.

the form of isolated sections of detached maxims, or on that of a detached miracle story, but the unity of a simple story of what this man had been, intended, effected, and done soteriologically. It was told with the aim given most simply and characteristically in Acts x. 35; viz. in this way to present:

The glad message of peace through Jesus Christ.

But this means, of course, that at the very beginning there was not a loose heap of sayings and other single stories that had been remembered, but actually a gospel, or rather a gospel-embryo. Perhaps it did not as yet contain a single saying of Christ. Such an embryonic gospel is offered by Acts x. 37–43. It recites none of the groups of sayings, but gives a characterization. That in turn does not mean it outlines a biography, but that, in the course of its message, it gives a vivid impression of a miracle-working redeemer.

Such little synthetic unities must have been the starting-point, for without them no missionary activity whatever could have been set in motion. They must have been quickly stereotyped. That happened of itself where missionaries developed a certain routine in delivering their introductory sermons. Those who wanted to win Jews and Jewish proselytes for the new message must have presented it in very similar fashion; they character-ized the authoritative person of the revealer who brought and guaranteed the further message of final redemption and salvation. Without first preaching about the new messenger himself one would have found no hearers at all for any sayings of his. They offered a thorough-going programme and outline, which however did not consist of separate logia, arbitrarily conjoined, but which lay at the basis when the logia were arranged and combined. It is this scheme and framework which alone explain the strange fact that in John we have a gospel which is almost indifferent towards the sayings-tradition as such, and which makes use of its own material in presenting the 'joyou message of peace through Jesus Christ.'

This material was not a mere sketch, but offered from the outset a record about a person of definite significance, presented in keeping with an immanent rule of arrangement such as is necessarily obeyed by every narrative intended to bring to knowledge 'the name,' i.e. the essential meaning of a person. It was not interested in, nor related to, chronology, but since happenings, actions, events, and cruxes of life belonged to the person who was to be presented, temporal succession and arrangement must result; and since the first missionaries had shared in the experiences, their memory of the actual sequence of events must naturally have co-operated in settling the arrangement.

What we have called St., Bussmann calls G. Concerning G as the basic document, he says on p. 28:

> The original text of G (i.e. the ancient narrative parent document) is constantly to be found in these sections in Luke (of which he has previously spoken). A reviser has altered this [original text] by his reflections and expansions, often in no insignificant way, as Mark and Matthew reveal. The revised text or the expanded recension of G was then edited by Mark and Matthew, each for himself and according to his particular style and literary purpose. This explains their mutual divergences.

This is approximately my view of the matter also; I would only add that doubtless Luke himself frequently recast the [considerably shorter] St. which he used, and hence the feature which Bussmann rightly recognized does not hinder the conclusion that many a datum of St. may have been preserved by Mark or by Matthew in a more original form than in Luke, who consciously writes more elegant Greek. Dealing with St. as a whole, Bussmann says on p. 111:

> Our conclusion is: Luke used G (i.e. St.) in the original form. Matthew used a recension of G as expanded by a Galilean. This recension was worked over by a Roman Christian to produce the second gospel (i.e. Mark).

I agree. Only one dare not assert—it seems to me—that exactly the same recension must have lain before Mark as before Matthew. We must regard St., as said above, not as any kind of finally edited writing, with identical copies, but rather as a manual which was growing in size. Perhaps it varied a great deal from one copy to another; indeed, probably it grew and changed in the same copy by marginal notations, glosses, and erasures. Not until incorporated in our three gospels, which ended the process, did it receive the character of an edition and recension. Thus the form of St. which lay before Luke cannot simply be called the original form. Certainly the form found by Luke was itself the result of a growth from still simpler previous forms and gospel embryos.[1]

After a narrative, which had characterized the redemptive person of Jesus in other respects, chiefly as regards his charismatic exorcizing and redemptive labours, St. intended to present and characterize him in Mk. iv. from the side of his teaching, and to show how and on what subjects he was accustomed to speak to the people. It characterized him by aptly brief, concise examples. It definitely intended to characterize him, and not merely to preserve additional narrative material found by accident; this is proved by the summary given in v. 33 (which was originally the conclusion and clearly the point of the section):

> And with many such parables spake he the word unto them, as they were able to hear it (i.e. to understand it).

Matthew proceeds in a similar manner. After the concise narrative of Mt. iv. 12-25, he introduces the Sermon on the Mount, consisting of materials drawn from the source Q; he attempts to piece together a unified discourse ostensibly delivered as a whole on one occasion. He tries to characterize, and does so with a discernible, definite object, which had not even existed for St. He characterizes Jesus' preaching from his own standpoint

---

[1] For example, it seems evident to me—to name but one thing—that the transfiguration scene, which even Luke found already present in St., is a later insertion, an interpolation which breaks an obvious connection of an earlier date.

and his own way of thinking. Matthew is the evangelist who belongs to an early Catholicism, then in process of formation, in which Christ and his message are beginning to be regarded from the viewpoint of the lawgiver, who brought the new Law of Christ in place of the old Law of Moses. Matthew, therefore, did not describe Jesus putting out on the lake in a boat, but, like Moses, on the mountain, the mountain of a new legislation. He did not represent him as beginning his work as a teacher with parables of the kingdom of heaven, but with an outline of righteousness.

That corresponds to the standpoint of Matthew, the first Church father, but not to history. Luke knew otherwise. According to him, Christ did not begin with teaching a new law, but with a text from Deutero-Isaiah, the one among the ancient prophets who preached a gospel. Jesus began with the 'besorah,' the good news. That corresponded to the saying in Mk. i. 15 with which the ancient parent document summarized Christ's message as a whole:

Believe in the 'good news.'

It is characteristic of Matthew that he did not repeat this saying in his summary in iv. 17. In Mk. iv the parent document passes from the miracle-worker to characterize the preacher, and to set forth the particular manner and content of his preaching; it characterizes him not as a teacher of maxims but of parables, not as a law-giver but as the preacher of a strange marvel, a marvel which grows and works 'of itself.'

By this we do not mean that Christ began his teaching activity with precisely these parables, but rather that the earliest Church retained the recollection of a teaching method and content, which it regarded as especially and primarily characteristic of Christ's teaching, and which were not the teaching of a law-giver. Mk. iv. 33 shows that St. knew of many parables of Jesus. It chose as examples of the didachē of Jesus the parables of the field with the seed growing of itself, and that of the mustard seed growing

87

into a tree. It is surely evident that these parables belong very closely together from the viewpoint of a dynamis already operative, and of a kingdom already dawning. It is surely evident that they did not come together by mere chance, but were intended to place before our eyes a quite characteristic and particular aspect of Jesus' teaching.

In support of this one may perhaps point to the following circumstance. The verses Mk. iii. 31 ff., which precede ch. iv, did not stand originally in St. They were not in Luke's copy of that source, at least not in connection with the preceding Beelzebub scene. Undoubtedly coming from a good and genuine tradition, they are joined by Mark to the Beelzebub scene in clear correspondence to vv. 20–21, which precede the Beelzebub scene. But in that case the account of the preaching of the kingdom of God in Mk. iv. once followed immediately upon the Beelzebub scene with its central saying preserved not by Mark but by Matthew: '. . . then indeed the kingdom of God has already come upon you.' This motif of already come, already operative, already perceptible, is therefore immediately continued in the parables of Mk. iv; hence these do not follow on the Beelzebub incident accidentally, but as a result of the correct feeling of their inner homogeneity and unity of meaning, in harmony with the viewpoint of the kingdom as already at hand.

2. Related to the utterances in Mk. iii and iv concerning the kingdom as something already operative, already coming, indeed already present in its beginnings, are other utterances scattered through the gospel narratives. They are not occasional and chance utterances into which, as it were, the other preaching of the kingdom tails off. They are not exceptions to which Jesus ascends now and then. They must not be isolated from one another in order to smooth them down with an exegetical plane. They possess a clear unity of meaning, should retain this unity, and are to be elucidated by one another. Moreover, they are not a product of a gradual creative

process on the part of a later church theology. Rather they clearly form a body of original thought, which did not first emerge from church theology and then gradually penetrate and become prominent in the gospel tradition. On the contrary, it was a body of thought evidently in process of being submerged because its original meaning was becoming obscure. This fact of perceptible submersion causes us to suppose that at one time there were other similar utterances which have now been completely lost; that in what is still preserved we have only fragments of an originally much larger amount, and that this stratum of Jesus' original conceptions was at first much more emphasized and much more in the foreground of his preaching than it appears to-day.

3. We can still perceive that we have to do with a stratum of thought which is in process of gradual submersion and exposed to reinterpretation and misinterpretation. Some of the signs may be given at this juncture.

Let us take the very deep and delicate, but crystal-clear parable of the seed growing of itself, in Mk. iv. 26. As we shall see later, it stood originally in closest connection with the parable in Mk. iv. 1–8, whose conclusion it formed and whose point it made clear. What happened to it? By means of interpolations which show that the organic connection of the two sections was no longer known, it was forced out of and torn from its connection, and it now stands there like a hieroglyph, to which when out of its proper context no meaning can be assigned with certainty. At the same time, in vv. 13–20 and parallels, an allegory was made of the section about the fourfold field, which belongs closely to the parable of the seed, and this allegory completely changes the point. The words of St., which are preserved in Mk. iv. 26–29 in their original form although torn from their original context, Luke has simply suppressed; not without justification, for in their isolation they had really become emptied of meaning. Matthew takes them over, but as an emptied vessel, into which he pours a quite new thought content that was

entirely different from the original intention. In xiii. 24
Matthew acts like Mark and puts the words of St. between
the parable of the fourfold field and that of the mustard
seed. But in Matthew the farmer who sows, and then goes
away and sleeps while the seed grows by pure divine
miracle without his or anyone else's work or concern,
becomes the householder who sleeps instead of watches
(which, in fact, he was never supposed to do); now comes
the evil foe and sows tares among the wheat (of which no
mention whatsoever had been made). The moral of the
story finally becomes: 'Do not uproot them but let the
tares grow together with the wheat,' a point which had
nothing to do with the original parable. In other words, a
saying of Christ's originally about the kingdom as already
present and operative has lost its meaning. Luke, therefore, omitted it completely. But the more conservative
Matthew was interested in the problems and needs of a
developing empirical Church fellowship, in the question
which was becoming acute as to whether one should allow
half Christians, sinners, backsliders, to remain in the
Church fellowship or uproot them. Thus he does not omit
but fills it with ideas due to a later situation, leaves a part
of its shell untouched, and completes the torso in his own
way.[1] Ancient material characteristic of Jesus is obscured
even in Mark, is becoming submerged in Matthew, and is
completely submerged in Luke.

Or let us take the passage in Lk. xi. 15 ff. and Mt.
xii. 24 ff. Its realism shows it to be no invention. It deals
with the struggle of the already dawning kingdom of God
against the kingdom and house of Satan. Let us compare
it with Mk. iii. 22 f. Luke and Matthew still read in their
copies of the ancient St.:

> If I by the finger of God (or by the Spirit of God)
> cast out demons, then has the kingdom of God already
> come upon you.

---

[1] We shall see later that he proceeds similarly with the parable
of the net.

THE LITERARY TREATMENT

These words are evidently the point of the entire passage. But even Mark no longer understood them, and just as Luke struck out the seed growing of itself because it had become meaningless for him, so Mark struck out this impressively original saying.

4. In this connection, i.e. in connection with the obscuring of the original meaning of the parables of the kingdom of heaven, one must understand the curious theory of parables which gradually arose and had already intruded into St., viz. that Jesus spoke his perspicuous parables, not, as St. so emphatically assures us in Mk. iv. 33, in order to be understood by the people, but that he might *not* be understood. This reflects the true state of affairs, viz., owing to influences which we shall soon investigate, the parables really were coming to be no longer understood, but were clouded by allegorizations and mystifications, and indeed some were suppressed.

5. This theory of parables utilized an ancient saying original to Christ himself, which is still preserved in Mk. iv. 11*a*, but now likewise misinterpreted in the sense of this theory. A brief word must be said on this point. The saying in question reads to-day in our text:

> To you is given the mystery of the kingdom of heaven, but to those outside everything is presented only in parables.

Thus Christ himself is represented as having set the use of parables in opposition to the real and adequate mediation of the meaning of his teaching; a monstrous idea, which is clearly contradicted by the self-evident saying of the oldest narrator as in Mk. iv. 33. Here it is said:

> In many such parables he spoke the word to them, as they were able to understand,

which clearly means that parabolic discourse corresponded to their power of comprehension. The saying, Mk. iv. 11, as it stands to-day, is evidently in consistent with itself. For even if everything was presented to the others only in parables, it was nevertheless presented to them, i.e.

91

THE KINGDOM OF GOD IN CHRIST'S PREACHING

given to them, even if only in figurative instead of literal
form. The difference would then be between lesser and
greater clarity in what was given, but not a contrast to
the fact of being given. This circumstance of itself suggests
that this way of comprehending and reproducing the
original saying of Christ cannot be in order. However, it
seems easy to recover the original form of the primitive
saying. Parabolē is the translation of māšāl. Māšāl actually
means parabolic discourse. But māšāl also has the meaning
of chidah = riddle. And that is what Jesus meant here:
To you (i.e. to those who bring seeing eyes) is given the
mystery of the kingdom of heaven, but to the others
(i.e. to those of dull mind and dim eyes) everything (that
I say about the kingdom of heaven) remains a riddle,
something not understood or comprehended. Therefore
'he that hath ears to hear, let him hear.' Thus the issue
is not that Christ spoke to some in parables (with the
actual purpose of remaining unintelligible), while to the
others he afterwards gave secret commentaries on the
parables. Rather, the meaning is that to those who had
eyes to see and ears to hear and who used them, the
mystery of the kingdom which was at hand, its quiet
growth, its taking effect and its operation, became visible
and traceable; while to those who did not hear the call:
'He that hath ears to hear, let him hear,' the discourse
about these matters was and must remain nothing but a
riddle.

6. The ancient saying, distorted in its present formulation by the above-mentioned theory, was certainly not
inserted in the place where it now stands until a later time.
That does not prevent it from being a saying of Jesus
derived from a good source. Even the interpolator felt
that it referred to the capacity to discern the already
dawning kingdom. Christ was concerned, particularly in
his parables of the kingdom of heaven, to bring a mysterious somewhat to men's hearing, sight, and feeling.
His discourses about it were not intrinsically claims,
admonitions, demands on the will, any more than they

were monologues. They were intended to effect something and to give something. Through them he wanted to open men's eyes to see a miracle which had been operative among them and in their midst 'since the days of John,' something which was taking place, and taking place now. That was the aim of his discourses on the growing seed, the germinating mustard seed, and the working leaven. Without this aim such discourses would really have no meaning. Without it they are really—all of them, and not merely the story of the fourfold field—mere monologues whose purpose one does not understand. We have the same situation as in the case of the Holy Spirit. In Jn. iii, Jesus speaks of the Spirit:

> which blows where it wills; you hear its sound indeed, but you do not know whence it comes and whither it goes; thus it is with every one who is born of the Spirit.

What was Nicodemus meant to understand by this account of processes completely independent of his will? Was the speaker even in this instance holding a mere monologue, i.e. an aimless discourse? Certainly not. The aim of this discourse was to help Nicodemus to gain open eyes for a mystery which was operative round about him, and to experience it. The same holds good in regard to the mystery of the kingdom of heaven.

THE KINGDOM OF GOD IN CHRIST'S PREACHING

PART IV

DETAILED CONSIDERATION OF THE MESSAGE THAT THE KINGDOM IS AT HAND

CHAPTER XI

THE KINGDOM OF GOD EXPELS THE KINGDOM OF SATAN

WE read in Mt. xii. 25–29:

> 25. Every kingdom divided against itself is brought to desolation; and every city or house divided against itself shall not stand; 26. and if Satan casteth out Satan, he is divided against himself; how then shall his kingdom stand? 27. And if I by Beelzebub cast out demons, by whom do your sons cast them out? therefore shall they be your judges. (Accordingly it is not, as you say, by Beelzebub, but by God's Spirit that I drive them out.) 28. But if I by the Spirit cast out demons, then (ara) is the kingdom of God come unto you. 29. Or how can one enter into the house of the strong man, and spoil his goods, except he first bind the strong man? and then he will spoil his house.

Instead of verse 29 as above Luke says in xi. 21 f.:

> When the strong man fully armed guardeth his own court, his goods are in peace: 22. but when a stronger than he shall come upon him, and overcome him, he taketh from him his whole armour wherein he trusted, and divideth his spoils.

Luke's version manifestly preserves a more original form than Matthew's, and likewise allows that Old Testament passage to shine through more clearly which Jesus uses here, and into which he puts the idea of God's final struggle and victory over Satan.

1. Kingdom here struggles against, and is victorious over, kingdom, the chshathra varya of the Lord over that of the chief and final foe. Material of very ancient Aryan-Iranian origin stands here in the midst of the gospel, and is palpably rugged and real. Here the

kingdom is power victorious, coercive power. It is also a realm of power, which replaces another realm of power —the kingdom, the house, the polis of Satan. It advances against the latter; victorious and growing, it pushes forward its boundaries against it in Christ's activity as exorcist. It expands its realm; its beginnings were small, but it grows ever larger.

The impressive Iranian idea of a divine warfare is also operative in the Book of Enoch. It appears more clearly in other passages of late Jewish apocalyptic, e.g. in The Assumption of Moses, x. 1, 2. Here, at the close of the prophecy of the final period, we read:

> Tunc apparebit regnum illius (Dei) in omni creatura illius, Et tunc Zabulus (Diabolus) finem habebit et tristitia cum eo abducetur. [Then His (God's) rule will be manifest through all His creation, and then Zabulus (the devil) will be no more and sorrow will be removed along with him.]

That is the plain Iranian message of the victory of the chshathra of the Lord over God's enemy, the conquest of the evil one in the great divine victory at the End. The victory takes place here through God's leader of the hosts, the archangel Michael.[1]

We find Iranian ideas of an eschatological warfare expressed in greater bulk and in greater detail in materials embedded in different passages of our Christian apocalypse, the 'Revelation of John.' (They were certainly not newly invented but found current by the Apocalyptist, who wove them into his special prophecy and adapted them to his particular aims.) In Rev. xii. 7 the seer views the end of things, the inbreaking of the final time. 'A great fiery dragon' appears,

> and there was war in heaven (whither the dragon had

---

[1] We likewise note the words 'et tristitia cum eo abducetur.' That is the purpose intended when someone comes with the message: the kingdom is near. This message is good news for sad and troubled people; it is besora and euangelion.

been compelled to ascend): Michael and his angels going forth to war with the dragon; and the dragon warred and his angels; and they prevailed not, neither was their place found any more in heaven. And the great dragon was cast down, the old serpent . . . he was cast down to the earth, and his angels were cast down with him.

Thus a great and decisive victory was gained at the outset, and the angels were already singing:

Now is come the salvation, and the power, and the kingdom of our God, and the authority (exousia) of His Christ.

But they closed with the words:

Woe to the earth and to the sea: because the devil is gone down unto you, having great wrath, knowing that he hath but a short time.

For although decisively defeated, the dragon now continued his attacks upon the earth:

and went away to make war with the rest of her seed that keep the commandments of God.

That is Iranian eschatology, applied and conformed to the supposed final fortunes of the Christian Church (at the same time, it fused with elements of Chaldean mythology, with which the Iranian tradition had long combined).

The fiery dragon is not, as Bousset thinks, an aquatic animal, for nothing can be fiery in the water. Rather it is the literal translation of Azhi dahāka (Sanskrit: ahi dahāka), which means a fiery, burning dragon.[1] Azhi

---

[1] The fiery dragon is at the same time the ancient serpent. Both are used here in the myth of the sun woman, and are applied again but in a different sense in Rev. xx. 2. In Rev. xx. 2 ff. Bousset himself referred them (indeed, he had no alternative), to Azhi dahāka and his war against Fretūn. But that the dragon in Rev. xx. 2 is of like origin with the fiery dragon here is indubitable. And no name is more suitable than fiery dragon on the one side, for azhi means dragon and dahāka means fiery, and the ancient serpent on the other side, for this figure does in fact belong to the most primordial mythology. The dragon and its conqueror Fretūn = Trita, are the most primordial of primordial figures.

dahāka, like the aboriginal monster against which Trita fought, had three heads (and seven tails). Acting under Chaldean influence, John changed it into seven heads. The Iranian tradition described the arch enemy as pressing into heaven. 'The Lord hurls down the evil spirit, who goes forth from heaven' (Söderblom, p. 267), and Azhi dahāka 'is cast down to the earth, to commit sin.' Here he rages against man and beast. In like manner with John, the fiery dragon comes to earth and rages in great wrath and persecutes the righteous. Also the remarkable 'third part' in Rev. viii. 7, 9, 11, 12; xii. 4:

> The third part of the earth was burned up, and the third part of the trees . . . there died the third part of the creatures which were in the sea . . . the third part of the waters became wormwood . . . the third part of the sun was smitten, and of the stars . . . and the day,

comes from the same source, for Azhi dahāka swallows a third of mankind, of the beasts, and of the other beings created by the Lord. His aim is the destruction of the world and the annihilation of the creatures (Söderblom, p. 268 f.). According to a later tradition he swallows Ahriman, and so with the devil himself in his body he becomes l'unique adversaire (Söderblom, p. 267). The warriors against him (as the combatants on behalf of the saoshyant, the coming judge, the saviour, judge, and founder of the new world) are Keresāspa or Fretūn (= Thraetaona āthwya = Trita āptya), beings originating from the oldest Aryan myths. In the Johannine Apocalypse the stratēgos of God, the valiant angelic hero Michael, represents a further development.

2. With equal clarity we can trace the same Iranian echoes in the Beelzebub scene of the Gospels.

In speaking about the strong man and the stronger one who comes upon the strong man, overcomes him, and takes from him his goods or his spoil, Jesus refers primarily to a passage from Isaiah xlix. 24 ff.:

> Shall the prey be taken from the mighty, or the spoil slip away from the powerful? . . . With him that con-

tends against thee (Israel) will I, Yahweh, contend, and
my children will I save, that all flesh may know that I,
Yahweh, am thy Saviour and thy Redeemer, I, the
Mighty One of Jacob.

Two strong men (gibbor) are spoken of in Isaiah. They
contend against one another. But Yahweh, the stronger,
smites the strong one, i.e. the adversary, and gives
deliverance. Isaiah meant the earthly oppressors of Israel
in this world; but for Jesus this scene of strife takes on
the deeper meaning of the divine struggle against God's
enemy himself.[1]

3. The meaning and the logic of his answer to the
accusation of being in league with Beelzebub is given
most clearly in Luke's record, which follows an older
form of St. than do Matthew and Mark.[2] Jesus says: Were
I to exorcize by Beelzebub, Satan would be arrayed
against himself, which cannot be. Therefore concede that
I exorcize by the finger of God. But if this is so, then
what I teach holds good, viz. that the kingdom of God
has already dawned, i.e. God's rule over Satan has already
come to pass and Satan himself is already deprived of
his power, i.e. his armour, since otherwise one could not
take away from him his spoil, the demon-possessed. As
long as the strong one sits in full armour and is not
deprived of his armour, and thus equipped watches his
household, no exorcist, not even I, can take from him
what he possesses. But just because the kingdom has
already dawned, because God has already achieved His
victory and stripped Satan of his armour (we might
continue: because Satan has already fallen from heaven,
but still rages with the remnants of his power here on
earth), it is possible by exorcism to take from him his

[1] Perhaps it had taken on this meaning in apocalyptic circles
before Jesus. The self-evident way in which he applies the words
almost warrants that supposition.

[2] In Matthew and Mark the logic of the verses Lk. xi. 21 f. has
already become blunted, and that from a cause which we can still
conjecture. See below.

spoil, i.e. those made captive by him and taken into his possession. The stronger one (i.e. God Himself), who had stripped him of his armour, now proceeds to take from him his spoil through the working of the exorcist Jesus, who was sent by God and is working with His (God's) power.[1]

4. We shall now give attention to a circumstance that is usually passed lightly over. What really is the reason that Jesus adds the clause 'ara ephthasen hē basileia' ['then the kingdom has come'] together with the entire detailed demonstration that follows? He had been charged with exorcizing by Beelzebub. This accusation he had refuted by showing it to be absurd, since in such a case Satan would be contending against Satan. The accusation was thereby answered. But what is the purpose of the subsequent remarks? They have no further reference to the accusation. We say: it was occasioned by, but advanced beyond, what preceded; it was intended to prove a thesis which Jesus had propounded long before and which had been as much doubted as his working by the finger of God. Only on this theory does the continuation become

[1] The peculiar obscurity which lies over the corresponding narratives in Matthew and also in Mark seems plainly connected with the fact that this story was no longer intelligible from the standpoint of the later community. For this community it was a matter of course from the dogmatic point of view that Christ himself had gained the real victory over Satan. This was not Jesus' view at all, and was not intended even in Luke. In Matthew and Mark, however, the words are so oddly veiled that one is almost compelled to gather from them that Jesus himself was the stronger one who had bound the strong one. It is plainly in connection with this tendency that in Mark the saying: 'then is the kingdom of God come upon you' is actually omitted. From the standpoint of later Christology this saying really was scarcely tolerable. For it clearly presupposed that Christ did not himself bring the kingdom of God, but that his own appearance was actually only a result of the fact that the kingdom had already come, that the powers of this kingdom were working in him and through him, but in such a way that he himself was part and parcel of this inbreaking entity of the kingdom, which was superior even to him.

intelligible. The word 'ara' introduces, like our 'really' or 'actually,' an assertion which is brought to the forefront. It means: accordingly what was asserted is correct. It presupposes the assertion as known and possibly disputed. In the present instance it means: Therefore what I teach and what I have taught, i.e. that the kingdom has come, is correct. It points to statements which Jesus must have uttered at an earlier time; to an assertion which was peculiar to him and which also had been doubted as paradoxical; to propositions such as the kingdom is in your midst; to other propositions which were implied in his parables of the kingdom of heaven; to a teaching which he had presented generally as his own peculiar teaching, and which he had certainly presented much more generally and frequently than our surviving gospel tradition leads us to suppose. In this tradition that teaching almost falls into the background. It was growing obscure, and doing so because, from the standpoint of the later Church, it was becoming paradoxical in a new way.

5. It is not Jesus who brings the kingdom—a conception which was completely foreign to Jesus himself; on the contrary, the kingdom brings him with it. Moreover, it was not he but rather God Himself who achieved the first great divine victory over Satan. His own activity lies in, and is carried forward by, the tidal wave of the divine victory. The victory and the actual beginning of the triumph of divine power, he not only deduces from his own activity, but knows of it because he has seen it. He has witnessed how Satan was cast out of heaven. This mysterious experience was the subject of a saying, which is a mere relic accidentally preserved from a context that was undoubtedly of larger extent. It reads:

I saw Satan fall from Heaven like lightning.

It is almost a miracle that such a saying should be preserved at all, for it contradicts all the later Christology. But the very fact that this saying, and likewise the words of the Beelzebub incident, were no longer possible from the later standpoint, and so could not have been invented, proves that both sayings belong to the most solid and aboriginal of Jesus' words.

6. In the power of the divine victory over the armed strong man, Jesus himself now works 'by the finger of God,' or by 'the Spirit of God,' i.e. with dynamis, exousia, charis, charisma. This dynamis of his is nothing other than the dynamis of the kingdom, the kingdom as dynamis. And this charisma and charismatic activity of his is nothing other and nothing less than the coming of the kingdom itself.

He does not bring the kingdom, but he himself, according to the most certain of his utterances, is in his actions the personal manifestation of the inbreaking divine power. 'If *I* by the finger of God drive out the devils, then the kingdom has come to you'—can one fail to hear the tone of these words? What do they express? Some say an eschatological feeling of power. But is this vague expression satisfactory? The words do not witness to a general and undefined feeling, but rather to a highly defined, concrete, and unique consciousness of mission with reference to the kingdom of God. They witness to the consciousness of a unique attachment to and union with the kingdom that supports this person, and simply removes and tears him away from everything in the form of 'law, prophets, and John' which was previously present as a mere preparation for the eschatological order, and which in comparison to that order must dwindle to a mere preparation, indeed at times to an actual contrast and opposition. They witness to the metaphysical background in which Christ believed his own person and activity were embedded. He was by no means a mere eschatological preacher, who originated certain thought complexes; rather his person and work were part of a comprehensive redemptive event, which broke in with him and which he called the coming and actual arrival of the kingdom of God. And that is the last and inmost meaning of this saying with its rich connotation.

104

7. The kingdom comes in and with him and his working, after it has first been realized in heaven by Satan's overthrow, in order that it might now become real 'in earth as it is in heaven.' And it comes chiefly not as claim and decision but as saving dynamis, as redeeming power, to set free a world lying in the clutches of Satan, threatened by the devil and by demons, tormented, possessed, demon-ridden; and to capture the spoil from the strong one; i.e. it comes chiefly as saving dynamis, as redeeming might. It is the realm of saving power which is ever expanding, ever advancing farther, in which the weary and heavy laden find rest for their souls. It makes claims, but that is not its new element; it demands decision and determination radically and fundamentally, but that is not its difference from the law and prophets. For, as we have already said, that had long ago been done by prophetic religion in the primordial words:

Ye shall be holy, for I am holy,

and:

Hear, O Israel: the Lord our God is one Lord. And thou shalt love the Lord thy God with all thy heart, with all thy soul, and with all thy might.

The radical nature and completeness of claim of these words, and their power to put one in the situation which calls for decision, cannot be surpassed or heightened by any consistent eschatology. They are words whose radical meaning even the Sermon on the Mount can only repeat, illustrate by examples, bring to the mind afresh, and press into the inner recesses of the heart and conscience, i.e. into the depth of the soul. It does not disclose that meaning for the first time. New, however, is the knowledge that saving power from above—unnoticed by and hid from dim eyes—is at work, and is quietly but irresistibly extending its realm of power in opposition to the realm of power of God's enemy.

8. Therefore it is also utterly false and contrary to the

original meaning of the person of Christ to understand him as a rabbi who uttered maxims and gained disciples, who was only later elevated to the miraculous Messianic sphere by the circle of these disciples, and who chanced to possess also a certain gift of healing which one hesitates to deny him completely, since other rabbis had the same gift. Wilhelm Schubert, not a theologian, showed deeper insight in *Das Weltbild Jesu* (published in the series *Das Morgenland*, vol. 13). His book is short but distinguished by understanding of the situation and environment, by intuitive penetration, and by excellent characterization. Schubert goes to the length of supposing (p. 32) that Jesus had long seen his unique and most important task in his exorcistic healings, expelling the dark tormenting powers. That seems to me to go too far and not to be demonstrable from our sources. But he is right in as far as Jesus was a miracle worker not by chance but quite essentially and in closest connection with his entire mission. He healed and exorcized, and showed separate concrete elements of both exorcistic and miraculous healing; Schubert is right in as far as Jesus sent his disciples throughout the country as similar persons to himself. Nevertheless his activity was not exercised in the manner of so many others who healed by miracle and exorcism at that time. Our gospels still bear witness to the latter, but Jesus, as the Beelzebub passage shows, knew himself to be, in this miraculous healing activity of his, the instrument of the dynamis of the inbreaking kingdom; on this side Jesus was altogether different from the others. Moreover it would be theoretically possible to assume that Jesus became aware that the kingdom was breaking in when his charismatic powers came to life and as they operated.

Looked at from a higher point of view, however, this means that Jesus' person and his consciousness of mission include something more than, something quite different from, his transforming of John's call to repentance into that for a 'decision to fulfil the divine will in its totality.'

He knew himself to be a part and an organ of the
eschatological order itself, which was pressing in to save.
Thereby he was lifted above John and everyone earlier.
He is the eschatological saviour. Only thus understood
are all his deeds and words seen against their right
background and in their true meaning. Directly or in-
directly, they are all borne up by the idea of a penetrating
and redemptive divine power. This idea had its immediate
correlate in the new God whom he preached, not the God
who consumed the sinner but who sought him; the Father
God, who had come near to men out of His transcendence,
who asked for a childlike mind and a childlike trust, who
freed not only from fear of the devil but from all fear
and anxiety, who filled the entire life with childlike
freedom from care. Thus also the akolouthia, the discipleship which Jesus demanded, did not signify adherence of
disciples to a new rabbi in the way that other rabbis
had had disciples and followers, but adherence to the
soteriological and eschatological saviour.[1] Finally, only
upon the basis of this understanding is there any possibility of rationally discussing the question whether Jesus
was himself conscious that his mission was Messianic in
character, or whether a society consisting of the disciples
of a rabbi elevated him at a later date to the rank of
Son of Man.

[1] This has been recognized by W. Bauer. In his essay, *Jesus de
Galiläer*, which we have frequently quoted, he says on p. 29: 'Jesu
had summoned men to let themselves be completely permeated by
the consciousness of the nearness of the divine sovereignty, to yield
to the conversion which alone leads to God, and to attach themselves
to His person as the God-sent Preparer of the new era.'

CHAPTER XII

THE KINGDOM OF GOD EXERCISES
ITS FORCE

1. 'THEN the kingdom of God has really come upon you,' says Christ in the Beelzebub passage, clearly referring, as it seems to us, to the fact that this is what he had always taught, and had done so in the expectation that his opponents, convinced by the accompanying proofs, would perceive the correctness of this teaching. But this in-breaking kingdom of heaven, as we have seen, was no static entity; it pressed in forcibly, it worked, and worked forcibly. To work forcibly, to exercise force as an operative power is the meaning of the Greek biazein, and more intensively of biazesthai in the middle voice (with the subsidiary meaning 'to exercise one's own essential force'). Instead of ephthasen hē basileia [the kingdom has come] as in the Beelzebub passage the same meaning could have been expressed by: ēdē biazetai hē basileia [the kingdom is already exercising its force].

Thus Christ actually says in Mt. xi. 12:

> From the days of John until now the kingdom of heaven exercises its force (biazetai), and those who exercise force capture it.

This saying must not be isolated, but interpreted in the context of Christ's fundamental outlook which we can comprehend. It is a part of the discourse in which Christ speaks of John, pays him high honour, and at the same time makes the sharp distinction between everything previous, including John, and that new and unheard-of thing which is breaking in. The saying signifies a change of eras, as does also the clause in the Beelzebub passage: ephthasen hē basileia [the kingdom has come], which clearly implies 'already.' The two sayings are obviously

parallel. Three periods are distinguished here in Mt. xi.
12–14: the period of the law and the prophets as mere
prophēteuein; the days of John as the days of Elias'
direct preparation; the period from the days of John as
commencement of that age which had been prophesied
and prepared. John was more than a prophet (v. 9*b*),
since he directly prepared the way for the coming of
divine sovereignty. He was Elias, the one who was distinguished from the other prophets by belonging to the very
boundary of the eschatological order. But he was no more
than Elias, one who could only prepare for it, but not
have part in it, nor be in it himself. And great as he was
(v. 11*b*), the least in the kingdom of heaven was greater
than he. For the period which had begun after the days
of the law and the prophets and after John had a
distinctive mark: what the former could only prophesy,
what the latter could only prepare, what both could only
await, viz. the kingdom of heaven, which up to then had
only been hoped for, only viewed by seers, shut away in
heaven, but motionless and inactive, was now stirring,
working, and working forcibly. Hē basileia biazetai [the
kingdom exercises force]. It grips and takes hold. It is
not present already in its completeness, but its working
can be detected. It still awaits its full revelation, but in
its preliminary dawning it is already present with mighty
preparations. That is the very characteristic of the period
'from the days of John until now,' i.e. the period of Jesus.
Even this period was not distinguished from that of the
law and the prophets and the days of John in that it was
already the complete eschatological order itself, but
rather in the fact that, as is said in precise terms, the
kingdom works, exercises force. It was not yet present
itself, but it was present as a power effective in advance.
This contrast of the periods by reason of the dynamis of
the kingdom corresponds exactly to the dynamic ephthasen
of the Beelzebub passage, and is therefore meant to be
understood by reference to it.

2. Biazetai. This could be meant in a passive sense:

the kingdom of heaven is stormed, is taken by force. The difference as compared with the meaning given previously would then be this. Hitherto it was only prophesied, only prepared; hitherto one could only hope for it, wait, prepare oneself and others for it; but now it is grasped, possessed, held fast as that which has come. That would not delineate the kingdom as purely future. Something which is only future cannot be stormed, grasped, held fast, but only something tangibly near and present. But biazein in the active and middle means to exercise force, one's own force, to be forcibly operative, to act violently. In the first case the second half of the saying would be a mere tautology, but in the second case it would be an excellent counterpart to the content of the first half of the verse. The kingdom of which Christ speaks in the Beelzebub passage does not suffer but exercises violence; similarly in the parables which we have still to examine. 'Biastai' in the second half of the verse does not mean those who have suffered violence but those who exercise violence; and biazetai is to be understood in the same way. The corresponding word in Hebrew is chāzaq in the hithpael. Jesus, who did not speak Greek, used some such word with the same connotation. Chāzaq means to be strong, then to become strong, grow, increase, become powerful, and especially obtain the ascendancy.[1] All of these related meanings are expressed in the word chāzaq, and since a preacher to the masses does not think in definite and narrowly limited concepts, but uses his words with a network of connotations, we too must listen for these connotations when Christ is speaking. But among the associated meanings we may presume, on the basis of Christ's apocalyptic ideas, that that of 'obtaining the ascendancy' received special stress. It corresponded most nearly to the eschatological idea; it corresponded in particular to the utterance in the Beelzebub passage. For it was one of the ideas of apocalyptic eschatology that other powers, indeed that Satan himself, had previously

[1] Judges i. 28: 'When Israel obtained the ascendancy.'

taken over control; but that the time would come when the kingdom of God would gain the *ascendancy* over them and him, and depose them. This was now beginning, and that fact formed the characteristic difference between the time of Jesus and earlier times.

3. 'And those who exercise force seize it.' Here we have the other side of the matter. The law and the prophets could only prophesy it, John only prepare the way for it, but now one could seize it, gain it, come to participate in it. Luke says in xvi. 16:

> And everyone presses his way into it by force.

Both phrases mean the same thing, for when one seizes a kingdom one presses into it, and when one presses into it one seizes it. (Jesus also speaks elsewhere of entering into the kingdom.)

4. On the one hand, the kingdom exercises force; on the other, those who exercise force seize it. This combination of contrasts sums up the whole of Jesus' preaching and its characteristic bi-polarity of thought. For on the one side, the kingdom comes and works and affects and seizes and grows of itself, without man's being able to do anything to help. And yet on the other side, only by summoning all one's power, and with the most strenuous determination, does one press into it.

> If thy right eye offend thee, pluck it out and cast it from thee;
> He who puts his hand to the plough and looks back is not fit for the kingdom of God;
> Strive to enter in through the narrow gate . . .
> Leave the dead to bury their dead and come and follow me;
> He who does not hate father or mother for my sake. . . .

These are forcible words, and only biastai, men who exercise force, fulfil them. They presuppose biastai, mithchazeqim, as their doers.

A new time, the time in which the kingdom is no longer at rest in a distant heaven but exercises its force; new men, who no longer tarry and wait but storm the kingdom which has come near—the essential difference between the time of Jesus on the one hand, and the days of John and on the other that of the law and prophets could not be delineated better, more concisely, more pregnantly, than by this saying. We might add that it could not be delineated more spiritedly than by the acute word-play on biazetai and biastai.

CHAPTER XIII

GOD'S SEED, NOT MAN'S DEED.—THE MYSTERY IMPLIED BY THE WORDS 'OF ITSELF'

1. Men who exercise force seize it. Only zealots, ardent for God's will, men of the strongest, most intense and violent determination are fit for the kingdom of heaven. And yet the kingdom of God and its righteousness are not created by human will, human achievement, or voluntary effort. It comes, it grows, it ripens, it bears fruit 'of itself.' That is the meaning of that most excellent of all Jesus' parables. It comes from the ancient parent document which, though defaced and obscured, has been preserved in Mk. iv. 3–8, 26–29. One must read these two severed sections in close connection and immediate sequence. They form not two parables but one, and vv. 26–29 give the point and explanation of vv. 3–8. That the section vv. 26–29 taken by itself is only a fragment; that it belongs closely to something preceding; that it presupposes and refers back to something that has preceded, is proved by the word 'thus' = 'in this way,' with which it begins, and by which it refers back to something preceding.

2. Someone had begun at an early date to gather the logia, the sayings of Christ, and to put them together in the document Q. The ancient 'parent document,' however, had an aim different from that of Q. It was intended to harmonize with the missionary preaching out of which it grew. The first function of the missionary preaching, however, was not that of handing on a master's logia or sayings, but of preaching the coming blessedness. Therefore it proclaimed the eschatological saviour with and in whose person, works, and words the final salvation came near to and was won by men. The aim of the ancient parent document was the same. In presenting Christ as

the saviour it need give only as much of the known sayings-material as was necessary for understanding his significance; no more and no less. Thus the document had to give a few characteristic examples of the method and the fundamental contents of his preaching.[1]

The saviourhood of Jesus, whence he came, how he separated from John, his own independent entry on the scene, his first deeds, the beginning of his preaching tours, the first gathering of disciples, the first extension of his activity, his work especially as a charismatic messenger of God and bringer of salvation, who healed by miracles, attacked Satan and his kingdom by his exorcisms, had already been portrayed by St. (cp. Mk. i–iii). This had been done simply, naturally, with no concern for exact chronology, in the manner of simple popular missionaries, yet not without a sense of arrangement of material and a definite feeling for what was characteristic.[2] Then St. went on to show by some examples the manner of Jesus as preacher, and its brief characterization places him clearly enough before our eyes. At the same time it chose materials which were intended to show what it regarded as the characteristic element in the new content of Jesus' preaching. St. does not begin with calls to repentance like John's, nor with a new law like the new Moses in Matthew, but with Jesus' specific and independent message, with the mysterium of the kingdom which was already mysteriously at work, already developing and growing, and which grew 'of itself.' Two parables sufficed for that purpose, the Seed Growing of Itself and the Mustard Seed; for its purpose was not to report the preaching of Jesus as a whole, but to characterize him as a preacher. At the same time it was meant to characterize him as one who, unlike

---

[1] This compact selection then became the starting-point for more discourse-material to force its way in, at first certainly as glosses and notes which were added on the margin of the copy, and which then pushed into the text at the next copying.

[2] It was particularly successful in contrasting Jesus as belonging to a new category with John whom it portrayed previously.

the scribes with their academic methods, could speak to
the 'am ha'arez. Hence it showed him to be one who,
although himself doubtless not ignorant of rabbinic culture
and learning, spoke to the people popularly, intelligibly,
and illuminatingly as in his lucid and clear parables, in
such a manner 'as they were able to understand' (Mk.
iv. 33). The admirably constructed section of St. originally
closed with this verse.

3. St. was subsequently divided up by interpolations
now given in Mk. iv. 10–25. That these verses are interpolations is generally conceded to-day, and is further
proved by the text still given by our Mark. For according
to Mk. iv. 1, 2, the intention was to outline a longer
discourse to the *people*, delivered from the boat. Verse 10,
however, interrupts this preaching from the boat, since
Jesus now suddenly stops and is alone with his disciples,
whereas the preaching from the boat nevertheless continues calmly in v. 26, and plainly goes on to reach its
evident conclusion in v. 33.

This circumstance shows further that v. 34 is a later
editorial addition. For it clearly points back to the curious
theory of the parables in v. 12 which belongs to the
interpolation, and of which we spoke earlier. Similarly it
points back to the curious theory in v. 13 that in secret
session Jesus gave to his disciples an allegorical commentary on his parables. The purpose of the gloss in v. 34 is
to add a postscript having the same theory, and so to
neutralize the clear but contrary import of what was said
in v. 33 on the aim of the parabolic discourse that Mark
found in St. Furthermore, the preaching evidently continues in parables in v. 26. Hence, even according to
Mark's very theory, it was held before the people and so
while Jesus was still in the boat, and not merely with
the disciples. If Jesus had now been apart with his
disciples in secret session, it would have been necessary
to give the allegorical commentaries, and these would
have been the chief matter.

4. The interpolation in vv. 13 ff. gives first a detailed

commentary dealing with the points of the parable one by one, and so makes a conglomerate of it. This is completely contrary to the style of Jesus. The commentary is at the same time an allegory, i.e. a form of homiletic application which later became general although foreign to Jesus himself. That it also misses the intent of the parable itself, indeed almost perverts it into its opposite, we shall see later.

5. The section in v. 26 begins with 'houtōs.' 'Thus,' 'after the manner suggested,' is the kingdom of God, as if, etc. . . . But a parable standing alone cannot begin thus, and parables of Jesus never begin in this way. The word 'thus,' 'after this very manner,' prompts us to ask: in what manner, how? But no answer is given if the section vv. 26 ff. is kept isolated. It connects with and presupposes something. It presupposes how and why that which is now to follow can be said of the kingdom of God. Quite obviously it presupposes precisely vv. 3–8. For from vv. 3–8 it is immediately evident that what is now said of the kingdom of God in vv. 26b–29 explains the fact and the manner of it.

6. While in the boat Jesus spoke the parable to simple folk in a plain but profound manner; not with the dark profundity of an esoteric and miraculous doctrine, but, clear as well as deep like all his parables, it ran as follows:

3. Hearken: Behold the sower went forth to sow; 4. and it came to pass, as he sowed, some seed fell by the wayside, and the birds came and devoured it. 5. And other fell on the rocky ground, where it had not much earth: and straightway it sprang up, because it had no deepness of earth: 6. and when the sun was risen, it was scorched; and because it had no root, it withered away. 7. And other fell among the thorns, and the thorns grew up and choked it, and it yielded no fruit. 8. And others fell into the good ground, and yielded fruit, growing up and increasing; and brought forth, thirtyfold, and sixtyfold, and a hundredfold. . . . 26. So is the kingdom of God, as if a man should cast

seed upon the earth; 27. And should sleep and rise
night and day, and the seed should spring up and grow,
he knoweth not how. 28. The earth beareth fruit *of
itself* (automatē); first the blade, then the ear, then the
full grain in the ear. 29. But when the fruit is ripe,
straightway he putteth forth the sickle, because the
harvest is come.

7. This parable is a strict unit in meaning and form,
there is nothing to allegorize, nothing to psychologize,
nothing to interpret in detail. We can understand its
perfectly simple and single point. This point is introduced
by the word 'so,' in such manner in v. 26. Two processes
are compared: the one ordinary, well known, its familiar
features repeated every year; the other a spiritual and
invisible process. The former was meant to be an analogy
to make the latter known, understood, and graphic, its
peculiar quality shining before the eye of the hearer.
Both processes, however, are processes of growth. What
was to be made clear was that in the second case, just
like the first, growth was a thing which resulted 'of itself,'
of its own urge and power of growth, and was, thereby,
independent of the doing, the willing, causing, or working,
indeed even of the knowledge and observation of man.
After the seed is sown, the man goes away, sleeps or wakes
at home, and does nothing. The seed is left to itself, and
its fate does not depend on the waking or sleeping, the
working or not working, of man. The grains which fell
by the wayside dried up, the sun parched them because
they lay too near the surface; the birds picked up what
fell accidentally on stony ground at one side, unknown to
the sower. The seed which fell upon cultivated land grows,
imperceptibly, quietly, unnoticed, 'he knoweth not how,'
and still less does he cause it. Quietly it puts forth blade
and ear and grain—it is not his doing. 'Of itself,' while he
is far away, doing nothing, unable to do anything; it is
remote from his action, indeed from his observation; the
earth of itself brings forth blade, ear, and ripe grain by
its own power working independent of man—'he knoweth

not how.' He does not know how it is done, how it happens. It is hidden from his eyes, it is a mystery.

In this mystery of acting 'of itself' lies the tertium comparationis, the analogy. Hence the word 'so,' 'in precisely the same way' in v. 26. 'So,' i.e. by this analogy, it is with the kingdom of God, as when, etc. The kingdom of God grows in the same way, quietly, secretly, unseen by dim eyes. It develops and grows by divine not human power; works and grows in a way that he does not know, mysteriously, in its own way, by its own power, automatōs. It ripens in 'fruits of righteousness,' in some cases thirtyfold, in others sixtyfold, in others a hundredfold—and all this as God's seed, not as man's deed.

The thing thus compared with a seed growing of itself is naturally not the kingdom of God as eternally present with Him in heaven. Rather it is the secret miraculous activity which 'from the days of John' 'exercises its force' quietly, mightily, irresistibly; and as it is eternally 'in heaven,' it is now on earth; it is breaking in, it comes, makes a place for itself, spreads victoriously, develops about men and in them, and is variously productive of 'fruits,' fruits of repentance and of the new righteousness. It is one and the same kingdom, which is also in heaven, but it is only when the kingdom which is beginning already, imperceptibly spreading, miraculously encompassing, inwardly and outwardly extending its realm of power, that it is 'so,' as when a man steps aside idly while the earth bears fruit of itself. It is logically eschatological, not from the standpoint of our 'logical eschatologists,' but from that of the miracle of the kingdom of God as Jesus envisaged it, and as he intended with his incomparable impressiveness and clarity to bring it before purblind eyes in this his finest parable.

8. To gain the right background for this parable, one must see it in the context of the entire tendency which Jesus' preaching manifests and which only becomes quite clear when seen in contrast with the other tendencies of his age. Viewed historically, Jesus' preaching was a

reaction against rising Pharisaic tendencies and the advance of their spiritual methods. It was anti-Pharisaism. This tendency of Jesus' message was directed against the Pharisaic mood and type of piety; it emerges in most perfect expression in a saying of Jesus, which, although true without regard to time and place, nevertheless is seen on its special contemporary background only in connection with Jesus' anti-Pharisaic tendency. The saying runs:

> He who does not receive the kingdom of God like a child shall not enter into it.

'Receive,' 'accept' like children—that is the new way of salvation which Jesus points out. It is the way which corresponds least to the Pharisaic mind and orientation, but diametrically opposes it, and this not in mere details, not in individual didactic propositions, but in its whole inner attitude of mind, which is indeed quite different. No better or more appropriate term could be applied to the specifically Pharisaic attitude than 'unchildlike,' 'contrary to the childlike nature,' and Jesus could not have contrasted 'the way of God' with the way of the Pharisees more appropriately than with the words 'like a child.'

What does 'childlike' or 'childlike disposition' mean? It is difficult, perhaps impossible, to define 'childlike attitude'; it must be intuitively perceived in its individuality, grasped intuitively rather than by definition; it must be felt. Its most prominent single feature is the deep and essential contrast of the naïve to the reflective, of emotional comprehension to theory and method, of the unconscious and spontaneous to consciousness, volition, affectation, and technique, of simplicity to punctiliousness and casuistry, of simplicity of heart to artificiality and professionalism, of natural openness and receptivity to distortedness and eccentricity, of immediate perception to hair-splitting and subtlety, of the *intuitio* to the discursive *ratio*. Punctiliousness threatened to appear in Pharisaic method; it consisted of a striving to become righteous before God by skilfully following a legal technique and subtly developing a legal science. The process became evermore unchildlike, theoretical, academic, and hair-splitting. The Law, the skilful handling of it, and punctilious legality, intervened between God and a heart in immediate contact with Him. The scribe and the one who knew and observed in detail the jots and tittles of the Law became the religious ideal of this tendency. 'To receive as a child' without hair-splitting erudition, in a simplicity of heart which neither understands nor uses techniques, subtleties, and learned rabbinic pettifoggery; above all, to receive, instead of desiring to cause, produce, compel—Jesus' word about the children sets this forth as the true way of salvation in opposition to the Pharisaic.

The meaning of the parable of the divine seed growing of itself is closely related in its tendency to the paradoxical saying about the childlike mind. It rests upon the same antithesis.

It speaks of fruit which must grow. John too had demanded the production of proper fruits. But he had demanded it with the terrors of the judgment—demanded it as something which a man should produce by an act of his own will through the repentance of the terrified conscience. In like manner, the Pharisees had insisted with earnestness and zeal upon righteousness and the fruits of righteousness. But they wanted to compel them, they wanted to take upon themselves the yoke of the malkūth of Yahweh and thereby of themselves compel the coming of the kingdom, to do so by a system of conduct refined and methodically regulated to the least detail, a régime which as such was a work of one's own decision, will, doing, and capability.

Neither the Pharisees nor John was aware that the way to God was the way of the child. Neither was aware that the kingdom of God and its righteousness were God's sowing, and that they grew in a way that man does not understand and that they are not a work of human decision or will, nor even a Pharisaic artificial system of human righteousness.

Of Itself, says the parable. Luther says: Non propriis viribus, meritis aut operibus [not by our own powers, merits, or works].

In the parable of the mustard seed which becomes a large tree the meaning of the parable of the seed echoes faintly from a new standpoint. It is, likewise, echoed in the parables of the treasure in the field and of the costly pearl, both of which fall into the merchant's hands unsought, unwilled, even undreamed of.

The new spirit breathes in the sayings about the childlike mind and the seed growing of itself; it threatened and eventually overcame the religious world of a rabbinic Judaism which was then developing. Jesus' authentic spirit breathes in these sayings rather than in his requirements and commandments. This fact was still known to the ancient parent document. Therefore, when its writer showed Jesus' manner of preaching, he chose this parable from the many and put it in the forefront.

This spirit was smothered by the legal reaction of the Jacobite school, which soon arose in Christ's own Church, and which then influenced the collection and formulation of Jesus' words. It obscured the original meaning of Christ's finest parable; it separated its parts, making out of its first part a moralizing allegory, out of its second part a mummy, and out of Christ himself a new lawgiver. But the Pharisee Saul—for the eye of an enemy has the keenest sight—perceived the true anti-legalist, anti-Pharisaic, revolutionary spirit of the movement of Jesus, and our parable is its strongest witness. Paul became its zealous persecutor. Rightly. For the new spirit attacked the foundations of Pharisaism. If the kingdom of God came and grew and developed in a way that man does not know, *of itself*, then the Pharisaic way of salvation by righteousness through works was at an end. Saul fought it until he himself succumbed. He did not succumb because he decided to recognize as Jewish Messiah a man from

Nazareth, of whom he was essentially independent, and knew only the name. That is nonsense. He succumbed because he was gripped and mastered by the new spirit. This, aroused by Jesus, and moving in his way, swept through Judaism, threatening it with disintegration.

CHAPTER XIV

THE MUSTARD SEED, THE LEAVEN, THE NET, THE TREASURE IN THE FIELD, THE PEARL OF GREAT PRICE

THE MUSTARD SEED

CLOSELY associated with the parable of the seed growing of itself is the parable of the mustard seed which grows into a large tree (Mk. iii. 31 ff.). Here, too, we have to do with something growing mysteriously.

1. Naturally, as a growing thing it is also opposed to everything which men can do or perform, but that is at best only a secondary question here and not the main point. The parable shares with the preceding in treating of a kingdom that is not merely future. A future kingdom cannot grow and in no possible sense can it be compared with a growing thing. In the present case, Christ puts something before men's eyes which is already in action around himself and his hearers as a miraculous process which they ought to perceive and rightly understand as being such. The point here, however, is not so much that the divine work goes forward 'of itself' as that it makes an unpretentious beginning, and on reaching completion has the widest of compasses.

2. What is it that grows up so mightily and extensively? In the parable of the seed growing of itself it may be designated as the new 'righteousness of the kingdom of God,' as that which according to Christ's thought should be in and with men, and which is present where God really rules in and over men; it grows not because men decide or act accordingly but because the spontaneous divine dynamis is an inner urge (comparable to the urge of the spirit and rebirth through the spirit). In the parable of the mustard seed which becomes a shade-giving tree,

something else is undoubtedly in mind. At a later date man thought in this connection of the visible fellowship of the Church which was spreading out, but that was too complete a transformation of the mystery of the kingdom of God as Christ wanted to describe it. Of course, he certainly had in view the concrete increase of the numbers who gathered to hear his preaching, and were gripped by it. Nevertheless, it would be too obvious and too petty a thing to say: In this parable, the kingdom of God is simply the increasingly numerous community of Jesus' adherents. Rather, we must put it suggestively in the following terms: it is the kingdom of God as an eschatological sphere of salvation, which breaks in, makes a small, unpretentious beginning, miraculously swells, and increases; as a divine 'field of energy' it extends and expands ever farther. The same sphere of salvation and power is also meant when the kingdom of God triumphantly expands in opposition to the kingdom and house of Satan, only now it is not related exclusively or specially to Christ's acts of exorcism, but to his activities as a whole, and without specification. His circle is throwing out ever-wider rings; already it spreads over Galilee, gripping and embracing ever more hearers; it is swelling to a movement which—marvellous to behold—is beginning to lay hold of the nation.

3. In this outer increase of people and size, Christ's eye beholds the miracle of the kingdom reaching out and extending; it is alive and growing as it breaks in. Why does he speak of it at all? Because he wants to give others the capacity to see and experience this miraculous process; that is his real aim in speaking. Unless this was his aim, all the parable did was to affirm: we began in a small way, but success is coming, and the circumference of our circle is increasing. That would have been correct, but also quite trivial. Even purblind and hostile eyes saw that. The point of importance was to perceive in this external phenomenon a secret process, the transcendent becoming an event in history; to trace behind and in the empirical

facts the mystery of the kingdom as already operative, and already growing; and to be aroused to a personal experience of it all.

THE LEAVEN

Mt. xiii. 33 and Lk. xiii. 21 add to the parable of the mustard seed that of the leaven, of which a little leavens the whole mass. The point here is the same as in the preceding case: to start from a limited beginning and spread throughout the whole. The ancient parent document omits the parable, not because it did not know of more than two parables of Christ—it knows and actually says that he taught with many such parables—but because its purpose was only to characterize, and perhaps because it regarded the meaning of the parable of the mustard seed as identical with that of the leaven. The latter is the prevailing opinion of exegetes to-day. Perhaps it is right. In that case the present point would be merely the extension of the kingdom. But to compare it with leaven which not only spreads, but penetrates and also transforms by its leavening power, points too strongly to a more special meaning. First little, then much; that also holds good here, but in the sense of the working of an inner process of transformation, which begins partim and ends totaliter. We read: 'until the whole was leavened.' Jesus speaks elsewhere of such a part which, by its nature and in its effects penetrates into the whole, and this in the sense of a process in man himself:

> If thine eye be single, thy *whole body* shall be full of light. But if thine eye be evil, thy *whole body* shall be full of darkness.

With such a meaning our parable would approximate to that of the seed growing of itself. In the latter spontaneous growth, in the former inner transformation—neither effected by human power. At the same time, in the former is the particular mysterium: a most unpretentious beginning, followed by the greatest of results.

THE NET

1. A somewhat harsh comparison may be permitted. Of things which are purely future we occasionally say: 'it is already in the air.' Similarly in order to symbolize the relation of the kingdom, which in itself is purely future, to its actually present beginning, we spoke above of the atmospheric pressure of the future kingdom which already makes itself felt as operative. Although future in its nature, it foreshadows itself mysteriously at the present time. For in regard to a thing, which is purely and strictly future, yet noticeable and traceable in its powerful precursory working, future and yet somehow present, the expression 'mysterium,' and the conception that such a mysterium is given to some in mysterious apprehension while closed to others, were so appropriate that they necessarily had to appear. At the same time, the aim of the discourses about this mysterium which was already in the air was not merely to present theoretical propositions about it, but to awaken a mysterious apprehension of it. Attention was to be drawn to the thing itself: in the exorcistic work of Jesus, in the spread of his influence, in the growth and broadening out from an unpretentious beginning.

Christ's eye saw it and its marvellous character, in yet other facts, and his hearers were meant to see it there too. The parable of the net speaks about such facts.

2. The new movement spread, took hold, carried with it, and brought together 'of every kind': apocalyptic dreamers and hotblooded zealots, irascible sons of Zebedee and the quiet in the land, those seeking mere healing and such as hungered and thirsted after nothing but righteousness, people of the 'am ha 'arez and strict disciples of the law, half proselytes and pure-blooded Jews, people who only wanted to practise magic with Jesus' name and such as asked about the highest commandment, repentant disciples of John, sinners and tax-gatherers, respectable people and weeping, sinful women. They were 'brought together of every kind.'

That was a fact marvellous to behold. That was God's power; the same miraculous power which was active when the devils yielded or when the divine seed grew up quietly and of itself.

> The kingdom of heaven is like a net which, when cast into the sea, gathers together 'of every kind' (Mt. xiii. 47).

not akin minds

3. This eye-opening parable, brief, concise like an epigram, agreeing in arrangement and style with the similarly epigrammatic parables of the treasure and pearl which immediately precede in vv. 44–46, has been preserved by Matthew, who immediately appends a detailed allegorical explanation by way of commentary (Mt. xiii. 48–50). Just as he misunderstood the close of the parable of the seed growing of itself and transformed it into an allegory of the existing church where the good grew with the bad like tares and wheat, so here also he allegorizes the parable of the net and makes it refer to the Church, which includes good and bad. He also finds an allegory of both in the judgment at the end of the age and the sorting out between the two classes. He makes Jesus reiterate the commonplace teaching that at the Last Judgment a distinction will be made between the righteous and the unrighteous, a teaching which contained nothing new, and which every one of his hearers had long known. At this stage, why the kingdom of heaven should be like a net and cast into the sea was no longer comprehensible.

The parable, however, does not speak about good and bad, but about men 'of every kind.' Kind = Greek genos = Hebrew min. When God, in Gen. i. 25, created all animals 'lemino,' He did not create good and bad animals, but animals of various kinds and each one according to his kind. Good and bad are not distinguished by belonging to different genera, but are within the same genus. Jesus does not speak of the good and bad and of their fate in the Last Judgment, but of a present miracle of the divine power, which, already breaking in, already working, suc-

Otto middle more meaning

ceeds in bringing together men of every kind who otherwise would never have met—a marvel to behold, a sign for seeing eyes. Here again the kingdom is comprehensive, a sphere; but the stress does not rest on that aspect now. Rather the stress rests upon the fact that it seizes, carries with it, brings together, the unwilling and varied elements into a unity; it biazetai, exercises its force, and already exercises it visibly.

Hence, an old and original saying of Jesus has, indeed, been preserved in this passage, but its original meaning is in process of submersion. Moreover, the passage speaks of the kingdom as already operative, which aspect of the kingdom was not understood at a later period.

THE TREASURE HIDDEN IN THE FIELD AND THE PEARL
OF GREAT PRICE

1. Jesus held to and preached the terrors of the Last Judgment; this accompanied the coming of the kingdom and was a necessary part of it. In view of the variety of associations which this term carried, and the elasticity of the meaning of this word, it would have been possible, indeed probable, for the kingdom itself to be occasionally represented by the metaphor of an inbreaking, consuming, or otherwise menacing terror. This was never done, and the fact is almost amazing. On the contrary, the kingdom was depicted as a good, winsome, and attractive thing. Such is the case in the parables of the treasure and of the pearl. Here also the kingdom is, as ever, God's sovereignty, God's power, the final condition, life with God, the supramundane goal, certainly also the great demand. It is, indeed, the kingdom of God. But the thing of which the parables themselves were meant to treat is the kingdom neither as a constraining power, nor as claim to sovereignty, nor as realm of power, nor even as a concrete supramundane condition, but as the blessing of salvation, the blessing pure and simple, and purely and simply a blessing. A blessing does not demand, it does

not work through command on the will, but by the fact that just because it is a blessing, i.e. something desired and most highly desirable, it awakens the strongest interest and thereby arouses search and exertion and surrender of everything. Then it is the goal, and this not as a function which imperiously presses to be fulfilled, but as a gift which, when its meaning and value are recognized, draws human will and effort to itself. It is not the summum bonum, the highest good, for as such it would be comparable to other blessings and only be distinguished from them in degree; rather it is a blessing which depreciates all other goods in comparison with itself and makes them mere means of acquiring itself. In the radical and exclusive requirements of their objective, these two parables stand beside the demands of the Sermon on the Mount; they differ from it in that they do not demand anything at all, but only describe what happens spontaneously as soon as this blessing comes home to the mind, viz. strongest effort in utter surrender owing to the interest that has been set alight, an interest which as such needs no command; indeed, being an interest it cannot be given by command.

2. In both these parables it is futile to ask whether the salvation is purely future or in some sense already present. This viewpoint does not obtain here. Whether purely future, or won proleptically, and no matter how recognized and understood, it awakens of itself an effort which excludes all other efforts, and gives the capacity for complete surrender for the sake of the one 'varyam,' the one thing desired and desirable.

Both parables were probably intended to bring out in addition a particular point. For it cannot be accidental that in both a particular feature recurs. Both speak not only of a general striving set in motion by a particularly prized blessing, but both agree in having the feature of an accidental discovery. The feature in common is that a blessing meets one and offers itself unexpectedly, without calculation, unforeseen, not computed by human skill or calculation, but independently of them. Thus it is with the kingdom of God as a blessing of salvation; one cannot compute it, know about it of oneself, and personally seek access to it. It must meet one, let one find it, flash forth of itself, not by a human quest.

CHAPTER XV

THE KINGDOM OF GOD IS IN YOUR MIDST

> And being asked by the Pharisees, when the kingdom of God cometh, he answered them and said, The kingdom of God cometh not with observation (or, with 'chronological calculation') : neither shall they say, Lo, here! or, There! for lo, the kingdom of God is in your midst (Lk. xvii. 20, 21).

1. A pithy logion, precise and immediately clear in a way surpassed by no other saying of Jesus. Its obvious, absolutely unmistakable point is in the words: Lo, the kingdom of God is in your midst. Whether the introduction containing the question of the Pharisees has only been spun out of this logion, or whether it corresponds to history makes no difference. What Christ says stands entirely on its own feet, is to be understood of itself, and is of itself unequivocally intelligible. What he had often said he said again now. The present saying is, at the same time, so noticeably analogous to Jesus' saying in the Beelzebub passage that both sayings are only to be explained in connection and by one another. In the former case, we read 'ephthasen eph' humās,' in the latter 'estin entos humōn.'

2. A contemporary expositor[1] of this passage begins his exegesis with the words:

> This much-discussed and much-tortured saying of Jesus. . . .

He then continues the torture. He says it has

> its point solely in the rejection of calculation of omens.

[1] K. L. Schmidt in *Theologisches Wörterbuch zum Neuen Testament,* p. 587.

If Jesus intended nothing further than to reject such advance calculation, why did he not rest content with denying it? Why does he add a positive statement of very weighty content, which he clearly enough introduces as the real point by using the word 'lo'? This statement is by no means identical with rejection. It is meant to be confirmation; it is meant to give a fact whose consequence is (a) that the apocalyptic methods of paratērēsis (observation) are not in place and (b) that there can be no talk of a Here and a There. Evidently (a) and (b) both actually result if he is speaking of the kingdom which—paradoxically and wonderfully enough—is already present in its first dawning. If that were true, then indeed all paratērēsis would be foolish. And then also all talk of Here or There would be foolish, for the matter in question was not something relating to place or space, but something dynamic, in view of whose nature a Here or There is not applicable. Only as thus understood is there any meaning in rejecting the Here or There. For in regard to the future kingdom, Here and There, i.e. local determinations, did have their place even for Jesus. The future kingdom had a thoroughly external aspect; it was to come with flaming lightning, with the appearance of the Son of Man, his angels, and the heavenly tribunal. From heaven yonder it was to descend here to the earth. From Jerusalem it was to go forth, and to extend itself over all the world from Zion, in the realm of the twelve tribes. And even the paratērēsis, as attention to the signs which indicated his coming and from which his temporal nearness was to be read, Jesus not only did not reject but he expressly summoned men to it by referring to the blossoming of the branches of the fig-tree from which the nearness of summer should be noted:

> Now from the fig tree learn her parable: when her branch is now become tender, and putteth forth its leaves, ye know that the summer is nigh; even so ye also, when ye see these things coming to pass, know ye that he is nigh, even at the doors (Mk. xiii. 28 f.).

That is paratēreisthai, i.e. to pay attention to signs of every kind regarding the future kingdom.

Our interpreter proceeds:

> The question whether the emphasis is intended, that the kingdom of God is already present at the moment of speaking is not open to debate.

No, that is no longer open to debate, but is expressed in blunt words and in the most definite fashion. And logical conclusions are drawn from it, which only receive their meaning and validity from it. He says further:

> especially since in the original Aramaic wording there exists no copula 'is,' 'will be.'

What the esteemed author means by these words is unintelligible to me. If neither 'is' nor 'will be' is present, then Jesus did not speak either of a future or of a present kingdom or of an existence 'among you' in any sense whatever. If no copula whatever is present, then he uttered completely meaningless words, for there are no sentences where there is no copula. It is a matter of universal knowledge that the copula is not actually expressed in Aramaic, but that the Aramaens nevertheless coupled things together is obvious, for otherwise they would have been unable to speak in sentences at all. Further:

> It must also be borne in mind that the Syriac translation requires a rendering which means 'in the midst of you' as a retranslation of the Greek entos into the Aramaic, which is related to Syriac.

Very well. Then Jesus said: The kingdom is in the midst of you, or in your midst, and that is just what we assumed. Further:

> The sons of Zebedee asked for the best places in the divine sovereignty, and Jesus answers that this is a matter for God alone.

There are places in a kingdom, but not in a sovereignty. That their distribution is a matter for God has nothing at all to do with the author's assertion that Jesus in speaking in this way only intended to reject calculation, but not to make any positive utterance. For the already dawning kingdom is only rightly understood as a matter for God alone. Finally:

> Yet Paul's message agrees with that of Jesus. Cp. Rom. xiv. 17: 'The kingdom of God does not consist in eating and drinking, etc.'

Is this included to mean that even for Paul the reference to the kingdom signified only something negative, or why does the author cite these words? Why does he omit the 'etc'? It reads in Paul:

> but righteousness, peace and joy in the Holy Spirit.

That is the positive side, and it has another purpose than that of saying what the kingdom is *not*. Paul's words, however, are as awkward as possible for the author. For peace and joy in the Holy Spirit are blessings of salvation in the present. They are the very things meant when we say: the eschatological order itself in anticipation, the final salvation as arrabōn and as aparchē.

It would probably be impossible to find a better example than this exegete of one influenced by a prejudice which has grown to be a dogma, and which compels the observer to see awry and to fail to appreciate the unique element of an original conception which is plainly to be seen in this utterance of Jesus besides others already examined.

3. 'It is in your midst.' The fact has long been pointed out that in Aramaic the copula—grammatically not expressed but, of course, added in thought—can designate the present as well as the future. So then, avoiding the obscurities of the author just cited, others have translated:

> The kingdom of God will be among you.

But the translator of our passage, when he rendered into Greek, knew equally well that the copula in Aramaic could signify present or future. The fact that he translated it as present, in this case, is noteworthy if only because in the circumstances obtaining at a late date a translation as future naturally lay nearer at hand. For the idea that the kingdom of God was already present was soon forgotten, for reasons still to be given. Further, by saying something to the effect that 'it will be among you,' Christ would have uttered a pure superfluity, for that the kingdom was to be among them some day the questioners themselves knew. They were asking when it would come. And finally, that it will come some day is no reason for the preceding words: 'not with observation and not Here and There,' which are substantiated by the clause beginning with 'for.'

In order to salvage a false theory, resort is made to supplying certain words, e.g. 'suddenly,' 'unexpectedly.' This word is put in a parenthesis and the parenthesis inserted into the text:

The kingdom will (suddenly) be among you.

It is a peculiar method of interpretation, which interpolates rather than explains. The word put in parenthesis would then be the real point of the discourse, and on it alone everything would depend. Christ would then have forgotten to express the real point of his discourse. What he really wanted to say he would not have said, and what he actually said he would not have wanted to say.

But could Christ after all say to opponents: The kingdom of God is in the midst of *you*? That is just what he did when, in the Beelzebub incident, he said to his distrustful opponents: The kingdom of God has come upon you, ephthasen eph' humās. (And it was no truer of the future kingdom that it was to come especially to the Pharisees.) 'You' here means neither the Pharisees in particular nor the scribes, but the same 'you' as are generally addressed by Jesus. The people are present at the Sermon on the Mount, and those actually there are only the momentary representatives of 'you.' 'To you' is a stereotyped phrase employed whenever anything is said about the coming kingdom. It appears in the Beelzebub passage, in the passage under discussion, and similarly when Jesus addressed his disciples before sending them out:

> Heal the sick, and say to them: 'The kingdom of God has come to you.'

4. What is the import of the passage under consideration? In any case, something paradoxical and intended to startle. It was meant to shatter the dogmatism of a finished eschatology and burst its too narrow limits. Jesus, like his opponents, knew of the future kingdom, that it would come, that God kept the moment in reserve, that one had to hold oneself ready for it in constant watchfulness, that one should be specially attentive as soon as the indications of its coming appeared, and that one should then know that it was near. The whole of this referred to the future kingdom. That was the first pole of his conception of the kingdom. The second was that the kingdom was already moving and so already present, in as far as it worked secretly in advance. Jesus did not reconcile the two poles. He no more adjusted the antithesis here than the strong inner bi-polarities of his teaching elsewhere. He said that those who exercise force seize the kingdom of heaven—and yet he praised the childlike mind which never acts violently but simply accepts and receives. He promised a heavenly reward for good work and insisted upon the treasure of good works in heaven— and yet in the parable of the workers in the vineyard he rejected all greed for reward. He related the parable of the growing seed which excluded all human work—and yet he demanded resolute personal action. He appealed to the court of the will and of personal freedom—and yet he was a predestinarian. Similarly, in the passage under discussion, he acts as if there were no future kingdom; every question that relates to that kingdom he confronts with the kingdom that 'is in the midst of you.' Perhaps he was at that moment engaged in controversy and so,

deliberately and with emphatic onesidedness, he brought out the opposite pole. What he says now only repeats what he had said in his parables of the kingdom of heaven in the Beelzebub incident. The paradox of his present utterance is in no respect more marked than in the point of the Beelzebub passage.

It follows that he remains a logical eschatologist, and this not from the standpoint of those who torture his words but from that of the mysterium-character, the mirum-character which the kingdom had for him. And it would be completely wrong to say that instead of a transcendent he was now teaching an immanent kingdom. The kingdom would be immanent if it were involved in the things of this world or in souls and grew out of them as their creation—a view we cannot conceive in Jesus. For him the kingdom was always purely and wholly transcendent, and only fully so when it descended with its dynamis, broke into the world sphere, and thus was 'in the midst of you.'

CHAPTER XVI

THE POWER TO SEE THE MYSTERY OF THE KINGDOM OF GOD AS ALREADY PRESENT

In summary of what we have already said frequently, and shall expound once more in the present section, we may begin with the following theses:

The kingdom, future and yet already dawning, is in truth a mystery. To grasp this mystery one needs the ability and the desire to see and hear rightly.

Jesus spoke definitely of this need. His clear utterances on the point were obscured by the false esoterism, expressed in the later and false theory of parabolic discourse.

On the one hand Jesus ascribed the hearing and seeing to men, and made it their responsibility; on the other he saw divine predestination operative in it.

1. We read in Mt. xiii. 10–17:

> 10. And the disciples came, and said unto him, Why speakest thou unto them in parables? 11. And he answered and said unto them, Unto you it is given to know the mysteries of the kingdom of heaven, but to them it is not given. 12. For whosoever hath, to him shall be given, and he shall have abundance; but whosoever hath not, from him shall be taken away even that which he hath. 13. Therefore speak I to them in parables (riddles), because seeing they see not, and hearing they hear not, neither do they understand. 14. And unto them is fulfilled the prophecy of Isaiah, which saith,
>
> By hearing ye shall hear, and shall in no wise understand;
> And seeing ye shall see, and shall in no wise perceive:
> 15. For this people's heart is waxed gross,
>   And their ears are dull of hearing,
>   And their eyes they have closed;
>   Lest haply they should perceive with their eyes,
>   And hear with their ears,

> And understand with their heart,
> And should turn again,
> And I should heal them.

16. But blessed are your eyes, for they see; and your ears, for they hear. 17. For verily I say unto you, that many prophets and righteous men desired to see the things which ye see, and saw them not; and to hear the things which ye hear, and heard them not.

In the parallel passage in Mk. iv. 10 the disciples did not ask why he used parables, but simply what was the meaning of the parables. Then Mark says:

> 11. Unto you is given the mystery of the kingdom of God;

'the mystery,' not, as in Matthew, 'the mysteries,' and the former is certainly the more original. Mark proceeds:

> but unto them that are without, all things are done in parables (riddles): 12. that seeing they may see, and not perceive; and hearing they may hear, and not understand; lest haply they should turn again, and it should be forgiven them.

Mark then gives forthwith the allegorical commentary on the first half of the parable of the seed. Mt. xiii. 12 says:

> For whosoever hath, to him shall be given, etc.

Mark detached this passage from the significant context rightly retained by Matthew, and introduced it separately farther on, and in the context of other material which he interpolated. The form which Mark reproduced is as follows:

> 24. . . . Take heed what ye hear; with what measure ye mete it shall be measured unto you; and more shall be given unto you. 25. For he that hath, to him shall be given; and he that hath not, from him shall be taken away even that which he hath.

This utterance is plainly the same as the one in Mt. xiii. 12, but is isolated and distorted. Nevertheless even Mark still understood its original and quite concrete meaning, for he appended it to the words:

Take heed what ye hear

(and with the words in v. 22, which, as we shall see later, likewise deal with the kingdom that is already in process of coming:

For there is nothing hid, save that it should be manifested; neither was anything made secret, but that it should come to light.)

2. Accordingly, an old and well-knit record in St., the meaning and connection of which became clear as soon as one read 'māšāl = riddle' instead of 'māšāl = parabolē,' had been preserved as a connected whole in the copy used by Matthew, whereas in Luke and Mark it occurs in fragments. Even in Matthew it has been falsely pressed into the breach that destroys the sequence of the parable of the seed; nevertheless, the interpolated record is itself an undivided whole.

The key and point of this discourse of Christ's is the saying in Mt. xiii. 16:

But blessed are your eyes, for they see . . .

beside which is to be placed from Mk. iv. 24:

Take heed that ye hear rightly.

Because he was compelled to interpolate these words, he had also to make the editorial remark found in Mt. xiii. 10:

And the disciples came, and said unto him, Why speakest thou unto them in parables?

This is plainly a mere editorial device, for it is artificial to ask why a popular speaker speaks to the 'am ha' arez in parables. He speaks thus, of course, in order and to the extent that simple folk can and should understand him. Everyone knows that; the disciples also knew it. Mk. iv. 33

says it plainly enough, and it was still known to Matthew also. Mt. xiii. 34 f. shows that he knew the true aim of the parables. The meaning and aim of parabolic discourse was made plain by the citation:

> I will open my mouth in parables;
> I will utter things hidden from the foundation of the
> world.

These words are clear and, when referred to the kingdom of God, they are as fitting as could be. (They correspond to Mk. iv. 22, which tells of what was hidden in order that it might be disclosed, of what was secret in order that it might become manifest.) In Christ's conception the divine design of salvation was to be identified with Christ's kingdom of God,[1] its coming, and the manner of its coming, and was 'hidden from the foundation of the world.' This secret element was not, however, to be still further concealed by parables. It was to be uttered, proclaimed before all the people.

Yet in v. 10 even Matthew gives the later theory of parabolic discourse, alleging that they were intended to conceal. But the original sense of the ancient logion is still obvious, and, as we have already said, it becomes clear as soon as parabolē is translated back into māšāl, the proper meaning of which is 'riddle,' 'speech difficult to understand.' The real trouble was that many did not understand Christ's parables. It was not because he confused the people by parabolic discourse, but because they would not or could not see and hear rightly. Therefore to them his speech must be a riddle. Hence the admonitory warning:

> Take care that you hear rightly.

3. We find here, then, the explanation of the profound saying which immediately follows in Mt. xiii. 12:

---

[1] Cp. Mt. xxv. 34: inherit the kingdom prepared for you from the foundation of the world.

> For he that hath, to him shall be given; and he that
> hath not, from him shall be taken away even that which
> he hath,

and we understand the logic connecting this saying with
the words of Mt. xiii. 11, which are preserved in a better
form in Mk. iv. 11:

> Unto you is given the mystery of the kingdom of God;
> but unto them that are without, all things are done in
> parables.

What is that which one person has, in order to obtain
ever more of it until he has an abundance, and which
another person has not, and this in such a way that not
having results in his losing even the little which he has?
It is just the capacity of being able to see and hear
spiritually, of being open to the mystery from above.
Isaiah is cited appropriately. Isaiah disclosed this
capacity; he rebuked his contemporaries for lacking it.
He distinguished between those having it and those
not having it, and he showed what happens to those
not having it. As B. Duhm says on p. 175 of *Israels
Propheten*, 1916:

> He who attends to God has it, but he who does not
> trouble himself about God gradually and progressively
> loses it. That is both cause and effect.

In fact, the saying, 'measure for measure,' does hold good
in regard to this capacity. The saying was probably at
first a detached logion, but Mark inserted it, not without
point, in iv. 24. For precisely in the measure that this
inner eye of mine is open, and that I have a sense for the
mystery, is the mystery given and measured to me. The
relationship is also a growing relationship; with all true
hearing and taking heed grows also the ability to hear
and to take heed, and correspondingly there is given to me
'more' thereof and 'in abundance.' But in that I do not
hear and do not take heed, and thus neglect my hearing

faculty, not exercising it, in that same measure it is taken from me, and finally even that 'which I have.' Therefore in Mk. iv. 24 this saying about the reciprocal measure stands in closest connection with the saying: 'Take heed what ye hear.'

4. The logic was similar when the ancient logion continued with the words preserved in Mt. xiii. 13. The translation of māšāl is indeed false, but otherwise the sequence of thought is clear. The words in our present text read:

> Therefore speak I to them in parables, because seeing they see not.

Since the word 'parables' is used to translate māšāl this sentence is meaningless. For if seeing they do not see, the only possible result would be that Jesus would turn from them in silence, but not that he would speak to them in parables or otherwise. If the theory of esoteric parables were correct, it could only read 'in order that they may not see,' but not 'because they do not see.' On the other hand, the word 'because' does hold good in all strictness if māšāl is meant as riddle, i.e. discourse hard to understand or not understood. To them, Jesus' speech was enigmatic discourse, because they lacked the ability to see and hear. That this was meant becomes still clearer when we insert the words from Mk. iv. 11, which are plainly more original:

> autois panta ginetai en parabolais.

In Hebrew that would be:

> Lāhem kol haiah bimešalim.

'Haiah le' means: to become something. Haiah limešalim means: to become riddles. No matter how clear a thing is in itself, it becomes a riddle or enigmatic speech to the stupid, to those without the faculty of understanding and feeling. From an original limešalim necessarily developed a mere bimešalim when the theory of esoteric parables came to exercise its influence, but even so, the expression:

> to them everything is given by riddles or in riddles

is still sufficiently clear.

5. Such not-seeing, not-hearing was clearly regarded by Christ in the first instance as a blameworthy attitude, a neglect of one's inner sight and hearing; and thus as the personal responsibility of the one concerned. He possessed the inner organ as such, otherwise there could not have been taken from him 'even that which he had'; but because he did not measure with the right measure, nor apply and exercise his faculty in the right measure, he became deaf and blind, and even that which he had, i.e. the inner eye itself, was taken from him.

In the second place, however, that which was at first conceived as subject to our will and which, therefore, was neglected at the cost of personal guilt, now admits of a predestinarian explanation. It was the case as early as Isaiah, and so also with Jesus. What from the first point of view was one's own omission, neglect of one's inner eye, one's own guilty failure, became divine determination when seen from a new standpoint.

6. In opposition to those to whom 'everything becomes a riddle, because seeing they do not see,' we find in Mt. xiii. 16 those to whom the mystery is given, those with blessed eyes and ears, who are pronounced blessed because their eyes and ears are opened, opened, as there can no longer be any doubt, to see and to perceive the kingdom in its dawning. This is clearly said in v. 17:

> Verily I say unto you: many prophets and righteous men desired to see what ye see. . . .

What the prophets and righteous men desired to see was the kingdom of the new age and its salvation. They desired to see this very thing, not a mere preparatory time in which one could only wait once more and wish to see it, but a time in which one experienced and took part in it. Now the time of waiting was past. With a single step, or, better with a seeing eye, a hearing ear, an understanding heart one was already in the expected state. And of those who in this way were already in it the least was, therefore, greater than the greatest of those who could only wait, prophesy, and prepare.

7. Hence what Jesus said about the true power of seeing the mystery of the dawning kingdom ran as follows:

> To you it is given to recognize the mystery of the kingdom. But to those outside, everything (which I say about it) becomes a riddle. For because seeing they do not see and hearing they do not hear and understand (because in spite of external hearing and seeing they close the inner eye and ear), my words are a riddle to them.

He adds the exhortation:

> Therefore take heed what you hear (pay attention to what is heard and open the inner eye and ear for that which in itself is given to every one, but which can be neglected and be lost). For to him who has (viz. to him who has the inner power of vision and uses it) will (ever more of it) be given, and given in abundance. But from him who has not (because he closes his inner eye) will also be taken away what he has (from him the eye itself, which he too originally had, will finally be taken away).

Such final loss was conceived in the first place as disobedience to the exhortation: 'take heed how you hear'; now it appeared under the mystery of divine determination and judicial hardening of those who do not hear.

With reference to them the prophecy of Isaiah was fulfilled:

> By hearing ye shall hear, and shall in no wise understand; And seeing ye shall see, and shall in no wise perceive.

From this view of the lot of such as had become inwardly deaf and blind, a lot at once their fault and their fate, the discourse then returned to its beginning:

> But blessed are your eyes, for they see and hear.

And the conclusion tells what these are in a position to see and to hear:

> For verily I say unto you, that many prophets and righteous men desired to see the things which ye see, and saw them not.

It was the salvation of the new age which was visible to him who could see the mystery of the kingdom as already present.

CHAPTER XVII

HIDDEN, THAT IT MAY BECOME MANIFEST

1. In Rom. i. 3 Paul distinguishes two forms of existence in Christ. One is that in which he appeared on earth, the other that in which through the resurrection he was instituted as the Son of God with power. 'With power' means only now in his full reality, the revelation of that which had previously been hidden under his bodily form. We find the same differentiation in Christ's message of the kingdom of God, and the same terminology is used to differentiate:

> till they see the kingdom of God come with power (Mk. ix. 1).

The kingdom present with power is the kingdom unveiled, revealed, in full realization. The particular addition 'with power' distinguishes and presupposes an earlier existence and presence of the kingdom which is not yet the same as the latter, and is not yet in existence 'with power,' but which is, nevertheless, already in existence and at hand; otherwise the addition of the distinguishing phrase would be meaningless.

2. As not yet present 'with power,' not yet disclosed and revealed, it is only latent, a krypton [hidden thing], which still awaits its phaneron gignesthai [manifestation], but at the same time a krypton only in order that it phaneron gignetai [may become manifest]. This is the fault of the isolated logion in Mk. iv. 22; its logic seems strange, and one usually passes it without attention:

> For there is nothing hid, save that it should be manifested; neither was anything made secret, but that it should come to light.

If the saying is read accurately, one notes that it deals particularly with the idea of an ultimate connection between being hidden and being made manifest. That is strange. In general it is by no means true that something hidden has been hidden in order that it might become manifest, and as a rule the statement is really impossible in this form. Plainly the speaker has charged the principle with a secondary meaning, derived only from the individual case which is to be placed under the principle. That is in itself a logical error, but welcome to us, for it exactly fits the hidden kingdom that it should be hidden only in order to become openly manifest. The leaven was hidden in the bread, not in order to remain a hidden thing, but in order that it might finally become manifest in its effect, viz. when the whole mass has been leavened.

3. Why did Christ utter the saying? What was its aim? It would have had none at all, if not that of making an inference from something already present to something coming. In the present case it meant that one should infer from the existence of the kingdom of God, which was already perceived by the seeing eye, that its full revelation was in prospect. The saying was a prophecy of what was to come, with proof of its correctness in something already experienced. It is analogous to the saying in Mk. xiii. 28 concerning the fig-tree which is already in the process of budding. From its budding, the one who sees, and takes notice of what is seen, should infer that summer is near. Similarly, from the already operative, developing, growing but hidden mystery which is perceived by him who has insight, we should draw the inference that it will be made plain, and this, according to the rule (which was made to do office for the purpose):

There is nothing hid, save that it should be manifested.

4. We observe once more how ancient and authentic words of Jesus about the kingdom as already at hand became obscure and misunderstood at a later date. Even Mark was not really at home with this profound saying. He attached it to Christ's well-known logion about the light which is not put under the bushel (Mk. iv. 21). A

pretended proof for this saying about the light is appended in the saying about the hidden thing; the meaning to be derived from the latter was that a man should not put his light under the bushel. But such an appendage is obviously unfortunate. For the light is certainly not something of itself hidden or concealed, and only to become manifest, but precisely something which is bright through and through, and of itself, and which men should be warned not to conceal. In Mt. x. 26 such loss of understanding goes still further. Here the word about the hidden thing becomes the vehicle of a full-blown esoteric doctrine, and is made to refer to a secret teaching which Christ is supposed to have whispered into his disciples' ears in the darkness. Similarly Lk. xii. 2–3, whereas in Lk. viii. 17 the ancient logion is still repeated in its pure form.

CHAPTER XVIII

THE REASONS FOR THE ECLIPSE AND DISAPPEARANCE OF THE IDEA OF THE KINGDOM AS DAWNING ALREADY

THERE are three reasons why Jesus' original teaching that the Kingdom was already dawning fell into the background and was lost to sight.

1. The later Christology displaced Jesus' own Christology, and thereby the idea of the regnum Christi as already present displaced that of the regnum Dei as already dawning.

2. The experience of the kingdom was explained as the experience of the spirit.

3. The conception of the church displaced the conception of the mystery of the kingdom.

1. Christ's preaching fits closely on the apocalyptic of late Judaism, and especially on that apocalyptic tradition to which the books of Enoch bear witness. (This I hope to set forth in more detail later.) Enoch proclaimed the eschatological figure of the new age as the 'Son of Man,' who was to appear in order to live and to rule with the righteous as their head and king in the time of the consummation. Enoch, however, did not simply proclaim him; the climax and high point of the Book of Enoch is the story of how Enoch was snatched up and exalted, and finally he himself was declared to be, and installed as, the Son of Man. To this corresponds Christ's consciousness of his Messianic mission, and this background affords the original explanation of that consciousness and its proper significance. That means two things:

The man Jesus bar Joseph of Nazareth knew himself to be the Messianic king, inasmuch as he was the claimant to the throne of the kingdom of heaven, but not inasmuch as and while he journeyed and taught here on earth, and expelled demons. The kingdom of heaven was not already, here and now, *his* kingdom. Only later would he inherit it. God was to bequeath to him, establish for him the kingdom. He was to establish it for him at the end of his course, in the moment in which he went to meet his death and his exaltation through his death. God was to establish it for him on the basis of his obedient suffering of death. Only after his Father had bequeathed it to him would God's kingdom be his kingdom.

But as long as he 'must journey' the kingdom of God as a regnum Christi did not yet exist. The kingdom of God existed and was some day to become the kingdom of 'the Son,' and was to become his own. But as such it was there in front of him. And as we have already said, Christ does not bring, achieve, or create the kingdom, but the kingdom comes of itself and brings him with it as the Christus designatus. Also it is not he who has won the great divine victory over the adversary, but this victory is only continued and completed on earth in his activity.

Those are the conceptions original to Jesus himself, and they still shine through the ancient traditional material. That they still do so at all is really amazing. For they strain away from, and indeed, are opposed to, what his church later thought of him, and necessarily thought of him from the moment that they knew him as raised from the dead and exalted to God. The old original traditions continued of course to exercise influence and could never be entirely eliminated. But soon and to an increasing extent the person whose Messianic consciousness of mission was determined by the conception that he was the Christ as Christus *designatus*, was displaced by that of the Messiah who had already appeared. His life and activity became the epiphany of a heavenly being who had descended to earth ready made, who concealed himself in the flesh, who emptied himself, but who was for that very reason something quite different from a claimant to a throne and a kingdom. This later Christology spread like a veil over the old traditional material, blurred its contours, and influenced its handing on and retelling.

The result is obvious: the conceptions of a kingdom that had already dawned, and the words of Christ which refer to it, were necessarily pushed into the background. Christ's activity could no longer be a part and a consequence of the kingdom of God which came of itself. And this very kingdom could no longer be an object of real interest. If one still spoke of the kingdom of God, one thought now of the heaven into which we should enter, of the future day that awaits us. That which had already come and was already present was the regnum Christi, i.e. the kingdom of the Risen Lord; no longer was it really the regnum Dei. The regnum Christi intervened, determining the present and drawing attention to itself.

2. This regnum Christi was at the same time the activity and rule of the spirit, which now came as the present gift of the exalted one. It was not only his gift, it was identical with him, for 'the Lord is the spirit,' as Paul says. But the spirit, the pneuma, is as we said identical with the eschatological order itself, possessed in advance, in the form of divine dynamis. Fundamentally, therefore, the spirit is identical with that which the dynamis of the already operative kingdom had already been. And it was only because of a circle which had originated through Christ's activity, and which had had such an experience of the present yet transcendent reality and had been touched by it, that an enthusiastic spirit-inspired fellowship could arise out of it. The experience of the kingdom developed and was only intensified in the later spirit-inspired experience. Of this fact Paul gives a faint hint when he says:

The kingdom of God is peace and joy in the holy spirit.

The experience of the kingdom is related to the experience of the spirit as the implicit to the explicit. But in that the implicit thus develops into the explicit, the explicit and its group of conceptions necessarily also becomes the rival of the implicit and of its more original and primitive images, drives these out of the circle of consciousness and of interest, makes them of marginal significance, and thus they become indistinct. What still maintained a place in the tradition no longer rang true; it fell apart, became associated with other and new conceptions, sank into allegory, or was regarded as a secret saying, for which one sought esoteric keys.

3. The sphere of the regnum Christi and of the rule of the spirit was the 'community,' which gradually crystallized into the ekklēsia or church. It was now the genuine reality which stood palpably before the eyes of its members and claimed their interest. Its existence was, of course, an effect of the fact that the kingdom had come, had gripped men and brought them together, and had extended its sphere of power in miraculous growth; and perhaps that is the reason why the parables which speak of that fact have been preserved at all. But precisely as a concrete ecclesiastical form and idea, the church was now also a competitor of the original idea of the kingdom, and necessarily overshadowed the latter in its primitiveness as well as with respect to its purely mysterious meaning, which was not related at all to empirical structure, organization, and sociological form. Similarly it threw a shadow over the texts treating of the kingdom that had already come. In so far as they constituted traditional material which could not be set aside, they might be utilized as ecclesiastical texts; they might be loaded and allegorized, as in Matthew, to refer to ecclesiastical problems; but in the presence of an ecclesiastical idea that became more and more explicit and fixed they became obscure and of minor importance.

Accordingly, the ancient thought-complex consisting of the original message of Jesus, a complex which itself had originally been a fertile soil for its own competitors, gradually retired before the ideas of the regnum Christi, the possession of the pneuma, and the rising conception of the church as competitors of the original ideas of the kingdom as already dawning, and of its dynamis. What still rises above the surface is like peaks which belong to a submerged mountain range, and which still indicate its scope and unity. Sufficient remains to teach us what Christ meant by the future which, by its secret spiritual working, even now surrounds us and is within us.

CHAPTER XIX

CONCLUSION

THE kingdom of God was for Christ always the future kingdom of the new age, and was conceived on strict eschatological terms. It was to follow on the Messianic woes and the divine judgment. But what distinguished his own eschatology from previous forms was, on the one side, that he already lived in the miracle of the new age which was active even in the present; that with clear vision he saw this as something already developing and growing around himself; that he knew himself to be supported by powers which, as aparchē, were already penetrating the world, and, supported and filled by these powers, he worked and preached; on the other side, that through works, speech, parable, and charismatic bestowing of power, he mediated contact with this miracle of the transcendental as a private possession to a circle of adherents who came into his train.

This is the fundamental datum from which one must begin if we are to see the person and message of Christ against the right background, and if we are to use both in order to grasp the meaning of Christ himself. I hope to be permitted at a later time to present Christ's person and message on this basis and so to deal more fully with his significance.

BOOK TWO

THE KINGDOM OF GOD
AND THE SON OF MAN

JESUS AS THE ESCHATOLOGICAL REDEEMER AND AS DISTINGUISHED FROM ALL MERE PROPHETS AND AS INTEGRAL TO THE ESCHATOLOGICAL ORDER ITSELF

Was Jesus the Christ of God? This is not a question raised by the history of religion, but a question of faith, and therefore does not arise in our investigation, which will proceed along religio-historical lines. For us, therefore, the issue is: Jesus was conscious of a mission; was that consciousness Messianic in character, and if so, in what sense?

This question is answered in the negative by a school of religio-historical thought, which, however, confuses criticism with scepticism, and so becomes dogmatic. It does violence to the sources, and proceeds in an unhistorical manner in so far as it leaves unexplained a datum which even it concedes to be historical, viz. that there arose not a school which handed on a thought complex as expressed in significant sayings of its master, but a church which knew that it was rescued for the eschatological order because it belonged to a certain saviour. The church did not produce, but was produced by, that Messianic faith, and without that faith it would not have come into being.

This school of exegetes declares emphatically that it does not hold with psychological explanations; nevertheless it psychologizes. A circle of people, like the disciples of an itinerant rabbi, were strongly impressed by him. The impression grew into the conviction that the rabbi was exalted from death to God (although the rabbi himself never said or thought of it, for the relevant words are supposed to be products of the theology of the church).

As a consequence, the church appears to have come to the further conclusion that he must be the Son of Man (although the rabbi himself is supposed always to have spoken of the Son of Man as someone other than himself). Moreover, it drew the deduction according to a logic which was unknown to that time. For the people believed that John had come again, but drew no conclusion from that fact as to the Messiahship either of John or of him whom it believed to be John redivivus.

A historical fact requires a sufficient cause. A sufficient cause for the Messianic faith of the church would be that the one around whom and through whom it gathered together had appeared in its presence with Messianic claims. Such claims are present in the gospel narratives and must be tested more closely. They are historical if and because they sufficiently explain the existence of the church's Messianic faith. Their historicity would gain in certainty if the consciousness of mission expressed in them accorded with two further criteria: i.e. (1) if it harmonized with the complete and fundamental import of the person as known to history, and (2) if it corresponded to contemporary conceptions already existing and previously shaped, conceptions with which the message was obviously related in other respects as well.

1. With regard to the first point. Records of any person's attitude, activity, and preaching gain in historical reliability in the measure that they yield a unity of import in such a way that the traits individually reported supplement one another and show themselves to belong together. This, it may be noted first of all, is palpably the case in reference to the content of the general message of Christ, as recorded for us. We have already mentioned this element at an earlier point. The message of the God who has again drawn near, who seeks sinners, forgives, and provides, does not stand accidentally beside the message of the kingdom, merely on account of Oriental optimism (this expression has been seriously used). Rather it is the exact reverse side of a kingdom of God 'quo tristitia

abducetur,' a kingdom which redeems from fear of the devil and all else, dawns with saving power, and is already operative soteriologically. It is not something self-apparent to an Oriental mind, but is the same mirum and paradoxon as that kingdom.

The same thing holds good, however, of the relationship between the message of such a kingdom of salvation and the eschatological person himself who is accompanied by the kingdom in its present dawning. Both belong together. That they do so is not apparent on the basis of some psychological reconstruction, but on that of eschatological logic itself. For the Son of Man belongs to the kingdom of God. The kingdom throws its shadows forward into the present; it is not yet here in power, but is already here secretly. Likewise: the Son of Man is not yet here in his power, but is already here 'before his power,'[1] like his shadow cast before him, as the one who some day will be the Son of Man in his power. And all this belongs closely together and every part requires every other.

2. With regard to the second point: Let us first disregard for the time being the sayings and doings of Jesus which have a definite Messianic form, consider such as do not bear this special form, at least obviously, and attempt to formulate their content. They do not testify to a mere 'eschatological feeling of power'—an expression which may mean anything or nothing. They testify to a definite and particular consciousness of mission; the minimum of expression for it is that which is given in the title of this section.

---

[1] The expression is from the Book of Enoch.

CHAPTER II

JESUS' CONSCIOUSNESS OF MISSION REGARDED APART FROM ITS MESSIANIC DRESS

JESUS spoke of a new thing now at hand, which neither righteous men nor prophets of the previous era had been able to see, but which was now to be seen, i.e. experienced. He knew that in distinction from every preceding period the new age itself was now in process of dawning; he made a clean cut, separating his own time, as that of initial fulfilment, from all earlier time. In addition, he was convinced that the kingdom able to vanquish Satan's kingdom was dawning in his own work, and he knew himself to be the instrument of its victorious power. The divine victory of the stronger over the strong was achieved in his exorcistic activity. The former fact alone really suffices to confirm what A. Schweitzer expressed by saying that Christ knew himself to be in a mystic relation with the transcendent figure of the Son of Man. For according to the logic of apocalyptic the Son of Man is the one by whom the divine victory is achieved. In this connection we must not overlook various other features in the picture of Christ.

1. Ye have heard that it was said to them of old time. . . . But I say unto you.

No *prophet* spoke like that, and it is not merely a case of opposing a new to an old teaching. Rather, the phrase 'but I' contrasts a new figure who was not present before, with an earlier figure who was merely prophetic. And 'I' is not merely the voice of an inspired word, overtaking and seizing the prophet as the burden of Yahweh, while at the same time making the prophet and his own ego

162

secondary; rather it is the expression of the speaker's entirely personal and inherent superiority over all previous authority and validity, over all that was said to them of old time, and over all those through whom it was said. That is expressly attested by the saying that 'here is a greater than Jonah and Solomon.' Jonah is the prophet of the earlier era and represents the prophetic revelation. Solomon is the sage of the earlier era and represents the treasure of the chokmah, i.e. of the wisdom and the Wisdom literature of the ancients. This had taken its place beside the prophetic tradition and also assumed the character of revelation. Both faded away before him who was 'more.'

2. Various utterances are united in meaning with the preceding, and are, therefore, genuine: (a) where Christ makes relationship to himself the condition for the same relationship to God, and where he identifies his own cause with the cause of God Himself; (b) where to the amazement of his hearers he actually invades God's own prerogatives.

(a) The former is to be understood when Jesus requires personal akoluthia [following] in the form of an immediate and complete attachment to his own person, with surrender of house, home, and possessions. Lk. xii. 8 is another passage of similar import:

> Every one who shall confess me before men, him shall the Son of Man also confess before the angels of God.

This saying is genuine, for no church would have invented at a later time a theology making a distinction so foreign to the feeling of the church, i.e. between the person of Jesus himself and that of the future judge. Furthermore, it is genuine because it corresponds to the criterion of unity. The consciousness of mission contained in the word 'me' is the same as that in the phrase 'but I,' and in both cases we have to do not with a challenging thought complex but with this 'I' which makes a demand and that quite personally. Likewise, in the saying of Mk. ix. 37:

> Whosoever shall receive one of such little children in
> my name, receiveth me: and whosoever receiveth me,
> receiveth not me, but him that sent me.

This is a word which no 'prophet' would have said. It
is the manner of one who knew and claimed himself to
be uniquely authorized—indeed, the representative of the
very deity.

Even our meagre reports still bear sufficient testimony
to the fact that the nimbus of the numinous surrounded
Jesus when he came forward, spoke, or laboured; thus
it corresponded to his consciousness of mission. The
numinous nimbus is attested in the impression, i.e. the
surges of feeling which Jesus evoked in his hearers. I have
spoken about that in more detail in my book, *The Idea of
the Holy*, pp. 162 ff. This impression of nimbus was not that
of the learned rabbi or the sage who by charm or profound
words aroused wonder. Some held him to be possessed,
others were filled with 'astonishment, fear, amazement'
(the latter occasionally even when he spoke comforting
gospel words). Both testify the same, i.e. his numinous
quality—we are tempted to say, his supernatural quality.
Anyone attempting to reconstruct history on the basis of
impressions must not omit to take this impression into
account. Perhaps it will not appeal, and this fantastic
element will disturb his wonder at the purity and loftiness
of the ethical maxims of the rabbi. But from a religio-
historical standpoint, however lamentable from a rationalistic standpoint, we are compelled to say that, especially
in an ancient environment, no personal impression is so
strong as the impression of the numinous nor so well
fitted to bind together a circle of those who receive the
impression.

The most definite expression for this numinous nimbus,
which must have surrounded Christ's figure and which
was perceived by his hearers, is given by Luke in v. 26:

> ekstasis took hold on all, and they glorified God; and they
> were filled with fear, saying, We have seen paradoxa to-day.

That is an impression of quite a specific kind. It is the impression that grips and moves men, when in an almost uncomfortable way—the element is perceptibly indicated by the high key of the words—a numinous figure, a numinous happening is thought to be there, indeed we might say where numen praesens is experienced.

(b) There are many sayings which testify to the numinous impression given by Jesus personally and by his attitude to the first disciples, but they have nowhere a greater force than at the close of the very incident of which Lk. v. 18–26 (and Mk. ii. 3–12 and Mt. ix. 2–8) tells,[1] viz. the charismatic healing of the paralytic with the accompanying act of charismatic remission of sins.

The ekstasis, the fear, and the paradoxon refer to the latter, for mere healings by Christ had long been known. Moreover, other miraculous healers of the time were known, and they did not cause such powerful emotional reactions as the heaping up and heightening of the terms would imply in the present instance. This heaping up of the terms of numinous awe was meant to imply that something entirely unique was present; this man had laid hold of the prerogatives of God Himself; he had presumed to do what belonged to God alone, 'to forgive sins,' and the earth had not swallowed him up for it; rather the subsequent healing had confirmed his pretensions. It was that which caused, and of necessity, ekstasis, amazement, and the feeling of the paradoxon.[2] They had perceived rightly. For undoubtedly Jesus here performed an act which pointed back to his consciousness of mission and his certainty of exousia and dynamis, which far exceeded anything of the sort that a prophet had ever possessed. Prophets could view the future, Elijah could do miracles, Isaiah could offer his king a miracle from heaven. But

---

[1] Here also the comparison shows that Luke goes back to older tradition. Mark and Matthew have greatly dulled this uninventable expression of emotional reaction to the numinous.

[2] Of the numinous thambos, the absolute 'surprise'; cp. *The Idea of the Holy*, p. 26.

none would have dared to claim for himself the authority to forgive sins.

Who can forgive sins except the one God?

Thus spoke the Pharisees in their hearts, only expressing what everyone felt and knew.

We had intended to treat first only those utterances in which Jesus' consciousness of mission is not expressly clothed in such Messianic formulas as that of the Son of Man. The passage just cited would then have had to be treated later, since it says

that the Son of Man hath authority on earth to forgive sins.

But as we shall see, Jesus confessed himself—and indeed necessarily—to be Son of Man only after a definite moment which was significant to himself, and confessed it even then only among his disciples. From such passages, the term Son of Man as a self-designation of Christ penetrated only gradually afterwards into other utterances, which as spoken by Jesus himself used nothing else than the simple 'I.' That is true of our passage, as is still plain from the very wording. For the saying that the Son of Man has power to forgive sins would not have appeared as a paradoxon. It was a matter of course that the Son of Man, the judge in the divine judgment, the representative and authorized agent of God, would have been able to forgive sins in God's name. At least it was not a paradox, and would not have required confirmation by a charismatic act of healing. It was, however, absolutely paradoxical, and only credible upon a testimony of God Himself, that this man from Galilee possessed such exousia.

Wellhausen thought that the phrase Son of Man was original in this place, but that it had the sense of man generally. But that men should be able to forgive sins, offences against heaven and against God, Jesus never taught anywhere nor did he even remotely suggest it. Moreover, he nowhere confirmed or proved general rules and their validity by a legitimizing miracle, as would be the case here if he had meant the general statement that men can forgive sins. He meant a prerogative which He personally had and which actually was amazing and paradoxical.

The historicity of the entire narrative has often been attacked. One cannot apply subjective standards of probability and improbability to records whose background is explicitly hagiological. Only by studying the background, comparing, and so learning the kind of thing that happens and that is typical, can we recognize the category or class to which the record belongs, and only then are we in a position to judge its historicity. I wish to say more about that in Book Four, when I shall examine Jesus' charismatic setting. For the present the following remarks must suffice:

The narrative which lies before us has quite typical analogies not only in accounts but in events which are repeated and are historically comprehensible. It is not a general miracle story at all, but one that describes a typical charismatic person, and shows him in the typical union of the charisma dioratikon [of penetrating vision], the charisma iaseōs [of healing], and the charismatic power of absolution. This is a typical union, repeated in hagiology and indeed as a historical fact. Since the latter is demonstrable, there is no ground for scepticism on account of historical considerations, which here as everywhere must be guided in judgment by assured analogies. Scepticism would be only caprice and merely decision according to fancy. The one in whose activity and person the dynamis of the dawning kingdom of God works, who therefore himself possesses the dynameis and the exousias and the charis, and—at a later time—the 'anthrōpos pneumatikos and theios' [the spiritual and divine man], which means likewise the chosen and favoured charismatic, who with the gift of diorasis [insight] also possesses the gift of physical and spiritual iasis [healing] (for forgiveness of sin is also an iasis), and who therefore is a physician of the body and of the soul at the same time, *he* may and can forgive sins, but men cannot do so. These essential connections have become plain by Karl Holl's researches in *Enthusiasm and Penitential Authority*. In their light the meaning and genuineness of the story of the paralytic shines out, and thus we see the basis of the ekstasis and the paradoxa on the part of the observers.

3. What was Christ's Christology? Naturally he had one, for he proclaimed the coming of the Son of Man, and applied definite conceptions to him. Moreover, he used the term of himself. His Christology followed the line of apocalyptic eschatology, especially that of the Enoch tradition, and it was genuinely his own, for it was poles apart from the Christology which soon arose, as was inevitable, in his church. His consciousness of mission was expressed in his Christology. Of that we shall speak later. For the moment, our first task is to consider some other conceptual forms in which his feeling of power, or rather, his consciousness of mission was clothed. These conceptions were not Messianic in the technical sense; nevertheless, they were characteristic of the person whom we provisionally described in the title of this section as 'the redeemer who is integral to the dawning eschatological order.' 'Spirit' and 'wisdom' are two of the relevant conceptions.

(a) Christ knew himself to be the one in whom the divine victory was achieved, and in whom the powers of the kingdom as saving forces were already operative. Jesus himself used the expression 'anointed with the spirit of God.' Luke, indeed, says:

if I by the finger of God drive out,

while Matthew says:

if I by the Spirit of God drive out,

and the former may well be the original expression. But the working of the divine powers in him was understood by Jesus as the indwelling of the spirit. Hence his warning about blasphemy against the spirit, which consisted precisely in failure to recognize the spirit in his activity. But in so speaking, he pointed to the meaning of his

168

person and message generally; he saw fulfilled in himself
the word of Isaiah about anointing with the spirit, as
prophesied of the Servant of Yahweh. Luke placed the
incident early, at the very beginning of his ministry,
cp. iv. 16 ff. In this passage Jesus is described as anointed
with the spirit, as having God with him, as a vehicle of
the spirit; words palpably meant to depict the contrast
from John who had just been portrayed as a preacher of
repentance. At the same time he is not characterized as
one among a possible many, but as the one in whom the
final prediction of prophecy was fulfilled, as the eschatological saviour who preached and brought salvation.
The spirit, the gift expected in the final age, was present
and was in him. He was anointed with it. Accordingly he
was actually a christos, an anointed one, even if these
terms did not yet mean the Christ in the technical sense.

The impression which he made upon his hearers corresponds to this view. Mark says in the parallel account:

> they were astonished at his teaching, for he taught them
> as one who had exousia.

Luke says:

> they were astounded at the words of charis which
> proceeded from his mouth.

And both mean the same thing.

> Charis has been understood here as charm. That seems
> to me impossible. For why people should marvel that
> charming words came from the mouth of Jesus bar Joseph
> it is impossible to see. Charis is grace, gracious gift.
> Accordingly in the present context it is the equivalent of
> charisma, and therefore of exousia in Mark, for this too is
> synonymous with dynamis, with charismatic, i.e. spirit-
> given, endowment of power. They were not admiring the
> charming man, but becoming aware of the charismatic
> and spirit-endowed man, the God-filled bearer of the
> Spirit. That was what they did not comprehend in the
> son of Joseph. Therefore they were astounded and shocked
> at the same time.

169

THE KINGDOM OF GOD AND THE SON OF MAN

(b) The place of the prophetic spirit had been taken in late Judaism by the mysterious 'wisdom' of God, sharer of His knowledge and His activity in creation and revelation. This concept of wisdom was the foundation of the later logos Christology in the gospel of John. (Even Justinian when he built the most magnificent church in the world for Christ the logos, dedicated it to Sophia, the divine Wisdom, that is, to the Christ as logos.) This logos Christology was afterwards developed into a dogmatic theology quite remote from the mind of Christ. Yet it actually had one of its roots in Christ's own consciousness of mission. Christ knew the Wisdom literature of late Judaism (whether exactly in the form preserved to us or in another form is a matter of indifference). He knew himself to be in relation to this Wisdom. In Mt. xi. 28 ff. he speaks in the very personā sapientiae:

> Come unto me, all ye that labour and are heavy laden, and I will give you rest. Take my yoke upon you, and learn of me; for I am meek and lowly in heart; and ye shall find rest unto your souls. For my yoke is easy, and my burden is light.[1]

This saying is peculiar in style. But that does not mean that it is not Jesus' own, for it is a *quotation*, and indeed from the Wisdom literature. No saying could be found or invented which would characterize the meaning of his person and message more exactly than this saying, and if it was put together, as many think, by some later person, he understood the figure of Christ and characterized it with a clarity which cannot be surpassed. The saying reveals one who in sharp contrast to contemporary teachers does not bind heavy burdens, nor, like John, terrify with threatening judgment, but who, as a saviour, invites to a

[1] Matthew unites this saying of Jesus with another given in vv. 25–27. As the parallel passage in Luke proves, this union did not exist originally, for Luke does not give our saying. Matthew found it as an isolated logion and attached it—very significantly—to the other. We must deal later with Mt. xi. 25–27, since it contains the Messianic term Son.

personal and saving fellowship. He does this with ancient
'words of wisdom.' But for that reason the assumption
that a later person interpolated these words is arbitrary.
Here and also in Lk. xi. 46, a passage whose authenticity
is indisputable, it is Jesus himself who opposes those who
load people with unbearable burdens. It is he himself who
requires gentleness and humility, reproaches the haughti-
ness and harshness of other masters, opposes his way of
God to their ways, and knows the Wisdom literature of
his people.

The meaning of the saying is in full agreement with
Jesus' application of the quotation from Deutero-Isaiah. He
knows that he is designated here. Similarly, Mt. xi. 28–30
is a citation from ancient and long-sacred scripture,
and Jesus applies it, like the passage from Isaiah, to his
own self. If Jesus knew the sacred scriptures of his people
and knew himself to be prophesied in them—and that
can hardly be doubted—scarcely any passages could seem
to him to point to himself so decidedly as that from Isaiah
and that from the Wisdom literature.

Mt. xi. 28–30 contains a saying of this class, and it occurs
in the original or in an identical parallel in Jesus Sirach
li. 31 ff. Here Wisdom cries:

> Come to me, ye inexperienced ones, come to school to
> me. What you lack, you can learn here. You are certainly
> very thirsty. I have opened my mouth and taught. Buy
> for yourselves wisdom, for you can have it without money.
> Put your neck under my yoke.

And the pupil of Wisdom in Sirach then proceeds to
confess and offer thanks:

> Look upon me. I have laboured and toiled for a short
> time, and I have found great consolation.

It is plain that Christ had this or a corresponding passage
in mind. His words are nothing more nor less than a
quotation of an old Wisdom writing, presumably known
also to his hearers, slightly remodelled and freed from the
somewhat intellectualistic traits of the original.

The significant thing for us in his words, however, is that he does not summon men to Wisdom, as a mere expert or teacher or even pupil of Wisdom, but that he, like Wisdom, calls men to himself. He speaks in the name of Wisdom, indeed as Wisdom herself. That does not mean that he shared the doctrine of incarnation as developed by later speculation, but it does mean that he —at least occasionally—knew himself to be so much the organ of the divine Wisdom that his own person was identified with that of the very speaker who used the divine voice—a feature which is never found in the ancient prophets.

> Some have attempted to interpret the words of Mt. xxiii. 37 with reference to Wisdom. Since Jesus did not work a very long time in Jerusalem, it is supposed that the reference is to 'Wisdom,' which had attempted to call Jerusalem to shelter under its wings. But according to Goguel's recent investigations, the case is probably much simpler. Jesus went up to Jerusalem for the feast of tabernacles. After working there for a rather long time, he went away. On departing, he referred to his return for the Passover festival, and lamented the unresponsiveness of the people of Jerusalem. He closed with the words (v. 39):

> > Ye shall not see me henceforth, till ye shall say, Blessed is he that cometh in the name of the Lord.

> Granted that even Matthew plainly interpreted this salutation eschatologically, as a greeting to the Son of Man appearing in glory, yet the latter is nowhere saluted with such an exclamation. It is rather the typical salutation given to pilgrims coming to the Passover festival. Jesus says that he will leave Jerusalem on account of its hard-heartedness, and only the Passover feast will bring him back. Here again Matthew has charged with mystery a simple saying original to Jesus.

> The passage is interesting, however, in another respect. 'Gather under his wings as a hen' is a quotation from Is. xxxi. 5: 'as hovering birds will Yahweh protect and

rescue, spare and deliver, Jerusalem's hosts.' But the protection guaranteed by Jesus is no longer, as in Isaiah, a protection against the political enemies of Israel, but against the coming judgment; the words as used by Jesus are of course meant eschatologically. But that reveals the meaning which Jesus gave to his own person in relation to his believers. He is on guard as the eschatological saviour; with his wings he gives shelter from the coming judgment. This reading of the words has a marked effect upon our understanding of akolouthia or discipleship; it is personal adherence to the saving eschatological redeemer.

CHAPTER III

THE NECESSITY OF A MESSIANIC
CONCEPTION

1. Such a consciousness of mission did not arise and does not receive its true explanation from apocalyptic or other historical antecedents, although its forms may be determined by and contained in such antecedents. But for a person to apply them to himself and to think of himself as referred to in them, the first requirement would be an immediate sense of vocation which belonged to the person and his very nature because he was what he was, and which was immediately felt and comprehended by that person. If consciousness of this vocation were present, it necessarily took on a concrete historical form. To one who was conscious of a mission of such loftiness, with these contents, in this situation, supported by ideas drawn from late Jewish apocalyptic, related to a kingdom which was coming and was already operative, indeed operative in him and through him, this form could be no other than that of a Messiah, and determined in particular by the idea of the apocalyptic figure of the Son of Man.

2. We have purposely chosen the vague expression that such a consciousness of mission necessarily had a form determined by the Messianic concept instead of saying that it had to be a Messianic consciousness. For according to the apocalyptic logic which Jesus followed, the Messiah-Son of Man belonged to the same category as the kingdom of heaven and was future and transcendent to the same degree as the latter. He dwelt in heaven and would come upon the clouds of heaven. A man, therefore, who journeys, teaches, and works in Galilee cannot yet be the Messiah-Son of Man. But just as the kingdom, purely future and transcendent, was nevertheless already operative, paradoxically present as an operative thing, already

present as apocryphon, the same held good in regard to the Son of Man. Schweitzer calls this relation of Jesus to the Son of Man mystical. Mysterious is the correct term. We can make shift to a certain extent with the expression: 'laid claim to be Son of Man.' That corresponds to Christ's own conception, for at his farewell meal he said that now his Father '*bequeathed* the kingdom' to him, i.e. he would now enter upon that dignity and power of the Son of Man of which he had previously enjoyed the reversion.

3. To this extent his work and especially his suffering was Messianic work and suffering. To express the paradoxical element of Jesus' idea of the kingdom we said that the future cast its shadow in advance. We can apply the same metaphor to the relation between Jesus and the Son of Man who as such was purely future. Or, perhaps, we may advantageously compare and contrast the later Christology of pre-existence. The concept of pre-existence is an attempt to explain the (fundamentally irrational) relation between a being empirically known to exist, and another being who is in existence apart from and prior to the empirical and temporal world (a relation which is rationalized by the idea of incarnation). The relation of Jesus to the Son of Man was conceived in this way at a later date. But Jesus' own conception was different. The idea of pre-existence was not in his thought. That idea puts a being, a life in (paradoxical) relation to a being which has always existed. We might apply the term 'post-existential thinking' to a mode of thinking which places one in (paradoxical, anticipative) relation to a being which has yet to come into existence. That very conception, though strange to us, was present ready-made, as we shall see, and it was present in the Messianic tradition which Jesus himself clearly followed, viz. that of Enoch's apocalyptic.

CHAPTER IV

THE SON OF MAN AND THE BOOK OF ENOCH

IT may appear fantastic that a man who lived here upon earth as an itinerant preacher should have held himself destined to be the Son of Man, and, indeed, to be already working and suffering as the Son of Man. We are prejudiced against the idea. This prejudice, and not real literary or historical proofs, is the reason why we reject the view and regard it as the fiction of the church of a later date. The prejudice is unjustified, for the conception had had a long history and lay close at hand. It must have come forward and have been seized whenever a man appeared who knew that he himself, his activity, his fate, that confession of and adherence to him, were of decisive significance for entering into that kingdom of heaven which was future, but which was even then dawning with his coming and his activity. That is clear as soon as we test the tradition which supported him and from whose ideas and presuppositions he started out. This tradition is preserved in the apocalyptic books of Enoch.

Here and there in a rather simple and unified basic document they contain a varied mass of strange materials: speculations (which clearly betray their origin in an Iranian and Chaldean source) about the world and the angels, and visions of the supernatural world and its mysteries. The particular subject and aim of the basic document were visions of the coming final judgment, the consummation, the blessed lot of the righteous and the damnation of the wicked, and, in addition, sermons and exhortations. The book is written for Jews and deals with the final deliverance of the Jewish people, but as against this nationalistic viewpoint the general contrast between righteous and wicked had long since moved into the fore-

176

ground. It was completed at the latest about the middle of the last century before Christ, and, as Beer says, 'it points to north Palestine' as its place of origin. It makes the impression of being a writing belonging to special circles, in which Enoch, if not actually already the hero of a cult, was the master and saint of a special religious sect. The book is found in two forms: an older, which never once mentions the speculations about Son of Man, but preserves instead other interesting speculative materials;[1] and a later, into which a mature speculation on the Son of Man suddenly breaks.[2] This literature is only interesting in regard to our present discussion because of its idea of the Son of Man, and particularly the idea of his relation to Enoch himself. But we shall now begin again at the point where we discontinued on page 44, paragraph 13, and avoided breaking up the treatment of the book of Enoch. We must give somewhat more detailed attention to the Iranian substrata of this literature, even if they have no special relation to our present question. At the same time we must bring out some features which are eschatological without being specifically Messianic, in order to show the more general connection of Christ's world of thought with the tradition contained in Enoch.

1. Enoch, the saint of hoary antiquity mentioned in Gen. v. 23, who was translated alive to heaven, has now become the preacher of the coming world judgment. The ancient myth in Gen. vi of the sons of God who came to earth to woo the daughters of men has been changed into a doctrine of the fallen angels and their ungodly conflict, a doctrine in particular of Azazel (= Satan) and his hosts. Behind and through this doctrine we can see clearly the

[1] The book of Enoch as preserved in Slavonic, German translation by Nathanael Bonwetsch, in *Texte und Untersuchungen zur Geschichte der altchristlichen Litteratur*, vol. 44, part 2. Cited as Sl. En. according to the pagination in Bonwetsch's translation.

[2] German translation by C. Beer, in *Die Apokryphen und Pseud-epigraphen des Alten Testamentes*, vol. ii, Tübingen, 1900. Cited as En. by chapter and verse. [See also Charles, *Apocrypha and Pseud-epigrapha of the Old Testament*, vol. ii.—TRANSLATOR.]

Iranian conflict of Ahriman and his hosts with Ormuzd and his yazatas. The angels of God, which are manifestly dependent on the good spirits of Ahura, and especially the six or sometimes seven great archangels, stand over against the fallen angels, and like them have their special spheres of authority.

Enoch is a preacher, and chapters xcii ff. contain a real book of sermons. Other hortatory discourses occur throughout the entire writing. They lack the elegance and charm of the parables of Jesus, but Jesus' maxims are plainly related to and dependent on this literature in style and construction. Moreover, the content of many sayings of Jesus is related to those of Enoch and some may almost appear as quotations.

2. The real basic theme of the book is given by its first verses, En. i. 3 ff.:

> The great Holy One (= God)[1] will march forth from his dwelling, and the God of the world will appear on Mount Sinai; he will become visible with his hosts and in the strength of his power appear from heaven. Then will all fear, the watchers will quake, and great fear and anguish will seize them unto the ends of the earth. The high mountains will be shaken; they will fall and pass away; the hills will sink[2] and melt in the flame as wax

---

[1] In the Old Testament also, Yahweh is at times called 'the Holy One of Israel,' particularly in Isaiah. (Only in later times is the term 'the holy ones'* also a name for the angels.) But this titular introduction of God as 'the great Holy One' is nevertheless somewhat surprising from the viewpoint of ancient Israelite style of speaking. It is, however, at once intelligible on the basis of mazdayasnian terminology. The genus to which Ahura belongs is that of the yazatas generally. Yazata, literally 'the one worthy of offerings,' can only be translated in Hebrew by qādosh. Yazatas are the supernatural venerable beings as a whole, the qaddishim. Yazata is therefore the obvious title for Ahura also. At the same time, as unique and as creator of all other yazatas, he is superior to them all in greatness, and in accordance with this double relationship could not be introduced with a better and a more technical characterization of his nature than as 'the great Yazata' = 'the great Holy One.'

[2] The earth is levelled up. That is part of Iranian eschatology.

before fire . . . and a judgment will take place over all. But with the righteous he will make peace and he will guard the elect. Grace will reign over them and they will all belong to God . . . and the light of God will shine upon them.

3. But the preacher is also the seer, cp. ch. xxxvii ff. Like Christ in Mt. xi. 27 he proudly claims a unique wisdom and knowledge, which have been bestowed upon him above all other men:

> Up to the present time there has never been bestowed by the Lord of Spirits such wisdom as I with my insight have received according to the good pleasure of the Lord of Spirits.

We do not really know at first whether it is only in the future or already in the present, but he looks at the dwellings of the righteous and holy ones. As a Jew he is thinking of those justified in the future judgment. But clearly a foreign trait is intermingled; in particular, the holy ones are mighty, active, and also primordial beings:

> they entreated, made intercession, and prayed for the children of men. Righteousness flowed like water from them and mercy like dew upon the earth. Thus it is among them from everlasting to everlasting.

These are not merely persons justified in the final judgment. In Jewish disguise they are the eastern pitaras and the Iranian fravashis in the spiritual world which preceded the earthly world. They are born of an original cult of manes and ancestors and are protective beings belonging to yonder world. Even in the religion of Zoroaster they were given a peculiar theological form, but also in Enoch they show some traits which do not fit in with the system. At this point Enoch also sees a strange and peculiar figure:

> the elect one of righteousness and faithfulness. I saw his dwelling under the wings of the Lord of Spirits. All righteous and elect ones glitter before him with the glow of fire.

A strange figure, quite certainly not born of Israelite conceptions, he is a high heavenly being, beneath the highest God, but in intimate connection with Him and surrounded by heavenly beings belonging to Him. He is merged into Jewish thought as the elect, and as a type of 'righteousness and faithfulness,' just as previously ancient fravashi figures were merged and explained as the souls of those formerly justified. Here, too, one cannot be sure at first whether this elect one will only exist in the future or whether, already become actual, he now dwells in heaven.

4. In ch. xl, Enoch sees God 'the Lord of Spirits' Himself, surrounded by His court, praised by four angels. The 'never sleeping ones' are to be distinguished from them. They too are angelic beings, 'spirits,' and their designation again is instructive. It is characteristic of the divine beings of the Aryan east that their eyes are always open, indeed that they never once blink. But still more characteristic is the name of God Himself: Lord of Spirits, which henceforth recurs continually as the real term for God. It is also said of Him:

He who fills the world with spirits.

This Lord of Spirits did not originate from the idea of Yahweh. Quite obviously He is the late Iranian Ahura. Spirit and spirits (Sanskrit, manyu and manas), like yazata, are technical expressions for the heavenly beings which are with Ahura in his spiritual creation and are before him; they refer to the six or seven great yazatas themselves and the accompanying host. They include also and in particular the fravashis of men which were created by Ahura as spiritual beings in his first spiritual creation. The empirical men of this world with body and soul are their earthly counterparts, and they only come into existence because and in so far as their fravashis, i.e. their spiritual, pre-earthly counterparts, are in the spiritual world with Ahura. (Therefore it can be said, even if the terms are not quite exact: 'he who fills the world with spirits.')

180

The conception of the fravashi as the counterpart in the other world of the empirical man recurs in the New Testament, when the maid Rhoda in Acts xii. 13 sees Peter. She believes him to be in prison, and upon seeing him thinks that she has seen his angel, i.e. the higher spirit-being associated with him. And it recurs likewise with Jesus himself, when he utters a warning against despising children, Mt. xviii. 10:

> for their angels always behold the face of my father in heaven.

These angels were indeed guardian angels, but the Iranian spiritual beings were also the guardian beings of their empirical and earthly counterparts. The angels of the children are also the spiritual counterparts of the children themselves. The otherwise strange argument receives a clear meaning only when considered in this light. To despise a child meant also to despise in him the noble being which always stood before the face of God, just as the Iranian spiritual beings were always with Ahura and in his presence.

In my view also, the name 'Lord of Spirits' should have a definitely eschatological undertone, and that again would fit the figure of Ahura. Ahura is a lord of spirits in quite a technical sense, in so far as the souls of the dead go to him and to his heavenly paradise through the judgment at the Cinvat bridge. Thus the spirits of the righteous, the holy, and the forefathers who have fallen asleep, are with the Lord of Spirits, and the entire tendency of the book of Enoch is to speak of God as the one who brings judgment upon the spirits. He conducts the judgment of the spirits, the judgment which in distinction from all present judgments will one day befall the spirits, the great judgment of souls at the end of the world. Later, the eschatological significance of the term 'Lord of Spirits' becomes still clearer.

5. The first of the four angels praises the Lord of Spirits Himself. Immediately after Him there comes again as object of praise that strange elect one (v. 5) in close

union with the other elect ones, and both are kept with the Lord of Spirits. The purpose of what is kept is only realized at the end, but it must already exist in some way and some place. Hence the elect one must be conceived as already existing.

Soon the seer looks also at the chshathram, the kingdom:

> after that I saw all the secrets of heaven, how the kingdom was divided, and how the actions of men were weighed upon the balance.

The kingdom is here a realm, for he sees in it 'the dwellings of the elect and the dwellings of the holy ones.'[1] The balance is Rashnu's, who together with Mithra and Sraosha at the Cinvat bridge, high in the air, tests and judges souls. It is the 'balance of the *spirits*, which does not err a hair's breadth for the sake of any man; it accounts princes and kings like the most miserable of men.' The conception of the balance of the *spirits* also points to the meaning of Lord of Spirits that we have suggested.

6. In that region above he also looked at 'Wisdom.' She had formerly descended to find her place among men, but when she found no dwelling place with them,

---

[1] Cf. Sl. En., p. 3:

> that he might see the dwellings of the Most High and (those) of the royal realm of the very wise God.

This 'royal realm of God' is clearly the heavenly world itself, as in the Wisdom of Solomon, x. 10. Obviously the kingdom in the latter passage is also eschatologically conceived; in Sl. En., p. 3, it is only the kingdom of God in heaven and as such.

Concerning the passage Sl. En., p. 3, we note further that it speaks of the royal realm of the very wise God. There was no special reason for emphasizing the wisdom of God. Why is the kingdom nevertheless and in manifestly titular manner called 'the kingdom of the very wise God'? 'The wise God' is literally Ahura Mazdā, and his chshathra cannot be otherwise designated in a title than as 'the kingdom of the very wise God.'

she returned to her place and took her seat among the angels (ch. xlii).

In Pahlavi Yasna xxxii. 4*c*, we read of wisdom:

> they (the godless) drive away Ahura Masda's wisdom and likewise his righteousness.

Then follows in ch. xlv–lvii a more detailed description of the judgment, what happens in it and what follows on it. First in xlv. 3, a prediction:

> On that day my elect will sit upon the throne of glory and make a selection among their deeds. . . . I will transform heaven and make it an eternal blessing and a light. I will transform the earth and make it a blessing.

That is the frašokereti, the 'miraculous creation' which Zoroaster had prophesied. After the mere prediction follows then the vision of the future itself, xlvi. 1 ff:

> There I saw him who had an aged head and his head was white like wool.

This Aged Head, however, is not Yahweh. He, the mighty warrior, is never described as an extremely old man. Nor are we dealing any longer with the original Asura, for Aryan gods were not represented as old men. It is the late-Iranian Ahura, and the traits of Zorvan, the post-Zoroastrian 'god of eternity,' had been transferred to him. This Ahura, influenced by Zorvan, emerges with much greater clearness in Sl. En., p. 23. Here the Lord desires to make the secret of his own deepest nature known to Enoch, who has ascended to heaven for the first time. He had concealed this secret even from the angels, i.e. his own original existence in its 'boundlessness and its incomprehensibility to all living creatures':

> they have not known my boundlessness and my nature, which is incomprehensible to all living creatures, but which I make known to you to-day.

He proceeds:

For before anything visible came into being I walked alone in the invisible realm. . . . And I commanded that in the highest region there should descend from the invisible a visible thing. And there descended the immensely great Adoel. And I looked upon him, and behold! in his body he had a very great light. And I said to him: Dissolve and let something separated from you become visible. And there went forth a very great light, and I was in the midst of the light. And as the light was moved in some way there went forth a great Eon, revealing the whole creation (which at first evidently has the light in itself in a spiritual way). And I said to the light: Go up and fix yourself in the highest region.

And I called a second time in the lowest region: Let a firm and visible thing go forth from the invisible. There went forth Archas, firm and heavy and very black. And I said: Open, Archas, and let a thing born from you become visible. And he was dissolved. There went forth a dark, immensely great Eon, bearing the creation of everything below. And I said: Go downwards and fix yourself and become the foundation of things below. And he went down and fixed himself and became the foundation of things below. And under the darkness there is nothing else.

And I commanded that (something) should be taken from the light and from the darkness . . . and it became water . . .

But from the invisible nature and the visible I created man, from both I created life and death.

Thus we can see light and darkness proceeding as two antithetic principles from the invisible, boundless, incomprehensible primitive deity, and they stand opposed as the upper and the lower. Water, the earth, and the world are results of different proportions of mixture. Also in man the opposites mingle and meet: life and death, visible and invisible. Obviously all this is Persian speculation centring on Zorvan. In this speculation the primitive eternal Eon, Zorvan, gives rise to Ormuzd and Ahriman, and these confront one another (a conception which Zoroaster himself would not have tolerated, for to him

THE BOOK OF ENOCH

Ahura Mazdā was the eternal one himself, and Ahriman was in no way Ahura's partner with a common origin from an eternal principle superior to him). Enoch laboriously worked these conceptions into the conceptions of Genesis. But the eastern origin of these speculations cannot be concealed. It was not Zoroastrianism but heterodoxy, if Zoroaster's pure doctrine is taken as the norm. Nor did it develop from Zoroastrian principles, but was part of those foreign Iranian elements which pressed in from Magism and other sources. In certain details (to which we shall return) it echoes speculations in Indian Aryanism, and it gives further proof that Indian, or rather ancient Aryan, speculative motifs were active among the Aryans of Iran. It is to be noted that the dualism which is here clearly present is at first only cosmic, i.e. on the one hand light and what is above, on the other darkness and what is below; it is a dualism concerned with the antithesis of life and death, but not yet with that of good and evil. (God applies the term good even to the creation of the dark, heavy, lower Archas.) In my belief, this exactly describes the original elements in the Zorvanite speculation.[1]

> 7. With him was another, whose countenance was like that of a man (literally, 'Son of Man,' 'human being').

Here the name Son of Man, which was to be a technical term for the mysterious figure of the elect one, begins to make ready. According to Dan. vii. 13 he is similar in appearance to a man, or literally to a 'son of man.' The latter does not mean that he was the Son of a Man, for son of man, or as we can also say, human being, was not intended to mean anything other than simply man and that the mysterious person looked like a man. The word is used at first only in comparison:

[1] Ahriman in the non-Zoroastrian tradition is not Satan, but either Hades or Pluto. This holds in Mithraic imagery, which did not originate from the Zoroastrian teaching but from Iranian tributaries. Hades and Pluto, like Archas, are gods of the lowest depths, of the darkness, of death, but they are not the arch-fiend.

> His countenance was full of grace like one of the holy
> angels. I asked the angel who accompanied me about
> that Son of Man. . . .

The one in question now not only looks like a son of man,
but he is already called 'that Son of Man'; Enoch asked:

> who he was, whence he came, why he went with the
> old man. He said to me: This is the Son of Man who . . .

Enoch saw a manlike figure, took it to be a man, and
asked who it was. The angel answered: This is not an
ordinary man, but the man

> who has righteousness, with whom righteousness dwells,
> and who reveals all the treasures of what is hidden.

Hence the term Son of Man, as Lietzmann says, is not
used as a title in this instance, but means a man. At the
same time, however, he is evidently a celestial man, of
a quite unique sort, and with quite incomparable titles
and predicates. Nevertheless, these remarks give no answer
to Enoch's further question: 'Whence came this man?'
Indeed, this particular mystery is only disclosed quite
late, and at the climax, in the final chapter of the writing.
Then he is revealed to be the son of the Lord of Spirits,
a fact which Enoch was not supposed to learn at the
earlier stage of the narrative. But the various predicates
in the answer to the question explain why he is with the
Lord of Spirits. The angel himself at once goes on to say:

> The Lord of Spirits has chosen him, and his lot has
> surpassed everything before him through righteousness
> for ever.

That is the reason why he is with the Lord of Spirits.
But Lietzmann appears to me to overlook that fact, that
in this instance the word is in process of becoming a real
title. At first sometimes accompanied by a demonstrative
pronoun, it sometimes occurs alone. The reader knew, of
course, who was meant. And so did the community, and
looked forward in reverence and hope to 'this Son of
Man.'

186

He goes with the Lord of Spirits, because, as the sum total (one is tempted to say as the essential idea) of righteousness and wisdom, he belongs to him and to the 'high, holy, and eternal world of heaven.' He goes with him in particular, however, because he goes with him to the final judgment. For he is the judge of the new age. So say the following verses, 4–8.

8. Whence came this idea of a Son of God, of whom it had also to be expressly said that he looked like a man, that he was the sum total of righteousness, and that he was the coming judge? Whence in particular originated the idea of such a being intermediate between deity and the world of angels and men? Certainly not from Israel. Compared with ancient Israelite conceptions, by far the most striking thing is that the Deity Himself retreats behind a functionary. The divine figure becomes remote and thereby majestic, but also almost a deus otiosus; He has transferred His contacts with the world, especially His judicial activity, to a vizier. That train of thought really began as early as Zoroaster, by introducing the hypostases of the yazatas, the amurto speñtas. It was completed later, when Mithra, expelled by Zoroaster, again pressed his way in beside Ahura. Compared with Ahura, he became merely a mediatorial figure, but that is exactly what gave him a religious relation, and led him to take over almost completely the exercise of the divine functions. Moreover, it was this very Mithra who had all righteousness, and later, accompanied by Rashnu and Sraosha, expressly became the judge of souls. In saying this, we do not mean that Mithra is to be specially understood behind the phrase, 'this Son of Man.' Other parallels from the east might be introduced; the figure of a being who had to do with the world, and who was subordinate to the primary, ineffable, remote, and aboriginal deity is of high antiquity among the Aryans. What ancient concrete figure was once the starting-point our text gives no hint, but it may be regarded as indubitable that the phrase 'this Son of Man' points back in some way to influences of the Aryan east.

9. He is called 'the Elect One.' This expression fits him into the Jewish manner of thinking, which says that he was provided beforehand, and foreordained by God as one that should come at the End. Nothing more than this is meant when we read of him in xlviii. 2 ff.:

> At that hour (the *final age*) that Son of Man was named with the Lord of Spirits and his name was named before the Aged One.

Further:

> Before the sun and the signs of the zodiac were created and the stars of heaven were made, his name was named before the Lord of Spirits. He will be (i.e. in the final age) a staff for the holy and righteous ones.

Taken strictly, the meaning is that he himself would not *really* exist until at the End. His existence is at first only that of the name, which is named before God in the earliest beginning. That would mean only an existence in the ordaining and creative idea of God. But this ideal pre-existence and pure futurity then pass over into a mysterious sort of present existence, as apparent in a strange and vague expression, v. 7:

> The wisdom of the Lord of Spirits has revealed him to the holy and righteous ones, for he keeps the lot of the righteous (viz. for the final age).

In order to be able to do that, not only may his name be before the Lord of Spirits, but in some way he himself is there even now, although with an existence which is only really manifest in the final age, i.e. an existence which is only then fully realized. He is also in some way at work already, and that as a mediator of salvation. Thus we read in xlix. 1:

> Wisdom is poured out like water, and glory never ceases before him from eternity to eternity. For in him dwell the spirit of wisdom and the spirit of him who gives insight, and the spirit of instruction and of power, and the spirit of those who have fallen asleep in righteousness.

Obviously, the latter can only take place if he already is present in some mysterious way with the Lord of Spirits. In that case the other utterances are somehow valid of him now. Then again, he is conceived even now as a source of wisdom, righteousness, and power. Indeed, it follows that men know him in some way even now, and experience his working. Verse 7 seems to be explicit:

> The wisdom of the Lord has revealed him to the righteous and holy ones.

There are already righteous and holy ones who know of Him. Indeed, the most noteworthy thing is that

> in him dwells the spirit of those who have fallen asleep in righteousness.

That can only mean that their spirit enters into Him to be kept there till the End.

These latter words are, in fact, gnostic and mystical. Like broken fragments they suggest the no longer recognizable, larger whole of some mythical conception. Few would think that anything of the kind could enter the mind of an Israelite. But on Aryan soil the conception that the soul after death enters into its ishta-devatā goes far back into Vedic times. Thus the believer in Vishnu enters into Vishnu, indeed into Vishnu's (spiritual) body, not in order to be lost in it, but really in order to dwell in it.

10. The transformation comes at the End with the 'Elect One' (ch. 1). It is the frašokereti. Paul speaks of it when he says:

> all will be changed.

The transformation concerns the entire world, but it concerns especially the righteous and elect; thus in ch. li:

> All will become angels in heaven

(As Christ says:

> they will be as the angels.)

189

And then, according to ch. li. 3:

> the elect one will sit upon *my* throne . . . for the Lord of Spirits has granted it to him and has glorified him.

That means: now 'he inherits the kingdom of his Father,' cp. Lk. xxii. 29 where Christ says the same of himself and enters into his glory. Further, lii. 4:

> All this that you have seen serves to demonstrate the sovereignty of his anointed, that he may be strong and mighty upon earth.

This passage obviously completes the synthesis between the eastern idea of the transcendent celestial being and the real Messianic idea of ancient Israel. The Son of Man is also the Christ. Traits of the Israelite Messianic ideal were then loosely attached to his portrait. Thus in ch. lvi–lvii prophecies mingle the transcendent world catastrophe with the final political fortunes of Israel and Jerusalem, and with the return of the scattered tribes, and these prophecies are immediately conjoined with the above remarks about the anointed one. It is the same mixture of naïve popular eschatology with transcendent celestial eschatology, which recurs in characteristic form in Christ's eschatology. Here again Christ continues the tradition which he generally recognizes.

11. In ch. liv. the great final battle against Ahriman appears in Jewish garb:

> These implements are prepared for the hosts of Azazel to seize them and cast them into the abyss of complete damnation. With rough stones will they cover their jaws, as the Lord of Spirits commanded. Michael, Gabriel, Raphael, Phanuel will seize them on that great day and cast them into the burning furnace, that the Lord of Spirits may take vengeance for their unrighteousness, because they became subject to Satan and misled the dwellers of earth.

It is not the Son of Man but the Lord of Spirits Himself who, through His angels, achieves this victory. The Son of Man only judges (lv. 4). Just as Ahura's messengers Vohu mano, Sraosha, and their fellow-warriors conquer Ahriman and his evil spirits, so now the Lord of Spirits through his 'angels of the presence' conquers Azazel and his hosts. The figure of Ahriman is here disguised as Azazel.

In Israel the latter was no 'devil' or prince of devils, but an ancient wilderness numen of a sinister sort, still found in Lev. xvi. 8, and strangely parallel to Yahweh himself. Two sacrificial rams are divided by lot between Yahweh and Azazel. Both are expiatory rams. The one is offered to Yahweh, the other is dispatched alive into the wilderness for Azazel. Such strange numina were only later transformed into devils (as even Ahriman was transformed into a devil only by the Asurians). In this way, the ancient wilderness numen received the rank of the enemy of God, a rank to which it had no original claim. Satan, as God's great radical enemy, did not originate from Azazel nor come from Israel. He was inherited from Aryan Persia.

12. Chapters lxi and lxii then recount the solemn installation of the elect one upon the throne of his glory, the weighing of all deeds in the balance (of Rashnu), and the terrors and the blessings which accompany his judgment. Chapter lxii. 14 gives the words which later become important for understanding Christ's Messianic act in conducting the Lord's Supper:

> The Lord of Spirits will dwell above them, and they will eat with that Son of Man, and lie down and rise up unto all eternity.

Verse 16 follows at once and presents the metaphor, recurring in Paul's eschatology, of the garment with which we are to be clothed, a metaphor known to be of eastern origin:

> they will be clothed with the garment of glory. And this is to be your garment: a garment of life near the Lord of Spirits. Your garments will not grow old and your glory will not pass away from before the Lord of Spirits.

191

13. In ch. lxii. 6 we read further of the Son of Man:

> The kings and the mighty ones . . . will praise him who rules over all,

in the final age,

> who was hidden. For the Son of Man was previously hidden, and the Most High kept him before his power.

'Before his power,' i.e. before the power was bestowed upon him at the end of days. Hence the existence of the Son of Man was twofold; on the one hand, he will exist in the future 'with power,' and on the other hand, he has not yet come 'with power,' but is still hidden with God 'before his power.' In the gospel this distinction recurs in reference to the kingdom which exists already but only comes at a future day 'with power.' Further:

> and has revealed him to the elect ones.

That is striking. The mighty ones know nothing of him, and he is still hidden with God, but the elect already know of him 'before his power,' for he is already revealed to them in spite of his concealment. The passage throws a light on the manner in which Jesus speaks of himself as Son of Man. The world does not learn his secret; as Son of Man he is hidden from the world, but God has already revealed the secret to the circle of His elect. Compare the words of Christ:

> Blessed art thou, Simon bar-Jonah. For flesh and blood have not revealed this to thee, but my Father in heaven.

Here the Most High had really revealed the Son of Man 'before his power' to the elect. Flesh and blood had not revealed it, nor had Jesus. For it was not the part of the Son of Man to reveal himself, but that of the Most High. The latter conceals the Son of Man, and He alone reveals him, and reveals him 'before his power,' not to all the world, but to the elect. That is the logic of Enoch's apocalyptic. Christ's attitude is in harmony with it.

192

14. The visions of the Son of Man, now also named 'Man's Son' without change of meaning, conclude with a solemn finale in lxix. 26 ff.:

> He seated himself upon the throne of his glory and the sum of judgment was given over to him, the Son of Man.

One sees how the phrase is here actually isolated and that it has become a title.

> And he causes sinners, and those who have misled the world, to vanish and be destroyed. All their works vanish from the surface of the earth. From now on there will no longer be anything corruptible.

He does the work of the Saoshyant, the 'adjuturus,' the coming helper and saviour whom Zoroaster had predicted. He saves in that he utterly expels God's enemy at the End, and in that he also causes everything corruptible to vanish from the surface of the earth.

> For the Man's Son has appeared and has seated himself upon the throne of his glory and all evil will vanish and pass away from his presence. But the word of the Man's Son will be mighty before the Lord of Spirits.

'But my words shall not pass away,' says Christ.

15. A strange tissue of mythical ideas and consequences rises before our view in this figure of the Son of Man. These ideas and consequences were originally distinct, and the object of religio-historical research is to discover the constitutive elements by analysis and derivation. On the one hand, there is a human yet supernatural intermediate being introduced between the highest deity who is situated at a distance from world and men; on the other side are the world and mankind. There is a warrior, derived from ancient myths of conflicts between gods and demons; a judge developed from old legends of judges of souls and a judgment of souls; a conception of a menacing final judgment; also an adjuturus and Saoshyant for those standing on the side of the gods against the demons; a matrix of ancient Israelite and popular eschatology; a

mingling of gods and a syncretism in times of contact between peoples and religions—that is how the 'science of comparative religion' sees it.

But the science of comparative religion would be a farce if it could do nothing more than carry on this analysing and see only the strangeness and not also the greatness and depth of the imagery. Syncretism? There is more here than syncretism. Here, arising from the living incentive due to the contact of two religious worlds in creative synthesis, a religious conception has originated which is really a conception, a vital conceiving, not a dead agglomeration of ideas. It is not merely a strange, but a quite wonderful, figure that arises, that of deity, highly exalted by sacrosanctitas, therefore untouchable, unapproachable, far from the sinful world; foreseeing from eternity and revealing in His own time the mediating figure of the Son. The latter is the sum total of the highest righteousness and wisdom, as well as a source of righteousness, of wisdom, of light, and of blessedness for those 'who hope in his name'; a saviour 'of most gracious countenance,' and one who is formed 'like a child of men,' both near to men and accessible to them; a saviour for the hopeful and obedient; a personal surety for the future and eternal salvation. Salvation as a future sojourn in his kingdom, and the latter as inner fellowship, 'to eat with him and stand up and lie down eternally'; his name already revealed, so that he who has hope lifts his eye to him even now, and he who hopes is certain even now of the salvation of those 'who are saved in his name'; a saviour-religion in the bud, and on the very point of bursting open; in fantastic apocalyptic dress, but more than fantastic apocalyptic; a stern message of looming judgment, and yet in its essence good news; a vestment of conceptions, worthy and kingly, and fully ready for the Coming One who in his inmost nature knows himself called to wear it.

16. Chapter 1 had spoken of the frašokereti, of the transformation for the holy and elect who shall experience the final age while yet alive. The righteous who fall asleep

previously enter at first, as we saw above, with their spirit into the Elect One Himself. The holy ones of the Final Age will be clothed with the garment of splendour as will those already fallen asleep. The splendour is the doxa, the glory.

This conception of clothing with a garment of splendour does not in itself lead to the idea of a revivification of the body and a reclothing with the abandoned body, but that of clothing with a radiant, fine, divine, texture of light instead of the earthly body. In Indian eschatology (which knows no resurrection) the corresponding feature is the šuddhasattva, the 'element of the pure,' which is also conceived as radiant. The soul is clothed with this when, having ascended through the different spheres to the divine throne, it has taken and passed its examination in faith. Then, in the same way, it receives a body, yet (as with Paul) not the material body of its earthly existence, but in very fact a spiritual body.

Such conceptions therefore do not bear the character of a corporeal but a spiritual eschatology. Only the latter corresponds to ancient Aryan tradition. Analogy says plainly that it was at first presupposed even by Zoroaster; for in his view also the disembodied soul receives individual judgment when it ascends to the Cinvat bridge in the air, and having received its verdict, it enters into paradise.

But Zoroaster is the very one who draws on traditions which were hardly of Aryan nature, and presents a corporeal eschatology which, in a naïve way indifferent to logic, he inconsistently unites with the spiritual type. He also teaches the resurrection as a revivification of the bodies abandoned at death, and their reunion with their souls. It is the Saoshyant who has the duty of accomplishing this awakening in the final age. And from this time it is precisely Parseeism that represents a corporeal eschatology which was before completely foreign to the west and especially to Israel.

Thus it is completely outside Israelite tradition, and

undoubtedly due to Parseeism, when Enoch, in ch. li (here only), presents the doctrine of a bodily resurrection:

> In those days the earth will give back whoever were assembled in her,

this means the dead, as corpses,

> and Sheol also will give back what it has received, and hell will give up what it owes. He will choose the righteous and the holy ones among them, for the day of their redemption is near.

This means the dead, in so far as they had entered as souls into the underworld. The meaning of the passage is obviously that they are then reunited with their awakened bodies. One is tempted to say that they are again clothed with them. This act of clothing then is evidently parallel to the idea of clothing with the garment of glory. For the latter also was certainly a body, but a new body, made of doxa, not the previous body. Two conceptions which originated quite differently are thus interwoven. The one derives from the idea of corporeal existence and also from that eschatology which, even if admitting marvellous changes, yet conceives the future world as a continuation of this earthly world; even the forms of life will continue in the manner of the previous world. Its stage is an earth purified from what is corruptible and evil. But the other conception presupposes a transfer into heaven and into a heavenly manner of existence in a condition of heavenly glory, with 'wholly other' forms and conditions of existence. Thus it says in Sl. En., p. 54:

> When all creation, the visible and the invisible, shall have come to the End, then every man passes into the great judgment of the Lord. Then times will be abolished, and henceforth there will no longer be years, nor months, days, hours . . . but the One Eon begins, and all the righteous who escape the great judgment of the Lord will be united in the great Eon. And the great Eon begins and they will be eternal. The great light will ever be

with them, a great and indestructible wall and the great and imperishable paradise. For everything perishable will pass away, but the imperishable will come and it will be the shelter of an eternal dwelling.

This sounds like an echo of Pauline's words.[1] Here all eschatology relating to corporeal existence, earthly existence, and nationalism seems to be outworn. The only reality is 'the high, eternal, and holy heaven,' of which Enoch has already spoken in another passage. When the kingdom of heaven is the theme, the same accents may be heard; similarly when we read that we are to be like the angels, and such words as 'Our Father, who art in heaven' and 'Thy will be done, in earth, as it is in heaven.' Yet naïve and primitive traits of an earthly, corporeal, and national eschatology are intermingled. Logical eschatology has this very character, for the logic of eschatology is indifferent to all logical consistency.

This intermingling of two fundamentally different eschatologies, i.e. an earthly and corporeal with a heavenly and spiritual, is characteristic even of the Iranian eschatology. It is repeated in the book of Enoch, dominates late Jewish apocalyptic, and is openly expressed in the eschatology of the gospel. Enoch characteristically intermingles ancient nationalistic ('Messianic' in the narrower and stricter sense) and universal eschatology not orientated with respect to Israel or non-Israel, but to men as righteous or sinful. This intermingling is a feature repeated in the gospels.

17. In conclusion, a few more passages where other Parsee ideas are suggested in the Enoch tradition.

(a) Ormuzd created a pure world, and from the

---

[1] Still more striking is the Pauline ring in the exhortation in Sl. En., p. 56: Walk, my children, in longsuffering, in meekness, in ill-treatment, in affliction, in faith, in righteousness, in promise, in weakness, in reproaches, in beatings, in trials, in deprivation, in nakedness, loving one another, until you go forth from this Eon of pains, that you may become heirs of the endless Eon.

beginning the arch-enemy opposed it. A corresponding passage in Sl. En., p. 30, says:

> and the devil understood that I intended to create *another* world, because everything on earth was subject to Adam to possess and rule.

Through Adam's rule and activity, the divine world was to come into being. But that world would not be as the devil wanted it. Hence he set himself in opposition to this plan of God's.

In different periods, according to Parseeism, the battle between the light and the dark is carried on and renewed. A corresponding passage in Sl. En., p. 112, reads:

> because the devil began to rule the third time: the first time before Paradise (i.e. immediately after creation the adversary had begun his opposing activity, just as Ahriman began immediately after the Creation to create his creatures opposed to the world of Ormuzd), the second time in Paradise, the third time he continued it outside Paradise until the Flood.

One sees in this case how Old Testament data are interwoven with periods of the devil's antagonism which occur according to an ancient scheme deriving from another source:

(*b*) Most striking is the passage in the Sl. En., p. 98:

> In the days of our father Adam, the Lord came to the earth to visit it and all the creatures which He Himself had made (in distinction from the creation of Ahriman, which He had not Himself made?). And the Lord called all domestic animals and all beasts of the field and all flying birds. . . . All souls of animals have a place and a fold and a hedge and a pasture in the great Eon. For the soul of an animal which the Lord has made will not be shut up until the judgment. But all souls (of animals) accuse man (at the judgment?). Whenever an evil man does secret shame to the soul of an animal, he does wicked mischief to his own soul.

CHAPTER V

ENOCH HIMSELF AS THE SON OF MAN

WITH ch. lxix the prophecies of the seer close in a brief summary of what precedes. The following chs. lxx–lxxi are called supplements. But they cannot be supplements, for otherwise a 'book of Enoch' would have concluded without having spoken of the thing most important for Enoch, viz. his rapture to God. They are not supplements; they are rather the climax of the writing, and are intended to announce at this point two great mysteries of the utmost importance to the readers of the book. They were to answer Enoch's previously unanswered question, which we cited above, viz.:

who was this Son of Man and whence did he come?

They were intended to reveal a mystery to those who hearken to Enoch's words, and to do so in order that they might hearken to him, the mystery that Enoch, who proclaims the Son of Man, will himself be the Son of Man.

The latter is the point which concerns us chiefly in this connection, and with it we return to our main object after the long digression in the last chapter. The point is of quite decisive importance for the question whether Jesus' consciousness of mission could, indeed must, have been Messianically determined; or whether and in what way he knew himself to be in mystic relation to the Son of Man.

1. The first verse of ch. lxx gives the theme for the entire section which now follows:

Thereafter Enoch's name was exalted in his lifetime from the dwellers of earth to that Son of Man and to the Lord of Spirits.

201

How this event took place in detail is now told in chs.
lxx. 2–lxxi. 17.

> He was taken up on chariots of the Spirit . . .

and indeed at first, as the ancient myth demanded, while
still in the body, and therefore not to the highest place
but only to a lower region 'between north and west'
(from which in ch. lxi two angels were sent out with
measuring lines). One does not really understand where
this lower region is situated. Enoch immediately sees
there

> the patriarchs and the righteous, who have dwelt in
> that place from time immemorial.

The preliminary region is thus a kind of limbus patrum.
Naturally Enoch first enters here, for he himself belongs
to the patriarchs.

In passing we only pause to note that Oriental ideas
obviously shine through the disguise. Real patriarchs and
righteous men from time immemorial did not exist for
Enoch, the ancient Israelite. He belonged to the seventh
generation from Adam. That is not time immemorial,
but a short time which Genesis measures to the year. From
time immemorial, however, the fravashis have dwelt in
the higher spheres. Behind them we can discover, cast into
theological form, the pitaras of the most ancient Aryan
tradition. They are the dii manes, rivals of the gods themselves, for whom Indian thought had difficulty in finding
a place in its theology. They have their own loka, the
pitṛiloka, situated in the Vedanta system above the
spheres of the moon and the planets, but beneath the
world of the highest God Himself, as is the case with
the limbus patrum in Enoch.

2. Enoch is transported while in the body. But he is
more than all patriarchs, and something higher is to
happen to him (lxxi. 1):

> Thereafter my spirit was hidden and it ascended into
> heaven.

Enoch's spirit was withdrawn from the earthly body, in order that he might now be able to rise above the limbus patrum into heaven. It is as spirit that he ascends into the real heaven, but at first only into a heaven still called lower, where God and His Son do not dwell, but holy angels of a particularly exalted kind:

> their garments were white, and their clothing and countenance bright as snow

(as with Christ in the transfiguration scene). In other words, they were clothed with the garment of glory.

The meaning of this intermediate station can scarcely be doubtful after the earlier statements of the book, e.g. 'They will all be angels,' and 'they are clothed with the garment of glory.' Still clothed in his body, Enoch was taken up into the lower place of the fathers. But here his spirit was hidden, i.e. separated from the body. As spirit he ascended to the world where the garments of glory are found. That means, it seems to me, that upon entrance into this higher sphere he himself now became an angel, and like the angels was clothed with the garment of heavenly glory instead of the body. Sl. En., p. 76, proves that we do right to conjecture that Enoch was transformed into an angel. The earlier visionary condition of Enoch, in which he viewed the eternal and the future things, is now described as a celestial journey which has already occurred (from which he returned again to the earth, and later experienced his final rapture). Then we read:

> And the Lord said to Michael: Take Enoch and remove his earthly garments and anoint him with good oil and clothe him in glorious garments (in garments of glory). And Michael took off my garments (i.e. the earthly element still clinging to me)[1] and anointed me with good ointment. And I looked upon myself and I was like one of the glorious ones, and there was no difference of appearance (between them and me).

[1] Hence the conception is purely animistic. The material body must be put aside.

It is plain that En. lxxi. 1 is meant to correspond to this procedure and describe Enoch's transformation into an angel.

3. Now Michael takes him by the right hand and leads him out, i.e. to a still higher stage. It is described by the somewhat vague expression:

> to all secrets of mercy and righteousness. He showed me every secret of the ends of the heaven and every storechamber of all the stars and lights, whence they (viz. the secrets) come before the holy ones.

Strange expressions, which indicate an ever more advanced ascent to ever more mysterious spheres. To these at first Michael is the guide who leads Enoch by the hand.

4. But now a still higher guide appears; the spirit itself. It guides him above all heavens into the heaven of heavens (lxxi. 5 ff.) :

> There(upon) the spirit transported Enoch into the heaven of heavens and I saw there in the midst of that light a building of crystal . . .

and above he sees the entire people of God, innumerable angels, thousands of thousands, surrounding that house and

> out of that house emerged Michael . . . and many, innumerable angels,

evidently to meet the newcomer.

> 5. And with him came the Aged One (God Himself). His head was white and pure as wool and His raiment indescribable.

The strange thing is that He comes without the Son of Man, who earlier, however, 'was with Him and went with Him.' The reason is given in what immediately follows.

6. Before we reproduce it, let us pause a moment to ask ourselves: Whence come these ideas, of which neither the prophets nor the Old Testament as a whole had the slightest notion? It is beyond doubt that Aryan material,

and indeed very ancient material, has been taken over, shifted and simplified in the process, and adapted—not without strain—to Jewish thought. Far off in the Indo-Aryan east, we find the clearest analogy to the process here described of spiritual ascent, of unclothing and reclothing.

In a compendium of Indian theistic dogmatics of later date but going back to ancient tradition, we find the ascension of the redeemed soul, from which I shall here give the parallels.[1]

Having gone out of the earthly body through the fissures of the skull, the soul begins its journey upward. It travels on a sunbeam first to the sphere of fire, being led on its way by heavenly patrons as soul guides; by a cleft in heaven it enters the sphere of the sun, and thereafter that of the moon; it receives new and higher guides, and passes over the brook Viraja (which frees it from the dust of earth). Here it lays aside even the still clinging 'fine body,' which is not material but nevertheless belongs to the earthly sphere. For the Viraja separates the prakṛiti, the realm of that which still belongs to nature, from Vaikuntha, the really supramundane sphere.[2] Thus stripped of its last earthly element it journeys on. Now it is taken by the hand by a strange figure, as Enoch was by Michael, and is likewise clothed by it with a heavenly, supernatural (aprākṛita) body (like Enoch with the garment of glory). Thus it may now enter into Vaikuntha, the real supramundane world, adorned with marvellous adornment, and just like Enoch, anointed with marvellous ointment. It now sees—not indeed, like Enoch, the theological marvels of the secrets of wisdom and righteousness, which are only new forms of what were originally mythological powers, but—a number of marvels. Heavenly women (whom we find again in theologized form with the Mazdayasnians) then come towards it. Just as the

[1] Cp. R. Otto: *Dīpikā des Nivāsa, aus dem Sanskrit*, Tübingen, 1916, pp. 63 and 72.
[2] The 'heaven of heavens.'

great angels of the throne came to meet Enoch from the house of the Aged One, so here the great Nityas, Ananta, Garuḍa, Vishvaksena, who likewise are angels of the throne of the Most High, come to meet the soul. It now sees, as did Enoch, the marvellous celestial palace and the divine throne made of marvellous substance. And it sees Bhagavat, the Lofty One Himself, as Enoch saw the Aged One.

These materials, already abridged and changed, but the same in essence, are found in India in more primitive form not merely at a late period but in the remote pre-Christian Kaushitakī-upanishad: the ascent of the soul, the journey through the higher spheres, the sphere of the moon as entrance to the lower celestial region, the sphere of fire, the ever higher spheres, finally the Brahmā sphere. Here too are all sorts of wonders. Here too messengers from the Most High God come to meet the soul, adorn the newcomer with the marvellous adornment, and anoint him. He must pass over a sea, and indeed with the 'manas,' i.e. no longer in bodily form but as spirit. If in life his mind was directed to Brahmā, he passes over; if it was not, he sinks.[1] Finally the soul comes into the highest world, and soon meets Brahmā himself.

That such ancient Aryan conceptions had analogues in Iran is not to be doubted. That they shine through in our book of Enoch is just as certain.[2]

[1] This judging sea is the parallel to the judging Cinvat bridge. One may conjecture that originally a Cinvat bridge passed over this sea also.

[2] The surviving material has been collected by W. Bousset in *Die Himmelreise der Seele*, Archiv für Religionswissenschaft, vol. iv, part 2, p. 155. It has escaped him that what is here preserved offers but fragments of continuous wholes which are extant in a more connected form in Indian tradition and must be very ancient there, for they have been strongly subjected to theological treatment even in the Kaushitakī.

In the Slavonic Enoch the place between the third and the fourth stage is of great antiquity. It is called 'between corruption and incorruption,' and in it arise two springs. That corresponds to the border between the still worldly spheres and the real supramundane

7. We shall now return to Enoch's experiences. With the highest spiritual beings the 'Aged One' Himself comes to meet Enoch. Enoch says:

> Then I fell upon my face.

And now again something new happens to him:

> my whole body,

i.e. the new one, which he received in the angelic sphere,

> melted away.

Even the angelic body no longer suffices for the high destiny towards which he moves. And what is more significant:

> my spirit was transformed.

A transformation of himself took place with respect to both sides of his being, so that he now had a new spirit, the spirit of power; with which he could utter praise:

> I cried with a loud voice, with the spirit of power,

sphere of freedom from death, Vaikuntha; along this border flows the brook Vijarā. In India the brilliant place Vaikuntha corresponds to the 'shining Garôdemāna' of Ahura.

In the Iranian eschatology a beautiful virgin comes to meet the soul before its entrance into Garôdemāna and leads it in. When asked who she is, she presents herself as the sum of the good works of the soul itself. One easily recognizes her as a theological treatment of the heavenly women who meet the soul in the ancient Indian tradition. They are not chiefly virtues but manifestly heavenly brides. They live again in the Huris of Muhammed's Paradise, and perhaps have always been preserved as such in the popular tradition of Iran. It is interesting, however, that even in Indian tradition a theological interpretation of such figures, which originally were more robustly conceived, has already set in. In the Kaushitakī, the women Mānasī and Cākshushī go to meet the soul as the beloved ones. They are the spiritual one and the contemplative one. Manifestly they too are conceived as the virtues of the soul. For the soul, when it must pass over the Arā lake, falls in and drowns if in its lifetime it has known and thought only about the present, but not about the future; if, in other words, it has not been a spiritual and contemplative soul.

i.e. with the new spirit into which his human spirit had just been transformed.

8. What it is that has happened to him in this way he himself does not know. The Aged One Himself reveals it to him:

He came to me and greeted me with his voice . . .

With His own mouth, not as elsewhere speaking through angels, the Aged One Himself utters the highest secret:

YOU ARE THE SON OF MAN.

Here, in the highest, most solemn moment is revealed the highest secret of the entire book: 'You have asked: "Who is this Son of Man and whence is he?" It is you yourself, Enoch!' That is the solemn installation of Enoch himself as Son of Man; it has been preceded by exaltation coupled with spiritual transformation, and is accompanied by the words:

Righteousness dwells over you, and the righteousness of the Aged Head does not forsake you.

In regard to the words just cited we may note that the Aged One does not say: 'my righteousness does not forsake you,' but the 'righteousness of the Aged Head does not forsake you.' His Majesty does not speak of Himself in the first person, but in the third person.

The Aged One proceeds:

He (i.e. the Aged One) proclaims peace to you . . .

It is the greeting at the installation from the lips of His Majesty, and He does not speak of Himself in the first person but again in the circumlocution of the *third person*: He proclaims peace to you, He, the Aged One, who is Himself the speaker.[1]

---

[1] Correspondingly, Christ does not say 'I' when he speaks of himself as the Son of Man, but inserts the title of honour, 'the Son of Man,' and uses the solemn circumlocution of the third person.

9. He proclaims peace to him

   in the name of the future world.

Why in the name of the future world? Because it is the place and the source of the peace which the Aged One desires for him who has been installed,

> for peace has gone forth from thence *since* the creation of the world.

This is perhaps the most noteworthy of all the utterances. From the very beginning, all peace has gone forth from something which does not yet exist at all, which is only future, which is the future world. If it does not yet exist at all, it is purely eschatological, the final order itself. Nevertheless from its futurity it extends its operation into the present and has indeed always done so, 'since the creation of the world.' Having a dynamis directed backwards, the final reality is already operative. We have designated this as 'dynamic post-existence.'

10. And now follow words which one must read with particular attention:

> And thus it will happen to thee eternally and from eternity to eternity (viz.) : All who shall walk in thy ways, thou whom righteousness never forsakes, their dwelling and inheritance will be with thee and they will never be separated from thee unto all eternity.

Enoch is here recognized as one whom righteousness never forsakes, i.e. the one who has stood the test as a righteous one and has not wavered. For the sake of this righteousness, which he has faithfully practised, he has been counted worthy of the dignity of the Son of Man. For its sake, there is now given him a further special promise: 'And thus it shall happen to you,' i.e. 'the following reward shall be yours.' In other words, as a reward for his righteousness those also who shall walk in his ways, i.e. his disciples, will now be granted dwelling and inheritance with him and in his presence, and will be with him from eternity to eternity. All this is given to him; i.e. a heritage and an eternal dwelling are given to the disciples for *his* sake and for the sake of his righteousness and faithfulness.

As we shall see, that is the rationale of Jesus' procedure in the Last Supper. Upon the basis of the righteousness and faithfulness which Jesus manifests in his suffering unto death, his Father bequeaths to him the heritage of the kingdom. Upon just the same basis, he himself can bequeath to his disciples power to partake or share in him, in his fellowship, and in his kingdom. Nor are these conceptions accidental and momentary fancies, still less were they invented posthumously in the theology of the church; they had long been adumbrated in the tradition which Jesus inherited.

11. We now add the words with which the entire book once closed, in chs. civ–cv:

> Your names are written before the glory of the Great One. Be of good hope, you will shine like the lights of heaven, the gates of heaven will be opened to you.

Here also we find a purely celestial eschatology. Here too both the primitive this-worldly and popular eschatology has vanished. Even the physical element has vanished, indeed seems almost to be attacked (ch. ciii. 1):

> I (Enoch) swear to you . . . I know this mystery (of the last things). I have read it upon the heavenly tablets and have seen the book of the holy ones . . . that joy and honour are prepared and written down for the spirits of those who died in righteousness. Your spirits . . . will live, rejoice, and be glad. Their spirits will not pass away.
>
> Woe to you sinners. . . . Do you not know that your souls are made to descend into the underworld? Your spirit will come to that place where the great judgment is held in darkness, chains, and blazing flames.

The passage explains why this book calls God 'the Lord of Spirits.'

12. We come to the close of our discussion of Enoch.

(*a*) First a few more words about the nature of the

religion we can see developing in these books. The conclusion of Enoch's discourses was formerly ch. civ. 10 ff. Here Enoch canonized his own work. He foresaw that sinners would come and twist his words and write rejoinders. He continues:

> But when all my words in their languages . . .

He presupposed therefore that people would have them in other languages than his own. That may show that several languages and thus also several literatures were known in these apocalyptic circles and that apocalyptic was found among people speaking several different languages:

> copy correctly, change and omit nothing of my words, but copy everything correctly.

That presupposes closed circles in possession of Enoch's tradition, circles of that character existing as societies with a definite constitution:

> then I know a further mystery; the books will be given over to the righteous and wise, and will occasion much joy, righteousness, and wisdom. The books will be delivered to them and they will believe thereon.

I.e. they are canonical literature.

> They shall summon the children of earth . . .

This religion is already conscious of itself as a missionary religion, and as one which is destined not only for Jews but for the 'children of the earth':

> and bear witness concerning the wisdom of these books. Show it to them, for you are their guides, and their rewards which shall come upon the whole world.

This is a missionary religion, which is in the very process of developing as a world religion.

(b) Then come the significant closing words (ch. cv. 2)

which the Aged One speaks and which one might have
expected long before:

> For I and my Son . . .

Here in the closing utterance of the entire book, the
highest mystery of the Son of Man is made known: the
Son of Man is the Son of God:

> will be united with them forever in the ways of truth . . .

The Lord of Spirits, together with His Son, enters into
personal fellowship with those who walk in the ways of
truth, and indeed

> during their lifetime. You will have peace. Rejoice, ye
> children of truth! Amen.

What does that mean? It means that the salvation of
eschatological reality shall dawn even now, 'during their
lifetime.' That is logical eschatology brought to its last
result, and, also, the final sentence of Enoch's entire message, the final and the highest outlook, sealed with oath
and Amen, of a book which claims canonical dignity as
the testimony concerning the Son of Man through one
who is himself destined to be Son of Man.

It means also one further thing, that the Son of Man is
active and operative even now, during their lifetime. As
peace comes from the new age even now, so the Son of
Man comes even now with his Father, in anticipatory
working, in order to enter into fellowship with the children of truth. He is hidden from sinners and adversaries,
but revealed to the elect. We must keep this in view later
when we examine Jesus' testimony about himself as the
Son of Man.

13. The conception of the Son of Man as found in late
Judaism belongs, we said above, to the most lofty conceptions that have ever appeared in the realm of religion.
It is not that, however, which interests us here, but that,
long before Christ's appearance, a certain idea was fully
developed in circles which had plainly been formed long

before him and to which he himself plainly belonged.
The idea was that a powerful preacher alike of righteousness, the coming judgment, and the blessed new age, a
prophet of the eschatological Son of Man, would be
transported at the end of his earthly career to God; that
he would be exalted to become the one whom he had proclaimed, in the literal sense that he himself would become
the very one whom he had proclaimed. But that also
meant that his activity even during his earthly life was
nothing else than the proleptic activity of this very
redeemer.

A man came after John who knew and saw that the
kingdom of heaven was near, or rather in process of
dawning already; that in his own activity it had 'come
upon you;' and that the conditions of entry into the kingdom of heaven were to confess him and become a personal
follower of him. He was supported, not by a general eschatological feeling of power, but by a consciousness of
mission which raised him above the prophets, Solomon,
and the greatest of those born of woman. He lived in the
ideas of Enoch's apocalyptic tradition. We assert that if
there is any such thing in history conceived as a complex
of ideas, and if powerful traditions do offer moulds and
settle outlines, then such a one not only could, but *must*
have known himself as the one destined to be the Son of
Man, and at work even now as representative of the Son
of Man. This idea was the form which his consciousness of
mission necessarily assumed under the conditions of his
age. We repeat: His consciousness of mission did not issue
from such a previously formed idea, but from the constitution and essence of his person. For the historian this is the
essence of a figure and a situation whose uniqueness
cannot be explained; but for the eye of faith it was a divine
disposition and mission. Under contemporary and historical conditions, however, it necessarily clothed itself in
that form. Not only occasional and individual sayings,
but Jesus' entire activity and attitude up to his last
logically eschatological and Messianic act, his action

at the Last Supper, correspond to this conception of him.

14. In considering the question as to whether a consciousness of mission could rise to the height of a transcendent conception of the Son of Man, it remains for us to weigh the following:

(*a*) The utterances concerning the Son of Man in the book of Enoch range to great heights, but the Son of Man is throughout a soteriological figure. He never becomes cosmological. His name was named before the creation of the world, but that also meant that he himself, even as the Son, remained a creature, predestined, and elected. He was hidden with God from sun and zodiac, but neither sun nor zodiac nor the world nor anything was created by or through him. The meaning of his existence and his pre-existence was simply to bring about the final salvation. Hence he who knew himself called to be the Son of Man in the sense of Enoch's tradition, knew himself called to do a redemptive work, not a cosmic divine work.

(*b*) We also repeat that Enoch as Enoch was by no means pre-existent. The conception is rather this, that he, the man Enoch, became and was elevated to something, which already existed hidden with God (as name or as reality), but which as such was not the already pre-existent Enoch himself. We have a remote analogy to such a conception in Paul in 2 Cor. v. 1:

> If our earthly tabernacle is dissolved, we have a dwelling with God, an house not made with hands, eternal in the heavens.

This building is the new spiritual body, which is to belong to our future existence. Accordingly that which we shall be some day, i.e. a heavenly being, has long been prepared in its bodily aspect as a house not made with hands, eternal in the heavens.

(*c*) In the scene where Enoch himself is exalted a still simpler conception comes to the foreground. We have pointed above to the remarkable circumstance that when Enoch came into the heaven of heavens and the messengers of God and the Aged One met him, the transcendent Son of Man, already mentioned as one who had long been with God, was, strangely enough, not present at all. Rather, the Aged One says to Enoch:

You are the Man's Son, who is born unto righteousness.

I.e. the whole conception that the Son of Man was really with God prior to the exaltation of Enoch here vanishes suddenly and completely. Only when Enoch was exalted and transformed was he born; only now was he actually made real. What was said of him at the beginning fully harmonizes with this, viz. that *his name* was named before God before the beginning of the world.[1] For as we saw above, that in itself means nothing else than that from eternity he was foreseen, chosen, and predestined; and that it is as 'name' (we would say as essential idea) that he was eternally hidden with and in God. These are simple Jewish ideas, but known elsewhere.[2] They express an ideal

---

[1] In En. xlviii. 2, the name of the Son of Man is actually given only in the final age:
> In that time this Son of Man was named in the presence of the Lord of Spirits and His name before the Aged One.

'That time' is not the time of the beginning but of the final age of which we now see a prophetic glimpse, and the giving of the name is manifestly the coming into existence, the being born, of the Son of Man himself. With that agrees the word of the Aged One in Enoch's ascension scene, from which one must also conclude that only then did the Son of Man come into existence.

[2] Joseph Klausner says in his book, *Die Messianischen Vorstellungen des jüdischen Volkes im Zeitalter der Tanaiten*, Krakau, 1903, p. 66:
> We turn to the name of the Messiah. The circumstances are peculiar. A Baraitha teaches as follows: 'Seven things were created before the creation of the world, the Torah and repentance, Paradise and hell, the throne of glory and the temple, and the name of the Messiah. For it stands written (Ps. lxxii. 17): His name shall endure for ever; before the sun his name arose. By this name of the Messiah is to be understood the concept of the Messiah. Expressed more precisely, it is the idea of redemp-

pre-existence, which is not only in harmony with the conception that this name will be realized at the pre-destined time by the coming to birth in the future, but which is actually required when a being is in question in whom the eternal redemptive counsel of God Himself is to be fulfilled. They are a simple explication of the Jewish ideas of divine election and predestination for a redemptive purpose. But this conception reduces at bottom to the idea of a chosen man who has been predestined by God in advance and who, in His time, will be exalted and glorified by God; it necessarily came into the foreground in the presence of the mythical speculations of pre-existence, as soon as the world and the speculations of truly apocalyptic fantasy receded from the foreground, and interest turned simply to the eschatological redemptive counsel of God Himself. And that was the case with Jesus. He was dependent upon apocalyptic tradition, but he himself can scarcely be called an apocalyptist. He is completely lacking in interest in the speculations and oddities of apocalyptic preaching. All his interest attaches to the eschatological redemptive counsel of God as such. As a consequence, he has no speculations as to the nature, the how, and the whence, of the Son of Man. He would come, and that upon the clouds of heaven. Whether he already existed, whether he had been with God eternally, whether he only

tion through the Messiah. This idea is pre-existent; the Jewish people is predestined to have a Messiah and to be redeemed through Him.'

Now in Enoch it is certainly not quite the same. It is plain that the basis is an ancient mythological figure, undoubtedly existing from the beginning with the deity itself. But it is just as plain that this figure is brought into the scheme of the genuinely Jewish ideas of election and eternal predestination; these ideas then come into contact with the mythical idea of real prior existence, mingle, and at the end emerge again. Hence the peculiar twilight over this figure; it arose from the fact that the seer really desired, and ought, to see purely future things, but at the same time he was the heavenly wanderer in the regions and dwellings of heaven and here saw realia, not simply futura.

216

came into being when he arrived, and only came into being in that Jesus himself was exalted to his place, of all that he said and knew nothing. He only said and knew that he himself would come as the Son of Man. *Destined* to be Son of Man, however, he was from the outset the Elect One of whom the book of Enoch continually speaks, and thereby actually was already the Son of Man, i.e. as the book of Enoch says, the Son of Man 'before his power.' Thus he could already work, and especially also suffer, as Son of Man, i.e. on the basis and by virtue of his destiny to be Son of Man. The conception of the Son of Man already at work and likewise 'before his power' was prepared in the book of Enoch, as we have found.

15. In conclusion we must note a further character, typical of figures of Enoch's kind. He is destined for the final glory of redemption, but at first he is not known to possess such dignity, and he comes as a preacher of righteousness. A redeemer belonging to this category, however, appeared long before the book of Enoch, in the figure of the 'Suffering Servant' in Deutero-Isaiah. He was conceived eschatologically throughout and was an *eschatological* redeemer; for chs. liv–lvi of the book of Isaiah prophesy and portray the glorious new age which Yahweh will soon inaugurate (lvi. 1):

> Keep ye silence, and do righteousness; for my salvation is *near to come*, and my righteousness to be revealed.

The editor of the book, however, joined this section directly on to Is. lii. 13–liii. 12, and especially the closing verse, which portrays the final victory of the Suffering Servant:

> therefore will I give him his portion among the many and he shall divide spoil with a numerous host.

Chapter lv. 4 points back to this figure. Accordingly he is to be understood as the bringer of judgment and the blessed final age. But this very Servant of God even during his preceding lifetime, is a preacher; most graciously and humbly he brings the besorah of God, and proclaims the message of consolation. But he too was unknown in his future dignity. Rather he was completely misunderstood. Only his disciples recognized him. He was cut off from the land of the living. But afterwards God would so glorify him that the peoples leap up astounded at the marvel which God performs on him. He shall 'live long, and the pleasure of Yahweh shall prosper through him,' i.e. the saving decree of God is to be carried out through him. He will be exalted and will be highly exalted, which undoubtedly means that he himself will be the future king, the king in the glorious kingdom which ch. liv ff. forthwith portray. Fundamentally different though this Servant of God is from Enoch they have it in common that, in both, a preacher of the approaching eschatological order walks upon earth, and is himself predestined to eschatological dignity. A further common feature is that both determined Jesus' world of thought.

CHAPTER VI

JESUS' MESSIANIC UTTERANCES AND ATTITUDES

1. HAVING his consciousness of mission, Jesus was connected with the Messianism of Enoch. What sort of Messianic self-assertions might we therefore expect from him, and in what form?

At first and in general terms there would of course be none at all.

Enoch was to be exalted and become Son of Man; he evidently preached in the power of this destiny, and he proclaimed the future Son of Man. But although he himself was the future Son of Man, he did not proclaim himself as the Son of Man. It was God and not himself who revealed the Son of Man as such. Similarly Jesus knew himself to be the filius hominis praedestinatus; therefore he summoned, worked, and acted as the one upon whom the choice had fallen; he worked proleptically with the powers of the Son of Man, with divine commission and divine anointing; but he did not deliver teachings in regard to his being the Son of Man, any more than did Enoch. Like Enoch, he preached the gospel of the Son of Man, the judgment and the salvation which would come with it; he said that he who confessed him would also be confessed by the Son of Man. Empowered by his call and correspondingly equipped by his nature, he *acted* as one who even now had the doctrine, the righteousness, the wisdom, the power, and the faithfulness—like the Son of Man in Enoch; but he did not teach that he himself was the Son of Man. He acted as the eschatological redeemer and saviour, to join, to follow, and to confess whom guaranteed both future fellowship with the coming Son of Man and entry into his kingdom. He went and sought the lost of the house of Israel. He released those imprisoned by Satan, healed the sick, forgave sins, preached the kingdom, threatened and comforted with the appearance of the coming Son of Man, preached the way of God as the way of repentance and of faith in the new besorah, opened men's eyes to see the powers of the dawning kingdom already operative; all this in virtue of the fact that the power of the future was operative in him and working in advance. All this was his calling. But it was not, and according to the logic of Enoch's Messianism it simply could not be, his calling to teach the secret of his person.

2. Similarly, Messianic doctrines concerning himself were not to be expected of him. It was the case, however, in certain circumstances, that a mystery actually lay over the person, the appearance, and the attitude of such a preacher, a mystery not invented in the church by later theology, but resulting of itself. The mystery was perceptible to his hearers, and, in connection with his preaching and miracle-working, necessarily led to groping interpretations of him as a miraculous figure, according to current ideas perhaps a prophet or one of the known eschatological witnesses. In the circle of the disciples, the conviction ripened that he was the expected Messiah. According to Jn. vi. 15, there were also wider circles among the people who, especially when impressed by his miracles, held him to be the Messiah and desired to force him to assume the rôle of the Messiah-king; there is no reason for mistrusting this saying. In the latter as in the former case the conviction arose spontaneously and not on the basis of Jesus' teaching concerning himself.

3. It is equally natural and to be expected that occasionally, not in the sense of a doctrine of reflective self-assertion, but as an incidental word bursting forth spontaneously, utterances of Jesus are to be found which unintentionally point to such a mystery, and which stuck in the memory of the hearers just because they were at first enigmatic and unintelligible. Thus in Mk. ii. 19:

> Can the sons of the bridechamber fast, while the bridegroom is with them?

This saying was uttered in the spirit of Enoch's Son of Man; he was closely united with his own, they 'eat, lie down and stand up' with him and share his joy. In conformity with Enoch's view, it reckons with a time when the one concerned—without any concrete explanation—will be taken away. But the saying does not teach anything, for it was not meant as a doctrinal utterance; rather it rose spontaneously from the circumstances. It is quite clear if we see that the speaker indeed knew himself to be the Messianic bridegroom, but was concerned neither to give a doctrine about himself nor methodically to suppress spontaneous expressions of his higher self-consciousness by deliberate and reflective self-discipline.

4. We said that Enoch did not reveal himself as Son of Man, nor did anyone else, not even the Son of Man. Rather God did it, and in His own time. Likewise it was not the place of men, nor of flesh and blood, nor indeed of Jesus himself (least of all the demons) to reveal him as the Son of Man. They would have encroached upon the exclusive privilege of God Himself. But Jesus did accept Peter's spontaneous confession: 'Thou art the Christ,' and he not only accepted it but broke out in exultant words about it:

> Blessed art thou, Simon bar-Jonah . . .

Why? And how does that agree with his previous attitude and with the Messianic logic which he follows?

The words that follow at once make it all quite plain; they are as consonant with the situation and as logical as possible:

> for flesh and blood did not reveal it to you, but my Father in heaven.

Here the eschatological logic is clear and speaks for itself. Jesus had no need to reject Peter's word, as he had rejected the word of the demons, for now God Himself had spoken.

5. No matter how insufficient the chronology in our gospel accounts nor how often ruined by displacements and inconsistencies, one thing is clear from Mk. viii. 27 ff. and parallels. The oldest tradition once distinguished in all strictness between a time when Christ did not speak about himself as Messiah even to his disciples, and another when he really did it and had to do it. The two periods were separated by a notable experience of Peter's. Christ now spoke of himself as Messiah to his disciples: he could do so now, for the phanerōsis [manifestation] had occurred from God's side.

Moreover, now he must speak. For now the hour of his departure drew near. If he was to be taken away, then his disciples, who were to carry on his work, naturally must know that he would be the Son of Man and that he would come as such.

But above all: now that the hour of his passion drew near, it was necessary for them to know that he would suffer, and do so not as a private individual, but as the Messiah; and they must know what the meaning of his Messianic suffering would be. Therefore he must speak now. His teaching about his Messianic position became of itself teaching about the divine necessity that the Son of Man must suffer.

6. He neither could, nor was he permitted to, reveal himself to his disciples. But if his work was to have meaning and continue, it must naturally have been a matter of importance to him that understanding should dawn on his disciples, and the hour of their confession should really come, and at the opportune time. This explains both his quiet waiting and the fact that he finally asked: 'But who think ye that I am?'

The issue has been raised whether Jesus here desired to teach by means of questions, like Socrates. This denotes a failure to see that the situation is typical of Jesus. The essence of it is the fact that he himself can teach nothing, but must await the divine instruction; secondly, that in the context of the eschatology peculiar to Jesus, and at the moment when the great final catastrophe of his Messianic life drew near as he journeyed up to Jerusalem, Jesus required to be assured that the disciples understood. That being the situation, it was clearly necessary that Christ should speak as he did, and that he should do so in the form of a leading question expecting an affirmative answer.

7. The fact that the Transfiguration follows immediately after God's revelation of Christ's Messiahship shows the crucial importance of the latter to Jesus and his circle of disciples. Whether it be history or legend, there is no doubt as to its meaning or the reason for its close connection with the confession of Peter. The reason was to confirm the inner revelation by an objective vision as an additional external testimony to a very far-reaching experience. Perhaps it is a legend. But even so, its insertion at this place would still be proof that the meaning of Peter's confession had been understood: a decisive act of God had taken place. God Himself had given the revelation.

8. Jesus now goes up to Jerusalem, through Perea, a slow journey filled, according to Luke, with preaching and instruction. By adducing historical traditions drawn from the fourth gospel, Goguel has shown it probable that Jesus went up in the autumn to the Feast of Tabernacles, spent some little time in Jerusalem, then went once more to Bethphage in Perea, and afterwards went to Jerusalem a second time for the Passover festival in the spring. Traces in the synoptists confirm this view. Accordingly, after the Galilean period there was a second shorter period of activity in Perea and Judea. In itself it would be very possible that since God Himself had borne witness to him, Jesus spoke at that time more clearly of his Messianic work to wider circles of his disciples. And in itself it would be conceivable that at his entry into Jerusalem he had received the homage of his believers

as Messianic homage. But to me the latter seems improbable. In Mk. xi. 9 we read:

> Hosanna, blessed is he that cometh in the name of the Lord. Blessed is the kingdom that cometh, the kingdom of our father David.

The acclamation is eschatological, but not specifically Messianic. For according to Ps. cxviii. 26, 'Blessed is he that cometh in the name of the Lord' is simply the exultant greeting at the feast, and was in general use to greet pilgrims to the festival. The words, 'Blessed is the kingdom that cometh, the kingdom of our father David,' only prove that people exulted to greet the great prophet who had proclaimed the coming kingdom. If they had regarded Jesus as the Messiah, then indeed they must have done homage to him as the king of the kingdom. Under the influence of the later Christology Luke actually makes them do so; he interpolates into the traditional pilgrim cry the words 'the king,' which are an obvious insertion. The original acclamation is undoubtedly preserved in Mark, but does not in itself say that people knew generally that Jesus was to be the king of the kingdom.

9. Doubtless, however, the tumultuous entry explains why the suspicion of the authorities, that they had to do with a Messianic claimant, was necessarily raised to the highest degree. The revolutionary act of cleansing the temple, doubtless an unheard-of attack upon the authority of the officials, was an additional point. So he was seized and delivered to the Roman tribunal as an insurgent, and specifically as an insurgent with Messianic pretensions. As such Rome had to judge him, since, no matter how he might conceive the future kingdom, he had condemned the empire of Rome to disappearance, and had brought into dangerous disorder the masses who had long been set against the Roman sovereignty.

Pilate knew nothing of a doctrine about the Son of Man. For him the only question was:

> Art thou the king of the Jews?

Christ answered:

Thou sayest,

and in that situation Jesus had no alternative to confessing himself king of the Jews. But before the Sanhedrin he confessed his Messianic rank in the form of the conception of the Son of Man as that was the familiar form in this case. He was the Christ, in so far as he was the one who would be the Son of Man:

ye shall see the Son of Man sitting at the right hand of divine Power, and coming with the clouds of heaven.

He was the Christ, i.e. the Elect of God, as the one destined to be the Son of Man. Enoch also would have had to answer in this way if the same question had been put to him in a similar situation.

CHAPTER VII

JESUS' DESIGNATION OF HIMSELF AS THE SON OF MAN

1. THE book of Enoch did not invent the mysterious figure found near God, for it already existed. Perhaps long previously he had actually been called 'the Man,' i.e. the transcendent heavenly man. This cannot be proved directly from the book of Enoch, for here this designation, as a special and mysterious title, obviously seems to arise from Enoch's question as to the identity of the human figure that the angel has showed to him. Almost always he is called 'that Son of Man,' with a reference to the earlier occasion, i.e. the figure that you saw in human form. But the latter phrase bore such emphasis in circles of readers and persons familiar with this and similar books, that when mention was made of 'the man,' with associations of the judgment, the coming world, the right hand of God, the throne, the coming with or upon the clouds of heaven, the words 'Son of Man' had the force of a title; and when an eschatological preacher spoke of the coming of the Son of Man and of his judgment it was known whom he meant, viz. the king in the coming world.

Jesus often spoke in this way; and even did it publicly, e.g. Mt. x. 23 and xvi. 27. These verses point to a figure accepted by theology and evidently known also to the people.

Here also a feature reappears which we already find in, and explain from, Enoch: the Son of Man according to Jesus was not simply the judge, but also belonged closely and intimately to his band of followers, and especially to those who were weary, wretched, suffering, and who were victims of injustice. The Son of Man called them his brothers (Mt. xxv. 40). Their cause was his own cause, and so closely was he connected with these his brothers that what was done to them was done to the Son of Man himself.

At the same time Jesus let it be known, and not only to his more intimate disciples, that in his activity he was the personal representative of that Son of Man. The cause of Jesus was the cause of the Son of Man (Lk. xii. 8):

> Every one who shall confess me before men, him also shall the Son of Man confess before the angels of God.

That means Jesus was the agent of the Son of Man; he worked and spoke with his aim and in his name just as Enoch also preached as the agent alike of the Son of Man and his righteousness, wisdom, and power of revelation.

2. We must clearly distinguish those passages which give full expression to Jesus' claim to the status of the Son of Man.

Such an expression was unavoidable in a situation like that before the Sanhedrin. Here Jesus confessed himself to be the Messiah and Son of Man.

These words are not due to an invention of the church at a later date. From the point of view of the church, they are simply impossible in their present form, because they include a view which Jesus accepted but which was not fulfilled. From the later standpoint they could indeed have been obscured but not fabricated (Mk. xiv. 62):

> I am: and ye shall see the Son of Man sitting at the right hand of Power.

The meaning is that the judges themselves will be the witnesses of the truth of his Messianic claim. They themselves will live to see and know him as the exalted Son of Man, and they *themselves* must then concede that Christ spoke the truth when he confessed, 'I am.' Such words could never be invented from the standpoint of a later community. Indeed, because Jesus' prediction was not fulfilled, the report very soon began to be felt as embarrassing to later writers. The embarrassment is clearly reflected in the accounts parallel to Christ's original saying

which has been preserved most nearly uncorrupted in
Mk. xiv. 62. Thus Lk. xxii. 67 gives first a notably tortuous
utterance: Christ is here represented as having said:

> If I tell you, ye will not believe. . . .

This remark is without meaning, for the point was not
that the members of the Sanhedrin should believe or dis-
believe his claim, but simply to establish what claim he
was making. Luke then gives the following words:

> From henceforth shall the Son of Man be seated at
> the right hand of Power.

That was, indeed, the unchallenged later conviction of
the church, but Luke broke off the real point, viz.: Ye
(i.e. ye judges) shall see the Son of Man sitting and coming
on the clouds of heaven.

It was known that this had not happened, that the
judges had not seen his coming, that the coming was
awaited in the more distant future. As a consequence,
Christ's very pregnant incidental utterance, as preserved
in Mk. xiv. 62, was made into a remark which was completely superfluous in Luke. It corresponded to the later
faith, but was without point in Luke. Christ's original
saying in Mk. xiv. 62 is all the more valuable to us. It is
authentic because it could not have been invented by the
theology of the church, and it gives a reliable attestation
to Christ's claim to Messianic rank.

The members of the Sanhedrin were satisfied when
Christ made the claim; they denounced him to the Roman
tribunal as one who asserted himself to be the Messiah.
Before this tribunal Christ acknowledged the claim and,
of course, incurred sentence, for the Roman tribunal did
not distinguish between an eschatological claimant and
an insurgent. Moreover, a man who proclaimed that a
kingdom was coming which would inevitably put an end
to all worldly power, even that of Rome, was, from the
Roman standpoint, a dangerous disturber of the masses
who must be crucified. He was crucified as a Messianic

claimant and without the Messianic claim the crucifixion of Christ is meaningless. The fact that he was crucified proves that he did not want to clear himself of the suspicion of being claimant to Messiahship, and therefore that he confirmed this claim before the procurator.

JESUS' DESIGNATION OF HIMSELF AS SON OF MAN INSTEAD OF THE SIMPLE EXPRESSION 'I'

1. THE gospel tradition contains a noteworthy fact. In numerous passages when he means himself, Christ does not say I, but uses the circumlocution of the third person and speaks of himself as 'the Son of Man.' He did this frequently when not referring in any way to his future position, but meant simply the man who was then speaking to the hearers. E.g.: 'The Son of Man has power to forgive sins'; or 'The Son of Man hath not where he may lay his head'; or 'The Son of Man came eating and drinking, and they say, Behold a gluttonous man and a winebibber, a friend of publicans and sinners.' How is this fact explained?

There has been much misinterpretation.

Our own thesis is as follows:

After the confession of Peter, and especially in contexts where Jesus was referring to his own suffering and his coming departure, he actually did frequently thus designate himself in a significantly solemn manner in the presence of his disciples. At a later time tradition introduced this solemn self-designation into utterances where the simple 'I' was original.

This view is supported, moreover, by the fact that frequently 'Son of Man' stands in one record where a parallel record still has the original 'I.' At times the change is made according to a general plan, and it may then be quite meaningless, e.g. in Mt. xvi. 13:

Who do men say that the Son of Man is?

where Mk. viii. 27 and likewise Lk. ix. 18 still say rightly:

Who I am.

One sees here how the change in Matthew has been made according to a general plan. For the question as to who men say that the Son of Man is, with the answer that he is Christ, is senseless, because that would be a mere tautology. It would be as if one were to ask who men said that the Messiah was, and then Peter's answer was that the Messiah was the Messiah.

That the circumlocution should be carried over from utterances of quite special character into sayings which originally contained the simple 'I' was obviously due to the influence of later Christology. In proportion as one became accustomed to see Jesus as the already incarnate Messiah who came forward from the outset with a public claim to be such, the exceptional Messianic circumlocution forced its way also into general use and took the place of the simple 'I.' The process was not conscious and intentional, but due to a subconscious motive. This explains the inconsistencies, the number of cases where the change was not made, and the divergencies of the records among themselves.

Moreover, the situation in the synoptists can be explained only on the assumption that in particular situations Jesus really spoke of himself in an emphatic manner in the third person instead of calling himself 'I,' and the fact that he did so is naturally the strongest proof that he was the one whom we have conceived him to represent.

2. After he had asked (Mk. viii. 27): Who do men say that I am, he proceeded (Mk. viii. 31 and Mk. ix. 31, following the intervening confession of Peter) to teach his disciples: The Son of Man must suffer, the Son of Man must be delivered up into men's hands and they will put him to death. He means himself. They are words of the greatest solemnity and of deep mystery. Even we can feel why the use in such a connection of the bare and usual 'I' should give place to the solemn circumlocution. Not this man who happens to be a carpenter's son from Nazareth, not the wise rabbi, not I, but the Son of Man must suffer, or I must suffer as Son of Man.

231

The use of a circumlocution generally, in place of the direct I, occurs elsewhere. Especially in Aramaic was it not unusual for a person to speak of himself in some such a way as 'this man' instead of 'I.' Such circumlocution appears frequently where a person of special dignity speaks to others, not as a private person, but in his official capacity. We found an example of that in the book of Enoch. The Aged One does not speak to Enoch as I, but applies to Himself his official name and speaks of Himself in the third person. Sufian masters occasionally speak to their disciples in the third person plural.

> The parallel of Buddha is noteworthy in this respect. Hundreds of times he says of himself simply 'I.' But often in his case too the 'I'-form disappears. He then speaks of himself in the third person and calls himself by his official name, the tathagata. That means 'the one who has thus walked,' i.e. the one who has walked as one should walk, who has walked the right way of salvation because he has found and taught it. One could translate: The master. Thus it is said here too, and indeed with especial emphasis and solemnity, not: I say, I teach, I do this, I will this; but the tathagata says, teaches, does, wills this. The same phenomenon appears in Buddha's case even when he speaks of his death (which means entrance into the mystery of Nirvana). As he lay upon his death-bed he did not say: 'The flowers have been strewn over my body,' but: 'The flowers have been strewn over the body of the Tathagata and have been sprinkled in honour of the Tathagata, the heavenly hosts make themselves heard in honour of the Tathagata, etc.'

3. We can understand therefore how it came about when the later records were made that the circumlocution was spontaneously carried over into situations or expressions where Christ himself only said 'I,' but which were of special solemnity or authority, and therefore were so much the more easily associated with that solemn circumlocution. The change appears in a passage such as:

The Son of Man has power to forgive sins.

This was done even by Mark, who in viii. 27 has nevertheless faithfully preserved the original and obviously correct 'I.' And we can understand moreover how this process of exchange, once introduced, gradually extended further, until finally it was done according to plan, and at times meaninglessly. Meaningless in truth were all cases where the circumlocution was used in situations before the confession of Peter, and not related to the narrow circle of the disciples themselves.

4. Naturally such a solemn circumlocution instead of 'I' was only possible in the mouth of the person in question and could only be due to his initiative. (It is absurd to say that a community which had always heard its master use 'I' would suddenly hit upon the idea of making him speak of himself in the third person.) But that again means that there really was a basic fund of original utterances of Jesus in which he thus spoke of himself ceremonially. Even the Christian community was fully conscious of this fact. In particular, Christ's appellation as Son of Man is always strictly confined to Christ's own words. If the narrator speaks of him he never calls him Son of Man, but uses the name Christ as was customary in the church. So also Paul: naturally he knew what the term Son of Man signified, and he himself lived in times when the Son of Man was a subject of speculation. His entire Christology, indeed, rests upon it and would not be possible without the speculations on the transcendent Son of Man. But he never says anything like Jesus Son of Man, but always says Jesus, the Messiah, or Jesus Messiah, or Messiah Jesus.

5. The transformation of the circumlocution into the simple 'I' no doubt set in very early, as also its thoughtless introduction into utterances prior to the confession of Peter. Thus Jesus calls himself Son of Man as early as Mk. ii. 10 and ii. 28.

Some have attempted to explain away these two passages, the latter perhaps with justification:

The sabbath was made for man . . . so that the Son of Man is lord even of the sabbath (Mk. ii. 28).

The argument is that since barnāš, child of man, actually can also designate simply man, Jesus meant to say simply: since the sabbath is made for man, man is lord also over the sabbath. That may be correct, but will not do in the case of Mk. ii. 10, as we have already seen. Rather the Son of Man is now inserted instead of Christ's original 'I.' This confirms the assumption we made above, that situations and sayings of Christ that were of special importance were the first to draw to themselves the solemn circumlocution. It is plain that in the completely unheard of, paradoxical act of forgiving sins, which far exceeded all human capacity, the circumlocution might as it were spontaneously displace the mere 'I.'

In Matthew the transformation became even less restrained. It forced its way into a saying like that of Mt. viii. 20. Here someone wanted to follow the master, and he pointed out that to do so meant to follow him into poverty and into homelessness. The birds had nests, the foxes holes, but he, who had left all, and who said of himself in another place:

But I must journey

had no enduring place. Here the mysterious designation Son of Man is of course unnecessary and pointless. But the change was already being made according to plan and the circumlocution was inserted by rote.[1]

[1] Some have attempted to eliminate even this saying. Son of Man is supposed to have meant simply man, and the entire saying is only an ancient saw, a proverb, which has been put into the mouth of Jesus with the intent of expressing the difference in manner of life between animals and man in general. The framework of the story is then merely spun out of this logion. But how could the idea be spun out of such a proverb that someone wanted to follow Jesus? And how could Jesus have warned him by this quite general sentence about the difference between the human and the animal manner of life? How such a saying could have been an ancient Wisdom saying is still less comprehensible. Such a saying might be fitting in dealing with Bedouin or gipsies. (In their own mouth it would naturally be

6. A ceremonial and formal method of referring to himself which Christ used in certain situations, but not until late and only in the circle of disciples, replaced the ordinary use of 'I,' and the replacement became schematic. But that it could begin at all presupposes that Jesus himself used the circumlocution. Its use began in connection with solemn words about his passion and delivery into men's hands. In these original passages there is, therefore, no wavering and no alternation between I and the Son of Man. Here the tradition is as hard as diamonds, and identical in form in all the records. Compare Mk. ix. 31, x. 33, xiv. 41; Lk. ix. 44, xviii. 31, xxiv. 7; Mt. xvii. 22, xx. 18, xxvi. 2–45.

That is how Jesus spoke of himself. He knew himself to be the one who had to suffer, not as an ordinary, chance, private individual, nor as a mere martyr, but as the Son of Man. In other words, he knew himself to be the Son of Man.

7. We must also place Jesus' exultant cry, which Lk. x. 21 ff. and Mt. xi. 25 ff. record similarly in connection with the occasions when Jesus calls himself the Son of Man. Here again Luke is nearer to ancient tradition than Matthew, for Matthew gives this assertion of Jesus about himself prior to the confession of Peter, where it is impossible, while Luke gives it after the confession of Peter, and as made privately in the presence of the disciples alone. Twice Luke records 'and he turned to his disciples,' a feature of which even Matthew was no longer cognisant. Matthew regarded the words as a Messianic proclamation made in public, corresponding to the later standpoint that Jesus came as the complete Messiah and appeared as such from the start. The words run:

still less suitable, for these do not feel their manner of life to be a lamentable burden, but pity the poor glebae adscriptus. They want to wander and rove, and despise the one who does not do so.) To a Galilean peasant, man, house, and home all belong together, and to tell him that he, as man, differs from a fox by having neither house nor home would not be an ancient Wisdom saying but, if I may be permitted to say so, a silly saying.

> I thank thee, O Father, Lord of heaven and earth, that thou didst hide these things from the wise and understanding, and didst reveal them unto babes: yea, Father; for so it was well-pleasing in thy sight. And he turned to the disciples and said: All things have been delivered unto me of my Father: and no one knoweth who the Son is, save the Father; and who the Father is, save the Son, and he to whomsoever the Son willeth to reveal him.

The phrase Son of Man is lacking here. In its place 'the Son' appears as a similar solemn circumlocution. That was the highest utterance about the Son of Man in the book of Enoch and here, also, it occurs only once. Norden has attacked this word in Luke, and indeed the entire passage, as gnostic. They are, in fact, 'gnostic' for they simply apply conceptions concerning the Son of Man to Jesus himself, and the Son of Man, who is the Son of God, does, in fact, bear gnostic traits even in Enoch. Harnack has established the probability that the words, 'No one knows the Son save only the Father,' are only a later addition and had no place among Christ's own words. That may be so, and that would substantially lessen the alleged difficulty of the passage. But it was not impossible for them to be said by one who believed the prediction of Enoch to be fulfilled in himself. The very nature of the Son of Man was an unfathomable mystery to Enoch; one could say equally well that only the Lord of Spirits knew it. And Enoch went on to say of himself:

> Up to the present time, never has there been bestowed upon men by the Lord of Spirits such wisdom as I have received according to the good pleasure of the Lord of Spirits (xxxvii. 4).

That Christ himself held his own knowledge of God to be unique and incomparable is proved by the bold words with which he placed himself high above the revelation given through the prophets and the wisdom of antiquity: 'Here is more than Jonah and Solomon.' (Cp. on this point Appendices IV and V.)

CHAPTER IX

HE THAT IS TO BE EXALTED

As the one destined to be Son of Man, Christ knew himself as the one who must be exalted. How did he conceive his exaltation and its connection with his death? Our thesis on this point is as follows:

He did not contemplate a bodily revivification and resurrection after his death, but that he would depart and be exalted like Enoch, and, from the time when he recognized that 'the Son of Man must suffer,' he thought of death itself as a direct gateway to exaltation. The Messianism of Enoch, which he followed, led to this consequence. His own original words still express the conviction, and it was the earliest conception of the Christian community.

1. Enoch was exalted to be Son of Man. Enoch, however, did not die, but was translated alive and hidden by God. We do not know whether in virtue of his prophetic knowledge Jesus knew from the very beginning about his suffering unto death. It is possible. But it is also possible that this knowledge only came to him later. If so, he at first reckoned that on the arrival of the Final Age and the great eschatological evils which were to prepare the coming of the kingdom with power, God would take him away and hide him until He sent him as the Son of Man appearing with power.

2. From the day when he saw that he must suffer, of course he reckoned with his death and with the idea that his translation, his hiding with God, and his exaltation to God, would take place through his death; and accordingly that he himself would not remain in death but would conquer death. This was his own conviction, and it alone is the basis of the possibility that Peter and the rest believed after Jesus' death that they saw him in

spiritual vision as living with God, exalted to God. But neither alternative signified a bodily revivification or an empty grave.

3. A conception of the bodily resurrection of the dead, of which Israel had known nothing, had come from the east and penetrated into the book of Enoch, although it is quite definite in only one passage. But on the whole the spiritual conception rules. In reference to Enoch himself the matter stands thus:

Chapter lxx recounts his translation in accordance with the ancient legend of Enoch, but in v. 1 we read:

> his name was exalted during his lifetime,

and

> his name vanished among men; from that day he was no longer numbered among them.

These are rather strange expressions, if the point was to tell of his simple removal. 'He was no longer numbered among them' means in itself only that henceforth he was no longer present and therefore that one no longer thought of him; even the expression 'his name vanished among men' does not really mean more. If one wants to describe bodily translation, one would not say: 'his name was exalted.' 'Name' does not signify body and corporeality but the essence of a thing or a man. One gains the impression that the ancient legend of translation was taken over in these verses, but that the attempt was also made to give it a more mysterious and speculative significance. The exaltation of the name was meant to signify something more and something higher than the ancient and primitive conception. The ancient conceptions were replaced by others derived from the mystical experiences of the visionary and the ecstatic. Enoch is portrayed even more clearly like that in the Slavonic Book of Enoch. When the ecstatic enters upon his upward flight, his body remains, but his spirit vanishes in a mysterious way: it 'is hidden,' and the result is that men no longer take any note of his

existence, and no longer know where and whether he exists.
Accordingly, we read in lxxi. 1 :

> Thereafter my spirit was hidden and ascended into
> heaven.

The adjustment to the ancient myth was achieved first
by the fact that Enoch was 'carried aloft' unchanged,
explicitly not as far as heaven, but to an undefined place
between two heavenly regions; then began the concealment of the spirit in separation from the earthly body,
and the ascent of the spirit into the real heaven. Here he
first became an angel and was clothed with the garment
of glory, i.e. an angelic body, and this was changed once
more when his transformation into the very Son of Man
ensued. All that had to do with ecstatic experience of the
spirit, but not with the physical realm. Enoch as Son of
Man had no body either as arisen and awakened, or even
merely as a transfigured but earthly body.

What is the case with Jesus? Jesus, like the Pharisees,
but as distinct from the Sadducees, recognized a resurrection, and, as far as it was conceived by him, it was certainly
corporeal. But what he said in controversy with the
Sadducees shows that in his mind the conception simply
combined with that of a life with God generally, a life
renewed from death. The vivification of the body had no
special emphasis, indeed was not really and necessarily
included in the conception. That is shown by his answer:

> the God of Abraham, of Isaac, of Jacob. God is not the
> God of the dead, but of the living. All live unto him
> (Lk. xx. 37).

Abraham, Isaac, and Jacob were dead. Nevertheless they
all lived unto Him. Accordingly they had received deliverance from the condition of death, and they were with God.
But they never rose from their graves. They had arisen—
if the word arisen is at all appropriate—from Sheol, but
not from the grave.

The story of the beggar Lazarus corresponds exactly.

At death he is taken up directly into paradise, while the rich man at death goes directly into hell, and does not break forth from the grave.[1]

Moreover, what Christ said before the Sanhedrin corresponds. Christ meant to say that the judges themselves would be witnesses of what God would do with him. If he had reckoned on a return from the grave, he would have said: You will be witnesses of my resurrection. Perhaps: You will see me raised again after three days.

> He is alleged to have said something of the sort on another occasion, in Mt. xii. 39 ff.:
>
>> As Jonah was three days and three nights in the belly of the whale; so shall the Son of Man be three days and three nights in the heart of the earth.
>
> The Matthew who said that was the dogmatic theologian of early Catholicism. We have Jesus' own logion in Lk. xi. 29 ff. Here Jesus appealed not to the whale, but to Jonah's preaching to the Ninevites and its effect; this was the true, spiritual miracle, and he did not speak of his resurrection.

We must draw special attention to the words that passed between Christ and the thief on the cross:

> Remember me when thou comest into thy kingdom.
> To-day shalt thou be with me in Paradise.

Is that pious legend? Maybe, but if so it is still more conclusive for our thesis. For then it proves that the conviction still existed for a considerable time in the Christian community itself that Christ's exaltation into Paradise and into his kingdom took place not from a grave but from the cross.

[1] Similar conceptions have been found even in the Old Testament. P. Volz says in *Die Eschatologie der jüdischen Gemeinde*, second edition, p. 117: 'It is most probable that in Ps. xlix. 16, and lxxiii. 42, and xvi. 10, the faith is expressed that the righteous one is received after death into blessed fellowship with God, not in the form of a resurrection but as an immediate entrance into the blessedness of the divine sphere.'

4. This actually was the first view of the Christian community, as has been proved by the researches of G. Bertram: *Die Himmelfahrt Jesu vom Kreuz aus,* in the Festgabe für Deissmann, 1927. He shows that the original conception was operative even in the fourth gospel:

> For the Johannine evangelist the death of Christ did not signify the deepest humiliation of Jesus, but his exaltation to be Son of Man was contained in it and combined with it (p. 211).

On p. 213 he shows that even in such a late writing as the epistle to the Hebrews there is no mention of either the resurrection or the resuscitation of Jesus. We must also note the investigations of M. Goguel in his work: *Trois études sur la pensée du Christianisme primitif,* Paris, 1933; section 1: Parousie et Résurrection, p. 36:

> Jesus therefore announced his triumph only in his glorious form.

Paul says in 1 Cor. xv. 4:

> buried and raised on the third day.

The combination of these words suggests that Paul was already influenced by the tradition of a resuscitation from the grave. But conflicting with that, he had another conception, which was in accord with Enoch's. According to Paul, fleshly bodies do not enter into eternity, for 'Flesh and blood cannot inherit the kingdom of God,' but 'we have a tabernacle, eternal in the heavens.' With reference to Christ, however, he says in Rom. i. 3 still more noteworthily:

> established as Son of God with power according to his holy spirit by the resurrection from the dead.

Christ's resurrection from the dead was accomplished, not according to his sarx, his earthly flesh, but according to Christ's holy spirit. The resurrection of the dead had nothing to do with the sarx, but with what was hidden in and behind the sarx, the holy spirit of Christ.

Lietzmann perspicaciously recognized that the term 'holy spirit' had a special significance in this passage. It is not the Holy Spirit which God will pour out at the end of the days, but the holy spiritual nature of Christ himself,[1] which had been hidden in fleshly covering. This nature entered at death into a condition of death, and a resuscitation was necessary for it to live again. But such resuscitation had to do not with his fleshly body, but with the holy spiritual nature which was hidden in Christ.

Lietzmann does not give proof that the conception of a holy spiritual nature in man was well known, but this proof can be furnished. In Susanna, Theod. xlv, we read in reference to Daniel:

> God awakened the holy spirit of a young man,

and, by virtue of this awakening of the spirit in him, Daniel can now discern what others cannot. What is here meant is the mysterious numinous quality in the inner life of a man which, when aroused from its slumber and its latent state, makes him capable of higher vision. Its forerunner was the mysterious watchman who was found in Israel's prophets and who made possible their relation to the divine secrets.[2]

Paul added 'by the resurrection from the dead' (Rom. i. 4). That proves that even the conception of the revivification of the body was not necessarily connected with such terms as resurrection and resuscitation.

At death man enters into the condition of death. According to ancient ideas he enters into Sheol. Here he still exists, but he does not live. If he is to come to life, he must be actually awakened, and arise out of Sheol from the condition of spiritual death. To this there is

---

[1] In the book of Enoch it would perhaps have been called his 'name.'

[2] At the same time this conception has in itself nothing to do with ideas of pre-existence, and in Rom. i. 3, Paul does not speak of the pre-existence of Christ. Daniel had this holy spirit in himself, but he was not pre-existent.

added the clothing with the body of glory. But nothing of this signifies the revivification of a corpse.

This very conception of a condition of death of the spirit, in which the spirit does not cease to exist but is, nevertheless, in a condition of death, recurs in En. cviii. 4.

> Their spirits will be put to death, will cry and lament in a boundlessly desolate place.

The godless are put to death, and death 'according to the spirit'; they are in Sheol. They still exist, indeed they cry out and lament, but as dead men. Their redemption from this condition could only take place by a resurrection of the dead, but this would concern only the spirit.

CHAPTER X

THE NEW DIDACHE: THE MESSIAH WHO SAVES THROUGH SUFFERING

1. MEN had long been familiar with the idea that suffering as such was to be compensated by some state of glory in the next world. The view was prepared for in Israel by the important discussion of the suffering of the righteous. Especially in the edifying sermons of the apocalyptists, it had long been crystallized out into the formula that he who suffers here will for that reason be glorified hereafter. It corresponds in general to the familiar antitheses in Christ's message: He who is poor here will be rich hereafter; he who hungers and thirsts here will be satisfied hereafter. And conversely, he who is rich and satisfied here, and partakes of the happiness and goods of the world, will be poor and depart empty. No doubt this was the subsidiary idea when Jesus said that he must suffer, but not his real meaning. For such views and teachings could not have confused the disciples nor have been incomprehensible to them: they would have been taken for granted.

Christ, however, does not say here: I must suffer. Nor does he relate his suffering to the general proposition that whoever suffers will be exalted: he says: 'the Son of Man must suffer.' His suffering has Messianic significance. His suffering was necessary, not merely as personal self-authentication, but as a Messianic act. It was not merely a piece of personal information about himself that Christ presented, but an unheard-of new dogma, the dogma of a Messiah who must suffer. And he did not clothe such statements in general maxims about suffering, but in an express citation from Is. liii. What completely confused the disciples was a new, a completely revolutionary Messianic doctrine, a new didache.

2. A first great inner alteration in Israelite Messianism

had been brought about by the introduction of the figure of the transcendent judge and saviour derived from Iranian elements. This figure was combined with the current popular idea of the Davidic Messiah, and took over some of its traits. The result was a first synthesis of two Messianic ideals which in themselves were quite different. It was a revolution in Messianism as such, and was reflected in the controversy which Christ had with the Pharisees about the Messiah. 'How can the Messiah, who is to be David's son, nevertheless be his Lord?' He was his Lord when he, unlike any other earthly king, was the Son of Man who was to sit at the right hand of God Himself.

It has been asked whether this question of Christ's was meant to signify the rejection of popular Messianism generally. To me that seems improbable. Christ was hardly so revolutionary that he would have completely and consciously rejected the conviction of the prophets and of the entire faith of his people. (Had he done that, one would have had to ask seriously whether he was a Jew at all.) He gave an affirmative answer to the question whether he was the king of the Jews, and was crucified for it. His followers at his triumphal entry hailed 'the kingdom of our father David'; accordingly the ancient Messianism must have been alive in the circles of his hearers, and this would be hard to understand if Christ had rejected it completely. More than that, it seems to me beyond doubt that Christ actually claimed to be a descendant of David. Paul called him the son of David according to the flesh, although his theology has scarcely any independent interest in this statement. He knew the brothers of the Lord. How could he have asserted Jesus', and hence their, descent from David if the conviction of Davidic descent had not existed among them? At a later date their descendants are supposed to have been taken before the Roman authorities on account of their Davidic lineage. But in any case Christ's question shows a change in the ancient Messianism and a problem which was not to be solved by the means of ancient Messianism. This question was the Shibboleth of a Messianism which

245

expected the Messiah to be the transcendent Messiah, the Son of Man, whether he came of David's seed or not.

The thesis that the Messiah was David's Lord might be very revolutionary for other circles, but it could not be felt as revolutionary by those in contact with apocalyptic Messianism, nor could it evoke confusion, incomprehension, or inner resistance. But the latter was necessarily the case in the highest degree in circles characterized by apocalyptic Messianism; these circles could not help feeling an incomprehensible inversion and revolution in the new and unheard-of teaching:

The Son of Man must suffer.

Ancient popular Messianism and transcendent Messianism had long been synthesized. Now a new synthesis appeared, of which no one had thought or could think: the synthesis of the Christ with the suffering and dying servant of God from Deutero-Isaiah. It was not only unprecedented; it must have seemed blasphemous. This fact may still be reflected in Mt. xvi. 22, where Peter dares to reproach Christ when for the first time he began to teach that the Son of Man must suffer, and where Christ repulsed him with the unusually sharp words of Mt. xvi. 23.

It is undoubted that the Messianic community, the so-called 'primitive Church,' which emerged from amongst Jesus' disciples, possessed this new didache; that it was distinguished from other Messianic believers chiefly by this article; that it thought of Christ as both the Son of Man and the suffering Ebed Yahweh (servant of Yahweh). Some prefer to think that here we have an invention of the Christian community, and, therefore, an anonymous creation of collective phantasy, to be explained as a 'sociological function.' Such a theory arose at the end of the last century, and seems to me to be closely connected with the tendency of that time to trace ideologies back to sociological functions of collective wholes and environments. But collective wholes do not create great revolutionary ideas, but rather great revolutionary ideas create new groupings with a new milieu.

3. According to our records, Christ's prophecies that as the Son of Man he must suffer were not meant as occasional sighs or marginal notes, but as a definite teaching, as a doctrina.

> He began to teach them that the Son of Man must suffer (Mk. viii. 31; also Mk. ix. 31).

The gospel tradition still shows with sufficient clearness that after a certain time Christ's preaching underwent a change occasioned by some new teaching. This new teaching is briefly summarized in the simple sentence: 'The Son of Man must suffer.' That corresponded formally to the rabbinic manner of teaching. The content of the thesis was formulated in a compact sentence which could be stamped upon the memory. But behind such sentences stood a teaching given in a more comprehensive oral exposition.

The original meaning of Christ's message was not changed by such a new teaching. It remained what it was, viz. a strictly and consistently eschatological preaching of the coming kingdom and its salvation, repentance as the way of approach, conversion, obedience to the divine will, renunciation of worldly goods; to follow and cleave to the redemptive saviour, to accept and receive with a childlike mind, in trust towards the heavenly Father, in love to God and men, in watchfulness and determination. His original message was not changed by this new didache but heightened and completed upon the basis of his prophetic perception that he had to suffer.

The suffering was not a tragic accident which befell him as a man. On one side, it was obligatory, and that meant, of course, not blind fate, but a necessity resulting from a divine decree. On the other side, it was a suffering which would befall him as Son of Man, and this meant that it was part and parcel of his Messianic calling. As Son of Man he must suffer. It was part and parcel of the Messianic

247

saving work committed to him. It was redemptive suffering. It was thereby the last consequence of his logical eschatology. The saving of the lost for the eschatological order was, as such, and as a whole, the meaning of his person and message. If suffering befell him, it was of a divine necessity; it was the completion of his general Messianic calling, and it fitted into the meaning which his person and message had from the start.

4. The idea that innocent and voluntarily accepted suffering could be redemptive for others was not new in Israel. It had long before matured in connection with the old and difficult problem of the suffering of the righteous. The new element was that redemptive suffering belonged to the calling of the Messiah. Perhaps such an idea would have arisen in Jesus even without Biblical guidance. But such guidance was clearly given to him in the figure of the Suffering Servant of God in Isaiah. From the beginning he had recognized this figure as a prediction referring to himself, and he wanted to be understood as its fulfilment. He had already reached the synthesis between the Son of Man and the Servant of God. In his new didache he now reached the synthesis between the Son of Man and the suffering Servant of God. Thereby he did not destroy his previous teaching but brought it to a logical conclusion. The new synthesis between transcendent Messianism and the Ebed Yahweh was so significant that we must discuss it in greater detail in the following chapter.

CHAPTER XI

THE SON OF MAN AS THE SUFFERING SERVANT OF GOD

1. MK. ix. 12 f. preserves the memory of doubts and questions which Jesus' new didache necessarily aroused in his disciples. It is plain that the connection of these verses with the Transfiguration is artificial, and they stand in an impossible context. They have been somewhat obscured by compression, but their meaning is still plain. Two cycles of thought, different in themselves, and thereby two questions different in themselves, have been inter-mingled in a much abridged form. The eschatological expectation of many, including even Pharisees, as we see from this passage, awaited the return of Elijah; and Elijah, as the precursor of Yahweh's own coming, was at times almost a rival to the Messiah. Our passage briefly sums up what Jesus often taught in greater detail about Elijah: 'That Elijah should come was correct; in John he had come; his significance was only that he restored all things, and accordingly he was only a preparer of the way.' We further perceive from our passage that Jesus saw in John's execution the fulfilment of a prediction (it is not clear what Old Testament or apocryphal words he had in view). Hence there is a connection between this question and answer and the other question:

> How can it stand written of the Son of Man that he shall suffer much and be set at naught? (Mk. ix. 12).

The disciples knew, and it was unquestioned, that the Scriptures had ascribed much suffering and contempt to one person, viz. the Servant of God. The meaning of Mark's words, therefore, can only be: How can such a saying about suffering and contempt be written of the

249

Son of Man? How is it humanly possible that such words could refer to the Son of Man? That was an utter paradox for the disciples (and for that entire age). How Jesus answered is still discernible from v. 13: 'The fact that Elijah would be put to death, you did not know and no one knew. That anything stood written about him and his fate, and that he was the subject, you did not notice. It was also a paradox that Elijah, the restorer, had to be put to death. And yet it was done to him, and done to him according to what stood written about him. The same thing is true of the Son of Man.'

2. In Mk. ix. 12 f. we have a fragment of those conversations between master and disciples which were necessarily connected with his new didache, and in which it was further developed. In the expression that the Son of Man 'must suffer much and be set at naught,' we have likewise an indubitably genuine saying of Jesus himself. It was fitting only on his own lips, not on those of the later church, because there is a perceptible contrast to the form of the remaining 'prophecies of suffering.' These were obviously filled out *ex eventu* with an ever greater development of the details of the later passion story as the church came to know it. But the saying in Mk. ix. 12 f., with its simplicity and in its vagueness, would not have been invented by the theology of a church.

3. In this original saying we have also the proof that Jesus was concretely aware of himself as the expiatory suffering Servant of God in Is. liii. His words do not say that he must suffer in any case, but that the Son of Man is the Servant of God. They are a quotation. Only so are they intelligible. It is impossible that someone who is reckoning on his own death would choose the bare words: 'He will be set at naught,' if they were not a quotation. Even the expression 'suffer much' would be strange on account of its general character, if it were not a quotation. But it becomes intelligible at once, if we look back to the manifold pictures of suffering which deal with the servant of God and which are so strikingly heaped up in Is.

liii. 2–4. One could not briefly sum them up otherwise or more simply than with the expression 'suffer much' in the sense of 'experience manifold suffering.' (The expression also shows that at that moment Jesus had no clear picture whatever of his end.) The same holds true still more of another expression which, if it were not a quotation of a well-known scriptural text, would be utterly flat. But 'be set at naught' stands word for word in Is. liii. 3 :

lo chashabnuhu, which means: 'we set him at naught.'

Indeed, even the word suffer seems to be verbal quotation. Delitzsch translates 'jeunneh,' and the same word stands in Is. liii. 4. Only on this basis does the term 'must' become fully intelligible. 'Must' here does not mean blind fatality, but inner necessity resulting from the calling and nature of him who is Son of Man, who is come 'to seek and to save that which is lost' (Lk. xix. 10). To save is the calling and purpose of the Son of Man. To save, however, is also the purpose of the suffering of the Servant of God. The Son of Man 'must' be the redemptively suffering Servant of God, if he is to fulfil his vocation as Son of Man, i.e. his vocation as Saviour.

4. But the 'must' which Jesus meant was not, therefore, a mere necessity, in some such sense as that it was only an ancient scriptural word that still held, and that had to be fulfilled. Scripture contained many oracles which were really intended to apply to the coming Messiah, and others which were commonly interpreted as referring to him but which Jesus passed by without attention. Mere blind oracular necessity existed for him as little as did the mere blind authority of the letter of Scripture. The 'must,' of the suffering of the Son of Man was not forced upon him by an oracle. It followed by inner logic when he saw himself as the eschatological redeemer and saviour, in the light of Isaiah's ancient redeemer who was most inwardly akin to him, and in the light of his fate.

5. In connection with this new didache, and plainly presupposing it as already announced, we have the passage:

251

> The Son of Man came not to be ministered unto, but to minister, and to give his life a ransom (lutron) for many (Mk. x. 45 par.).

Here again we have a clear synthesis of the Son of Man and Isaiah's Servant of God. The saying speaks of the Son of Man. At the same time it characterizes the coming of the Son of Man by the conception of a humble ministry. Such ministry was to reach its climax in voluntary self-surrender unto death. It is only the latter point that gave *full* force to the saying as an exhortation to humble and voluntary service, but, measured by the customary idea of the Son of Man, even the first point was something distinctive and new. To his own people the Son of Man was a majestic, kindly being, and by no means a humble, ministering figure. The typical humble, ministering person was not he, but the Servant of God in Isaiah. It is the latter who is pictured with all features and colours as wholly humble and at the same time as the one who voluntarily submits to disdain.

In the saying of Mk. x. 45, the striking expression 'for many,' again strangely vague, is simply a quotation from Is. liii. It is 'the many' who are strikingly emphasized and repeatedly mentioned in Is. liii. (and here in an intelligent way):

> Verse 11: As a result of the affliction of his soul he will procure righteousness for *the many*, and will take upon himself their iniquities.
> Verse 12: therefore will I give him his share among *the many*,
> Verse 13: he bore the sins of *many*.

Again, the manifold expressions which Isaiah used for the expiatory and saving power of the sufferings of the Servant of God, could not have been reproduced more compactly and clearly than with the words:

> to give his life as a lutron (= *kopher*).

That was new teaching. But as such it had, nevertheless,

been long prepared for in the general character of Jesus' message and person; from the beginning he belonged to the category of a 'charismatic evangelist,' and, as such, repeated and fulfilled that of Isaiah's redeemer.

6. The gospels say that this teaching was misunderstood by the disciples. It is upon this fact in particular that Wrede founded his thesis of the Messianic secret. He alleged that the idea of a Messianic secret was only invented at a later date, and he held that it was imported into the gospels at a later time, because only later times would have transformed an itinerant rabbi into a Messiah. Adolf Jülicher showed the impossibility of Wrede's hypothesis in his painstaking work: *Neue Linien in der Kritik der evangelischen Ueberlieferung*, Giessen, 1906. Our gospels in general show the disciples as by no means so devoid of understanding as Wrede represents. Christ pronounced their eyes and ears blessed, because they could perceive what others had not been able to perceive. With reference to the suffering of the Son of Man, the gospels do, in fact, recount the disciples' inability to understand, but here they recount more than a mere lack of understanding. Peter dared to oppose his master with reproachful words, when the latter began the new and offensive teaching for the first time (a fact which no later person would have dared invent, and which was even passed over in silence by two of our evangelists). Neither fact, the disciples' lack of understanding nor the vigorous resistance to this new Messianism, was invented subsequently; they are as consonant with the situation as they could possibly be. The point, however, is to understand rightly this lack of understanding and this resistance. What was it that the disciples did not understand, and what impelled Peter to utter his reproach?

That the righteous suffered—this ancient problem had long engaged the profoundest spirits of Israel. Faith had long before given the answer that the suffering of the righteous had its meaning in that it ministers to the salvation of Israel. (See W. Bousset, *Die Religion des*

Judentums im neutestamentliche Zeitalter, II, 9.) In the Mechiltā, an ancient commentary on Exodus, it was regarded as a matter of course:

> All the righteous, the pious, the prophets, and the fathers have given their lives for Israel.

Moses offered to suffer in place of his people: 'Destroy me rather than them.' Likewise David offered himself when the angel of wrath was destroying the people by pestilence. Jonah's flight was interpreted as intended to give his life for the salvation of his people. Of Elijah it is said in Sifrē: because he was jealous for his God and made expiation for (wayekappēr) the children of Israel, because he gave his life unto death (Dalmann). In particular, it was known from the martyrs of Maccabean times that a martyr's suffering of death had a special intercessory and expiatory power on behalf of the people of Israel. Thus the very feature, which, to moderns, is the strangest thing about this 'must suffer,' was, for the circle of the disciples, certainly neither problematic nor unintelligible, but as natural as possible. For this reason Christ did not offer anything like a theory of atonement, confusing by its novelty. Indeed, he never once gave any sort of commentary by adding such words as: the Son of Man must suffer for the salvation of Israel; that was quite obvious if he (as Son of Man, the redeemer, and the future king of Israel) had to suffer at all. And speaking as a great and upright rabbi, or as a mere prophet, but not as the Son of Man made manifest to his disciples, if he had said to them: I shall suffer, and suffer for you and for your benefit, they might perhaps have doubted, but such words would have been neither unintelligible nor offensive to them; and no Peter would have been able to reproach him for using them.

The confusing, and even dogmatic, statement: 'The Son of Man must suffer,' must be understood quite differently from the above. This statement was un-believable, unbelievable until the End, until the events themselves confirmed it. It was more; it was offensive for the circle and to individuals who believed in the Son of Man (perhaps it was for this very reason that Judas became a traitor). According to Enoch's apocalyptic, the Son of Man was the king of heaven himself, and one intended for that throne was destined to judge the adversaries and enemies of God. But it was quite in harmony with Enoch's Messianism that Jesus should come as a preacher of righteousness, equipped with the miraculous powers of the already dawning kingdom, and even now show himself powerful in deed and word. If he had preached that the Son of Man would be translated at his own time, that would have been understandable and without offence for apocalyptic circles. If he had 'given' his *followers* the prospect of suffering and hardship, of persecution by the unrighteous and death at their hand after his translation, even that could not have caused them either to marvel or to take offence, for the idea that Messianic woes awaited the adherents of the Messiah was part of this Messianism. But that he would be delivered into the hands of the unrighteous just because he was the Son of Man, and indeed that it was imperative in the sense that it belonged to the essence and vocation of the Son of Man himself, all this was so hard a saying, and so much opposed to the religious faith of these very people, that one must marvel that there was not more than one Judas among them.

Let a person make the attempt for himself; let him read the book of Enoch and give himself up to its impression, in order to feel how monstrous it must have been for one who believed in Jesus as Son of Man that the synthesis should be made between one who claimed to be Son of Man and the despised, God-smitten man of suffering from Is. liii. At the same time, we shall possibly see that this synthesis was not made bit by bit in the gradual growth of posthumous apologetics in some unknown church, but that it was due to an incomparably original conception on the part of one who could also conceive that the kingdom of God was at hand and was actually coming as He Himself conquered Satan.

255

CHAPTER XII

THE ASSOCIATIONS OF THE TERM 'LUTRON'

1. 'To give his life a *lutron* for many.' The Greek word, lutron, is the equivalent of the Hebrew word, kopher, and is so surrounded with associations belonging to Israelite ceremonial, so deepened and enriched also by Is. liii, that the term can scarcely be represented by a word taken from the world of our own experience. We might translate it with some such a phrase as a means of expiation. But then we should have to discuss its significance more closely for such a phrase would not suffice to reproduce the emotional content of lutron. We shall now briefly attempt such a discussion. Our object in doing so is not to examine the theory of atonement, but only to suggest what a Jewish hearer, familiar with his own cult and ritual and knowing his own sacred Scriptures, must have meant by it, and that not in concepts or theories, but in emotional intuitions.

2. Christ did not put forth a theory of satisfaction for the simple reason that he had none. Lutron does not cover a definite and definable theory, nor even a definite concept, capable of being fixed by a clear-cut definition. It covers a complex of associations of different character and different origin. This complex one can trace to a certain extent. The Hebrew word, kopher, corresponds to the Greek word, lutron. Both may mean recompense, e.g. recompense as a payment or disbursement to another, to ransom a captive, or to release oneself from a debt due to somebody. In this sense the word can be used in a wholly secular manner of the dealings of buyers and sellers with one another. The literal meaning of the word in such a case is always the releasing of oneself from a business debt which one owes to another and has to discharge.

But originally the word kopher did not come from the secular sphere of commerce but from the numinous sphere of the cultus. It means release from an obligation which is the obligation of *sin*. Moreover, the idea of release from sins goes back to a still more primitive conception. Kopher comes from kaphar, in Piel kippēr. This means cover, conceal. In ritual language it is the concealment of a misdeed, a stain, a sin between a man and his numen, so that these evils vanish from before the eyes of the deity. Then there comes in the additional, indefinable idea of a consecration which restores and sanctifies, and which removes the unholy element contained in pollution by sin.[1] And it is only by this connotation that kippēr, in the sense of propitiation, expiation, and atonement, receives its genuine ring and meaning. (Concerning this wholly irrational element cp. R. Otto, *The Idea of the Holy*, pp. 56 ff.) All this is important for understanding the meaning of lutron, for comprehending what the Servant of God did when he gave his life 'as a guilt offering,' and what Christ meant and intended by his procedure at the Last Supper. If the Son of Man gives his life as a ransom for many, he gives it as a means of their consecration and sanctification. One must give weight to this consideration before pondering rationalized ideas involving an element of vicariousness. With this irrational, deeply numinous element are associated ideas of forgiveness and pardon which arise from the social relations of men with one another. If a fault is covered by expiation, it is also forgiven, pardoned. But the clear and rational conception of pardon and forgiveness does not simply step into the place of the mysterious expiation, but now has a depth which can only belong to divine forgiveness. Perhaps it is more correct to say that forgiveness is the highest element in a rational conception, and can be used only as an expression for something which is fundamentally incapable of rationali-

---

[1] 'The effect was a double one: Sin and impurity were thereby taken away; consecrated character was thereby imparted.' (P. Volz, *Die biblischen Altertümer*, 1925, p. 13.)

zation at all; really, it is only a symbol, indeed, the final symbol for the irrational acts of expiation and atonement.

3. The fifty-third chapter of Isaiah, with its idea of the propitiating, suffering, and dying Servant of God, belongs to the same category of ideas or rather emotions. This suffering of his would be described in ritual language as a kopher, a lutron. But the circle of associations which this word covers is greatly enriched, deepened, and changed, and it is highly charged with meaning from this source. The Servant of God is understood to suffer humbly, voluntarily, and also innocently when he takes upon himself a heavy divine decree; his suffering operates for the salvation of others in that, like a guilt-offering, it 'covers,' consecrates, sanctifies, expiates. In the same category is the idea that he takes upon himself a punishment, merited not by him but by others. This idea is very profound in itself, and it is also embedded in other associations which appear of equal worth and which, like it, hover indefinitely between reality and symbol. The first feature to be mentioned is that of healing, and it is particularly striking.

He bore our sicknesses; by his stripes were we healed.

He is an expiator of sin, in so far as he is also a physician of sins. The holiness of his suffering passes over as spiritual healing power to the sinful. Further:

We all went astray, each one turned to his own way.

The self-surrender of the master has the effect of bringing his disciples to teshuba, to conversion from a wrong way. At the same time it leads them from a wilful choosing of their own way to a fraternal fellowship in the only way— that of the master. The suffering of the master is propitiatory, because its effect is to convert and unite. Further:

> Through his knowledge he procured righteousness for many and (in this way) took upon himself (and removed) their iniquities.

His understanding, viz. of the divine will, which he shows by recognition of the divine will in humble, patient endurance of what is sent by God, has also the effect of bringing his disciples to the right understanding and thereby to righteousness. Thus he removes their iniquities. Further:

> Yet he acted (as intercessor) for the wicked.

In a righteous man's intercession for those who belong to him there lies atoning and expiatory power. Every one of all these rich and deep associated ideas would suffice as the basis for a doctrine of the atonement. Their interaction on, and their rivalry with, each other prove that here we are not dealing with anything theoretical or capable of being made the subject of theorizing. All of this shows that the ideas fuse in the ancient, ritual conception of the guilt-offering, or the āšām:

> When he shall have made himself into a guilt-offering.

The guilt-offering was a special kind among Israel's offerings. The idea of a vicarious punishment was not definitely present in such an offering, and it would be wrong to see the sole meaning of this guilt-offering in the idea, profound as it is, of voluntarily suffering a punishment deserved by others. It would be false to take it thus, in a one-sided way and at the cost of the associated ideas, and then go on to see in this meaning the key of the whole section; and then further to rationalize and flatten it into a juridical doctrine of vicarious punishment. Rather, just this manifold variety of associations which spring up very spontaneously, crowd together, and in part encroach upon one another, gives us the right key and shows us the true state of affairs. An element wholly irrational at bottom is here encircled by groping interpretations, which are all justified in their way as ideograms; yet plainly neither individually nor as a whole do they give any idea of what is meant, namely, the atoning power of suffering when assumed voluntarily, humbly, and innocently for the benefit of those who are bound together as disciples in imitation of, and attachment to, the one who thus surrenders himself. Much less do they yield a theory of God, a concept of the deity, from which can be construed the *a priori* necessity of an expiation for sinners. The most important consideration is that they have not been thought out at all on the basis of a concept of God, indeed, they have not been thought in any way. Rather they have been born from the experience of sinful men who, by the holy, innocent, self-surrender of their master, have experienced a power which atones, washes from impurity, releases from the burden of guilt, heals from spiritual sickness, liberates from error and self-will; and to whom thereby the unapproachable transcendent numen has become a God of the berith, the saving covenant.

The same holds good in regard to Jesus and the lutron. He offered no theory of atonement. He did not give a new and different concept of God in place of a previous concept of God as Father. He simply expressed the idea that, by the humble and voluntary surrender of life on the part of the Son of Man, the many would gain what the disciples of the Servant of God had gained by the suffering of their master, viz. the possibility of entering as reconciled individuals into a berith of God, which inheriting the kingdom of God made possible and assured to them. This also reveals the significance of his procedure at the Last Supper; it was an eschatological and regal act of the Son of Man, who was also the atoning, suffering Servant of God.

Let us pause a moment to make a comparison in the sphere of the history of religion—a task which would call for a more thorough grounding than a short note can give.

Two profound conceptions of the relation between mankind and the transcendent divine reality were born on Aryan soil. On one side was Plato's perception that all truth which supports human life is rooted in the eternal divine idea, exalted above becoming, change, and corruption. On the other side was the powerful, mystic, ancient Indian conception of the Eternal One, in which all multiplicity, separateness, and fragmentariness of worldly existence vanish and which is one with the deeper self of man.

Equal in rank, if not even stronger and deeper than either, was the Aryan and Iranian conception of the sublime divine warfare against the power of ungodliness, and of man's duty to struggle on God's side against God's enemy.

But even this Aryan idea only gained full depth when it was filled and penetrated with the content of that word which is the really primal word in the religion of Israel:

Ye shall be holy, for I am holy.

It was upon the basis of this word as primal and as expressing its deepest understanding that Israel came to perceive also that only he can be holy whom God sanctifies:

I the Lord which sanctify you am holy.

This understanding was completed in the fifty-third chapter of Isaiah. This chapter is unique in the history of religion, and expresses an experience which is wholly irrational and not elucidated by any theory. A group of disciples experience atonement and sanctification in the humble voluntary suffering of their master in obedience to God.

This deepest element, before which everything else in the history of religion falls into the background, was not discovered by Greeks, Indians, or Iranians; it was born in Jewish souls.

BOOK THREE

CHRIST'S LAST SUPPER AS THE CONSECRA-
TION OF THE DISCIPLES FOR ENTRANCE
INTO THE KINGDOM OF GOD

CHAPTER I

THE NEW TESTAMENT ACCOUNTS OF CHRIST'S LAST SUPPER

1. THE New Testament gives us four records of the Last Supper: Mt. xxvi. 26–29, Mk. xiv. 22–25, Lk. xxii. 17–20, 1 Cor. xi. 23–26.

In addition, Acts says that the first church possessed and regularly exercised a form of celebration peculiar to it, with the name klasis tou artou, fractio panis, the breaking of bread. We may grant that the church practised klasis tou artou, that it was the point of departure for the later ecclesiastical eucharist, and that the four records noted above refer to the eucharist, but we do not grant that the original fractio panis of the primitive church was understood in essentially the same sense as the later eucharist, and as the records of the Last Supper ascribe to it. Rather, the breaking of bread only gradually acquired the later meaning under the influence of the theology of the church, and the four accounts of the Last Supper themselves contain a mythology adapted to the ceremonial. This developed at a later date, out of the theology of the church and was put forward as an 'aition' or explanation of the rite which had gradually taken shape.

The later ritual and the four records in their present form can only be understood when the ceremonial is held to refer to the death of Christ in the breaking of his body and the shedding of his blood, and also to refer to a 'diathēkē,' i.e. a covenant which was established when Christ sacrificed his life in the breaking of his body and the shedding of his blood. The covenant had a special connection with his blood. His blood as shed in death was undoubtedly meant and hence was thought of in closest connection with the body as broken in death; the covenant was not accidentally connected with Christ's blood as such, but with it as shed in death; hence the covenant was equally connected with his body as broken in death, and both the breaking of the body and the shedding of the blood were only the two sides or elements of the single act of which Mk. x. 45 and Mt. xx. 28 speak, viz. that the Son of Man had come to give his life as a lutron, a means of atonement, for many.

2. All four accounts, in the form which we are accustomed to read to-day, speak of such a covenant, i.e. one connected with the blood of Christ. But it is a question whether we must not forthwith make an exception of one account, viz. that of Luke. When we inquire as to its oldest critically determinable form, i.e. in the oldest western codices, the texts of the Itala, and that of the Codex Cantabrigiensis in Greek and Latin, we find it gives the account only up to and including the words, 'this is my body'; but these codices lack the following words of our present usual Lucan text. Thus they lack the account of giving the cup after the distribution of the bread, and also the words: 'this cup is the new covenant in my blood, which is shed for you.' The phenomenon is easily explained if these words were originally lacking, and were later supplied from the other accounts, especially from Paul; but if these words had stood originally in Luke, we cannot explain why they could have been omitted later by anyone, while all the other accounts were left uncontested. But that means that the original text of Luke did not contain these words. It follows that there once existed an ancient account of Christ's Last Supper, in which these words were not as yet to be found, and in which there was no mention of a cup after the distribution of the bread.

3. Lietzmann, in his work, *Messe und Herrenmahl*, thinks that Luke did know of the cup after the distribution of the bread, with its accompanying words about the blood of the covenant, but that he brought it forward and placed it before the distribution of the bread. When this rearrangement was made the words accompanying the cup of the blood covenant were lost.

266

In actual truth, Luke is strikingly different from all other accounts, in prefacing the distribution of bread in v. 17 with an account of the blessing and distribution of a cup without reference to blood or the shedding of blood. We shall have to speak of this more in detail. But if the account had actually come into existence for some liturgical or practical reasons, and the original cup after the distribution of the bread had been put in advance, then the words about the new covenant and about the shedding of the blood would, of course, have been lost. There is no sense in speaking of shedding of blood before the breaking of the body; only when the breaking of the body had been symbolized by the broken bread could anything be said about a cup of the blood. The shedding of blood presupposes that the body had already been broken, that this fact was the cause. But it is impossible that such significant and weighty words as those of the covenant blood could have been lost once they had been coined. If so, Lietzmann's whole assumption collapses, that the introductory cup in Luke was really a cup after the meal which Luke placed earlier. But the reverse process would be quite intelligible, indeed almost unavoidable, viz. that a simple introductory cup was later interpreted from the meaning of the breaking of the bread and in an analogous manner, and then, as was inevitable, transposed to the second place in the ritual. Later we shall discuss the fact that traces are still found in Paul himself of such a subsequent change of order, viz. putting into the second place a cup which originally stood first.

Luke's record says that Christ blessed and distributed a cup (v. 17) accompanied (v. 18) by a word of farewell, but without reference to the shedding of blood. Afterwards he broke the bread, distributed it, and accompanied the breaking and distribution with the words: This is my body. Luke found nothing in his source about a cup after the distribution, and hence, nothing of a cup of the blood covenant.

4. But did Luke's source contain nothing at all about

founding a covenant, and did he make no such record?
Was there originally no idea of founding a covenant?

On the contrary: it was found in Luke's source and
it has been preserved by Luke himself, in v. 29:

> kai *diatithemai* humin kathos *dietheto* moi ho pater mou
> basileian.

Diathesthai means in Hebrew karath berith = diathēkēn
poieisthai. The word occurs twice in v. 29. The English
language has the term 'to covenant,' thus: I covenant to
you as my father has covenanted to me. But if we desire
to do full justice to the Hebrew equivalent for diatithesthai,
i.e. to karath berith, we must use a circumlocution, e.g.:
I make or found for you the covenant of the kingdom,
that you may eat and drink at my table in my kingdom,
and sit upon thrones. . . .

5. This fact, that the idea of founding a covenant was
not completely lacking in Luke, was pointed out by Franz
Dibelius in his work: *Das Abendmahl*, Leipzig, 1911. But
the crux of the matter is to recognize that these words
of Christ's in v. 29: 'I appoint unto you a covenant, viz.
the kingdom, that you . . .' have been preserved by
Luke, although he gives them at a great interval after
the distribution of the bread. Originally combined with
vv. 17–19a, they formed a typical, compactly joined,
unified paragraph on the Last Supper similar to the three
other accounts. In that case, this pericope, when compared with the records of the Last Supper in Matthew
and Paul, bears a fully archaic character, and was not
derived from the other three accounts. Further, it did not
originate from the theology and the customs of the church,
but preceded them, and it reported an event which had
no organic connection with the life of the church but only
with that of Christ himself. Finally, the three accounts of
the Last Supper in Mark, Matthew, and Paul, and the
later eucharistic practices, may one and all be understood
as transformations, under the influence of later, but still discernible motives, of what was given by the original record.

CHAPTER II

THE ORIGINAL ACCOUNT

1. WE must distinguish between the original Lucan report and the still earlier pericope on the Lord's Supper, and we should recognize that this latter was divided by insertions made by Luke (or perhaps by one or more of Luke's predecessors).

We obtained Luke's original account by rejecting v. 19b–20. The rejection was founded upon the witness of the ancient western tradition. Wellhausen, and others following him, would go still further with reference to Luke's record and reject v. 19a. That is caprice, for such rejection is not supported by any MS. It is also contrary to sense, for in this case Luke would have told of a meal at which no one received anything to eat, and Luke, who is closely akin to early Catholicism, would then have given no aition or explanation of the sacrament of the church, which is unthinkable.

Luke's gospel originally said:

> xxii. 14: And when the hour (for the meal) was come, he sat down and the apostles with him. 15. And he said unto them, With desire I have desired to eat this passover with you before I suffer: 16. for I say unto you, I shall not eat it, until it (!) be fulfilled in the kingdom of God. 17. And he took a cup and when he had given thanks, he said, Take this, and divide it among yourselves: 18. for I say unto you, I shall not drink from henceforth of the fruit (genema, peri) of the vine, until the kingdom of God shall come. 19a. And he took bread, and when he had given thanks, he brake it, and gave to them, saying, This is my body.
>
> [Verses 19b-20 were not in Luke's source.]
>
> 21. But behold the hand of him that betrayeth me is with me on the table. 22. For the Son of Man indeed goeth, as it hath been determined (by God): but woe

unto that man through whom he is betrayed! 23. And they began to question among themselves, which of them it was that should do this thing.

24. And there arose also a contention among them, which of them was accounted to be greatest. 25. And he said unto them, The kings of the Gentiles have lordship over them; and they that have authority over them are called benefactors. 26. But ye shall not be so: but he that is the greater (eldest) among you, let him become as the younger; and he that is chief (of the meal) as he that doth serve. 27. For which is greater, he that sitteth at meat, or he that serveth (at table)? is not he that sittteth at meat? but I am in the midst of you as he that serveth.

28. But ye are they that have continued with me in my temptations;

29. And I appoint unto you a kingdom, even as my Father appointed unto me, 30. that ye may eat and drink at my table in my kingdom; and ye shall sit on thrones judging the twelve tribes of Israel.

31. Simon, Simon, behold, Satan asked to have you, that he might sift you (Simon and the disciples) as wheat: . . . etc.

Following his early source, Luke recorded vv. 17–19a, up to and including the words: This is my body. To these words he joined vv. 21–28, which latter verses are an interpolation either by Luke or, at an earlier time, by his predecessors. They are still clearly discernible to be interpolations as are even the motives for interpolating.

2. Let us consider the breaking up of the early, unified pericope, consisting of vv. 17, 18, 19a, 29, 30, by interpolating vv. 21–28.

(a) First, vv. 21–23. They contain a warning to the traitor, and cannot have stood originally in this position. According to Mk. xiv. 18 ff. and Mt. xxvi. 17 ff. Jesus did not speak the words to the traitor after, but before the breaking of the bread. Beyond question, this is correct. No matter what the original meaning of the story of the Last Supper, the narrator's intention was always to record something specially intimate and solemn, such as concerned only Jesus himself and those who really belonged to him. Therefore, it could not possibly have been reported in the original story that Judas had shared in the meal, nor even that he was included in the words: I appoint unto you the kingdom, even as my Father appointed it unto me. But the section about Judas was interpolated into the meal for the obvious, 'dogmatic' reason, viz. the fulfilment of an ancient, alleged prediction. In Obad. 7 we read:

> the men that were at peace with thee have deceived thee, and prevailed against thee; they that eat thy bread lay a snare under thee.

As soon as it became customary to find ancient prophecies fulfilled in the details of Christ's passion, nothing lay nearer than to present the traitor, contrary to the older tradition in Mark and Matthew, as eating Christ's bread with him, and then to make the words to Judas follow the distribution of the bread; in this way the ancient prophetic words were fulfilled in the most literal manner possible.

(b) Similarly, the section which follows the words to Judas, about the ambitious strife of the disciples with one another (vv. 24–27), cannot have stood here originally. It is found in Mark and Matthew, but, like the section on Judas, in a totally different position (cp. Mk. x. 45 and par.), viz. following on the incident of the sons of Zebedee.

Making a comparison, we see at once that it is now fully motivated, but, in the Lucan context, completely unmotivated. But again we can easily understand that it was editorially interpolated in a supper incident, for, according to Luke, Jesus had already twice reproved this very desire to have the chief seats at a supper as an example of culpable ambition (Lk. xiv. 7 ff., xx. 46).

Thus, obviously, at the basis of Mk. x. 42 ff. is an early pericope which inculcated humility. An attempt was made to adapt this pericope along the lines of Lk. xiv. 18 and xx. 46 till it recorded a meal. This circumstance again affected the transforming of the early material in Mk. x. 42 and produced the oddly confused record of Lk. xxii. 27, in a way which does not appear in the clear words of Mk. x. 45. Christ was not among the disciples 'as he that serveth'; like them he reclined at table and like them he was served by the attendant. By adapting the ancient pericope at the basis of Mk. x. 42 and by inserting it into an unsuitable place, the editor ruined it; but when we grasp this fact, we can the more readily grasp the singular mutilation and disfigurement in the much clearer and very tersely formulated words in Mk. x. 45:

> For the Son of Man also came not to be ministered unto, but to minister.

Mark's significant words:

> and to give his life a ransom for many

had to be cut off as soon as the pericope Mk. x. 42 ff. was forcibly transformed into an account of the Last Supper. For the idea of a ransom for many was precisely the meaning of the distribution of the bread, and by the act of distributing the meaning had just been fixed. The words about a ransom could no longer be retained when the Marcan section was placed after this act. (On the other hand, the very circumstance that the saying was now cut off proves that the act really had this meaning.)

At the same time, it is obvious that the account of the conflict was inserted at this point because of the words which precede in Lk. xxii. 23: 'and they began to dispute with one another.' A dispute had already begun among them. Each opposed the others contentiously and sought to avert from himself the suspicion of betrayal. Verse 24 then proceeded:

> egeneto de kai philoneikia [there arose also a contention].

This means that after the first there at once occurred a second dispute; thus an editor attempted to make some sort of a narrative by merely stringing material together. We see at work the same redactional concern as in Lk. xxii. 28, except that the latter is clumsier than the former.

(c) For, finally, it is even less possible that Lk. xxii. 28 stood originally where it now is:

> Ye are they that have continued with me in my temptations.

The temptations of Christ had not yet taken place at all. On the contrary, shortly before he had been greeted in festive fashion at his entry into Jerusalem. He had succeeded in cleansing the temple and had not been attacked. He had taught unchallenged in Jerusalem and in the temple. Up to this time neither he nor his disciples had had any peirasmoi [temptations]. And further, he soon says the very opposite in Lk. xxii. 31, when he places the peirasmoi in prospect for 'you' as only in the future; he gives to his chief disciple the prospect not of attacking but of succumbing to the peirasmoi. According to Mk. xiv. 27 he said in general terms:

> You will all be offended in me.

Lk. xxii. 28 is manifestly an editorial supplement, an attempt to provide the necessary transition from the element of censure in the preceding verses to the words about inheriting the kingdom. These words, completely isolated by the preceding insertions, could not possibly have followed immediately upon the words of censure. They had to be introduced somehow; that is the function of Lk. xxii. 28, and, as we must say, it is obvious and awkward.

3. Verses 29–30 were therefore once connected immediately with the saying: this is my body (Lk. xxii. 19). Hence the early pericope once ran:

> 17. He took a cup, gave thanks and said: Take this and divide it among yourselves.   18. For I say unto you: Henceforth I will no more drink of the fruit of the vine, until the kingdom of God comes.   19a. And after he had

s

taken bread and given thanks, he broke it and gave it to them, saying: This is my body (= this is I myself); and I appoint unto you in covenant the kingdom, as my Father has appointed it unto me in covenant, that you may eat and drink at my table in my kingdom, and sit upon thrones, judging the twelve tribes of Israel.

4. This early pericope has an archaic character which is at once clear when it is compared with the parallel records. Luke embedded it in his account of Christ's passion as did Matthew and Mark also with their sections on the Last Supper. It should be clear without more ado that Luke's account is more ancient than those of the other two narrators, and equally that the ancient account is in any case not a myth explaining the cultus such as might have been invented later.

No matter what the motives, if one invents a myth to explain a rite which arose later, the invented myth will not contradict the existing practice of the rite itself. Least of all could one invent it in such a form as carried in itself elements which would actually destroy the meaning of the rite as existing in the church. The existing rite, as a rite of the church, related to the church and to its needs and aims. The cult-myth would therefore necessarily have these in view, and would have to be constructed from their standpoint. But that is not at any rate the first and direct meaning of the ancient section we are reviewing. Clearly, its climax is an utterance, not to a 'community' generally, but to the special circle of eleven disciples whose circumstances are described and who were gathered round Jesus as he was about to meet his death. To them, and of course only to them, he promised that they should sit with him upon thrones to judge the tribes of Israel. The fact that the ancient section reached its climax at this point shows how fully it accorded with the then situation, and also that it could not have been invented by anyone holding the church's point of view.

Of course Christ did not inherit the kingdom from his Father for the eleven disciples alone, but also for the elect

of the final age generally. The Son of Man had come to
give his life as a ransom, not for eleven men, but for many.
It was, therefore, of course quite fitting and consonant
with the general message of Christ himself that the fractio
panis, filled and weighted with the significance which it
had received when Christ fulfilled its meaning, should
not be continued as a rite for the eleven only, but at once
became a rite of the church; it was celebrated as a testament not only for the narrowest circle of disciples, but for
all children of the kingdom. It would be contrary both
to the material content and to common sense that a rite
already existing in the church should have been given an
artificial explanation in words which in no way mentioned
the church, but only a very small group; and even then
its primary and direct meaning referred quite strictly to
the time when Jesus bade his disciples farewell.

That the latter is the case may at first appear destructive
of practice and custom in the church. Nevertheless, we
may be thankful that Christ's actions and words have been
preserved in their direct and primary meaning. For in
these records we find a reliable account of something
which Christ actually did. The account is historically
reliable because it refers to a condition of affairs which is
definitely not that of the church; the account therefore
bears in itself the guarantee of a genuineness beyond invention. The 'covenant promise' of the kingdom is even to-day
transferred from the circle of those who were immediately
and primarily intended, to 'the many,' and this is done
with the same inner justification as it was done in the first
church by the very disciples whom it exclusively concerned
when uttered.

5. There is still a little to be said that may be of value
for the particular aim of comparing the other three reports
of the Last Supper. On the one hand, we find that all
the essential constitutive elements of the other accounts
are contained in the archaic account; on the other hand,
we touch upon a very essential and, indeed, indispensable
element when we say that the later narratives, when

compared with the earliest record, are actually the poorer, as regards the strictly eschatological implications of Christ's act in distributing the bread, which meant the body, as described in our primitive section. This must be further discussed. We do so by considering the three elements which constitute the basis of our primitive section, and by asking their meaning. They are:

1. The introductory ritualistic blessing and distribution of the cup.
2. The ritualistic breaking and distribution of the bread as a single act accompanied by the explanatory saying: This is my body.
3. And in immediate connection and logical union with this saying, the diathēkē, i.e. the covenant promise of the kingdom of God.

But before we take up these matters in detail, the question is still to be asked regarding the whole of what Christ did, whether it represented a purely exceptional act without analogies and parallels, or whether it fitted into a category, and if so, into which one. It is important to know the category because of the associations which at once result when typical traits or traits of a certain category are found in Jesus' act, and because these associations help to make clear the meaning of the act itself.

CHAPTER III

THE CATEGORY OF CHRIST'S ACTION
AT THE LAST SUPPER

1. THE pericope dealing with the Last Supper, like many other sections, certainly stood by itself at one time. The narrators fitted it into the context of the Passion story, and then at once interpreted it as an account of a Passover meal. That is the case in Lk. xxii. 18 ff. He inserts it with the introductory words:

> 15. With desire I have desired to eat this passover with you before I suffer: 16. for I say unto you, I shall not eat it, until it be fulfilled in the kingdom of God.

At least v. 16 in the above quotation is a mere editorial adaptation to the words with which v. 18 opens the ancient account of the Last Supper as contained in the pericope now inserted:

> I shall not drink from henceforth of the fruit of the vine, until the kingdom of God shall come.

Christ can scarcely have expressed the same idea twice in such quick succession. And indeed it is not v. 18 that is assimilated to v. 16, but v. 16 to v. 18. That the saying of v. 18 is original is proved by the fact that Matthew and Mark also hand down its substance, but preserve nothing of Lk. xxii. 16. To this we must add that the outlook in v. 18 is reasonable, but in v. 16 not. For v. 18 has in view the future Messianic meal, which from the time of Enoch was a feature of eschatological speculations. But in v. 16 we read that the Passover meal should some day be repeated or fulfilled; an idea not found anywhere else. Verse 16, however, assumes the latter conception and thereby proves itself to be added by an editor who desired to

277

motivate v. 15, but who no longer had any clear conception of the genuine ancient Jewish ideas of the Messiah.

The entire assumption that Christ's last meal was a Passover meal and is to be understood as of that category must be abandoned. The reasons for this have been given recently and, as it seems to me, conclusively by Lietzmann in *Messe und Herrenmahl*.

2. The Last Supper belongs to some other category, viz. that of the religious festive meal, a cheber or a chaburah with sacramental character and with ritualistic peculiarities.

Pious Jews had long had the custom in some form of using a longish grace spoken after a meal; in addition, brief consecrating words of thanks (berākoth) were spoken over the bread and other foods, and likewise over the wine, when there was any on the table. From the private meal, however, we must also distinguish certain fraternal meals, in which several chaberim united as members of a chaburah.[1] Such fraternal meals had a religious and consecrated character. 'As early as the

[1] Compare the old but excellent work of Abraham Geiger, *Urschrift und Uebersetzungen der Bibel*, 1857, p. 121, on the cheber, the hetairiai, which arose at first as priestly brotherhoods. He distinguishes them from the priestly societies of pagan neighbours with their voluptuous, sacrificial meals in common. Presumably Ps. xvi. 4–5 is in point here, where the redeeming cup of Yahweh is opposed to the cup of the idolaters, but the latter is manifestly regarded as analogous to the former, and as a means of becoming a chabēr with Yahweh. Geiger further says on p. 122: Later ' "associations" were formed whose individual members were united with one another and which held consecrated meals in common.' And on page 123: 'Of particular significance were the common meals of these societies, sussitia, chabūrah. The most solemn meal of that sort was the Passover, which was eaten in fellowship, in a phratria (brotherhood) of at least ten, at times even of twenty persons. But in general all meals which were held in fellowship were meritorious, and consecrated by a religious character.' That such community meals were then particularly practised in associations which came into being, and that they tended to separate off certain rising associations, is proved by the example of the Essenes.

Greek period the Jew maintained the fraternal meal, consecrated by religion, which for him replaced the offering':
O. Holtzmann (Berākōt, 1912, p. 80). They are found in
Sadducean and Pharisaic circles. In particular, we may
conjecture that they existed in the secluded groups of those
who looked for an apocalyptic Messiah, the 'quiet in the
land,' from among whom Jesus and his disciples originated.
We may assume that even in these circles it became the
regular custom to offer the petition which was later taken
up into the usual Jewish grace:

> May the Merciful One count us worthy of the days of
> the Messiah and of the future life,

and possibly also the other petition:

> May the Merciful One send us the prophet Elijah, to
> bring us the message of happiness, of salvation, and of
> comfort.

In religious societies such as those of the Essenes, these
fraternal meals actually took on a sacramental character.
The associations which surrounded festal meals show up
clearly in Paul; and in his case they were certainly not
'Hellenistic' but corresponded to Jewish feeling and had
been inherited from the old Pharisaic chaburah. Not only
Paul but also the rabbis speak of the 'table of the Lord,'
and Paul's idea that by the fraternal eating of the one loaf,
many become one, and especially the idea that the eating
of the bread connects those who eat closely with that one
who distributes it, are exceedingly ancient connotations
which, even when unexpressed, accompanied such a
religious festive meal and were vividly and immediately
felt.

The brief consecrating sentences which were spoken
over the food, especially over the bread and the wine if
one had it, were in the form of simple words of thanks,
eucharistiai. But at the same time they were words of
consecration. The participants felt that the words blessed
the bread and wine; the eucharistia was also a eulogia,

a blessing, by which the food and drink were withdrawn from the secular realm and consecrated. That corresponded in general to the idea of the berakah. It was not only a word of thanks, but also a word of power (hence the Jewish berakoth actually became magical and exorcistic formulae, and could be widely utilized as such). It can scarcely be wrong to assume that he who partook of food which was blessed, received his part in the blessing which had been spoken over it. This inhered immediately in the idea that one ate and drank at the 'table of the Lord,' that one was a chaber, koinōnos, comrade of a meal consecrated by berakoth.

3. Bread necessarily formed part of every meal, and often enough the meal must have consisted of little else than bread. Wine was not a necessary part, and among the poorer classes it must often enough have been lacking or have been replaced by water. This circumstance still holds good in the later Christian eucharist. Breaking of bread: thus it is called by its oldest name, without special mention of wine, and among certain ancient Christians it was observed without a chalice, among others by water. But when the chaburah possessed wine, this was used in the kos shel berakah, and, long before the Christian eucharist, it played a role as 'the cup of blessing.' At times it appeared alone. Even to-day among the Jews on particularly solemn occasions a cup is blessed independently of a meal, e.g. at a wedding or at a circumcision. It is, as its name says, a cup of blessing, has portentous significance, and was doubtless meant originally not as an empty ceremony, but as imparting a blessing, a means whereby those for whom it is consecrated may drink in a blessing. To explain this custom, the Jews still appeal in giving religious instruction to Psalm cxvi. 13, 'the cup of David.' For 'David' says here:

I will lift the cup of salvation (kos hajeshuoth) and proclaim the name of Yahweh.

And the same 'David' says still more clearly in Ps. xvi. 4 f.:

280

I may not drink their (i.e. the idols') drink offerings of blood, but Yahweh is the portion of my inheritance and of my cup (menath kosi).

In contrast to this, we read of the godless in Ps. x. 6:

Fire and burning wind is the portion of their cup (menath kosam).

'A portion of inheritance' was such a portion as one obtained through inheritance; similarly 'a portion of a cup' was such a portion as one obtained through drinking a cup.[1] The godless drink in fire and burning wind, but David drank in Yahweh's salvation. The latter is meant also by the blessing and drinking of the kos shel berakah, the potērion eulogias or, as Paul says quite in harmony with, not Hellenistic but very old Jewish conceptions, the 'cup which we bless.'

We note here further that the cup in Ps. xvi. 5 clearly

[1] Ps. xi. 6 proves that the expression menath kos in the sense of 'portion of a cup' is, as Gunkel says quite correctly, a 'congealed way of speaking,' i.e. a fixed term. From this portion of a cup in Ps. xi. 6 one cannot possibly separate the term menath kos which recurs in identical form in Ps. xvi. 5. Now the parallel in v. 4 proves that this kos is conceived as a cup of offering and libation, and the above-mentioned late custom of pouring in the case of the Qiddush cup further proves that the cup in question was a libation cup. Verse 6 in Ps. xvi then needs no artificial conjectures; it is immediately clear. A menath which one obtains by cheleq is here distinguished from a menath kos. Cheleq is an acquisition in a natural way, e.g. spoil, income, reward, wages for work, distribution of landed property, portion of the area and tribe, or inheritance. In opposition to this was the menāth which one obtained in a supernatural way, i.e. by a cup of redemption, and thus as the deity's special gift. The Psalmist meant to say: 'in every way and in every sense Yahweh is my menath.'
The cup of Yahweh was already known in ancient Israel. In *Der Ursprung der Israelitisch-jüdischen Eschatologie*, p. 135, Gressmann said:
At the main festival, which took place after the vintage, the hosts entered the banquet halls of the sanctuary (1 Sam. ix. 22; Is. xxx. 29). There they ate and drank and were joyous before Yahweh. When then the festal cup, the cup of Yahweh, was passed from hand to hand . . .

possesses certain associations which we also find in Paul. In reference even to these it is superfluous to seek for traces of Hellenism, for they are just as much Israelite as Hellenistic. In Ps. xvi. 5 'David' clearly places the cup of Yahweh over against the cup of idols, or as Paul would say, demons. Obviously 'David' believed that whoever drank the cup of someone had a menāth, an inheritance, a koinōnia, with him, i.e. became his koinōnos. In 1 Cor. x. 21, Paul says:

> You cannot drink the cup of the Lord, and the cup of demons.

'David' in his time meant nothing else. And if Paul did not actually quote 'David' here, yet he thought entirely in 'David's' terms. At the same time what he said carried a connotation which must have been familiar to ancient religious sentiment generally and especially to that of the Jews; it must have been as familiar to the readers of Corinthians as to the primitive church, and have been no less customary to the eleven and Jesus himself because they were Jews, and chabērim of a religious meal. This associated idea is that participation in consecrated food bestows a menāth, a koinōnia, a sharing in the blessing, in the possession of salvation, in the consecration, the sanctification, and the holiness with which the previously secular food was sanctified.

The relation of the cup that was blessed to the cup which 'David' offered in Ps. cxvi. 13 remains clear in the eucharist as recorded in the Didache. Here the cup of blessing is expressly called 'the vine of David.' What was prophesied in the case of David's cup is now fulfilled—that is the meaning—through Jesus, the Servant of God. He has revealed the vine of David. Presumably over and above this is to be added the idea of a special eschatological cup. According to an ancient conception, David himself was to distribute the cup at the Messianic meal.[1] That this

---

[1] On this point compare R. Otto, *Sünde und Urschuld*, 1932, p. 103.

idea had been developed from Ps. cxvi. 13 may be regarded as proved by the circumstance that the Jews even to-day appeal to this very passage telling what David did, and regard it as explaining the custom of the kos shel berakah.

4. From such usages, certainly very old, the special rite of the Qiddūsh [sanctification] has developed. It was known and practised before Christ. At that time, however, it had forms that were less fixed. The schools of Hillel and Shammai used to dispute, for example, whether the ceremony of blessing of the bread should precede the blessing of the wine or vice versa. Qiddūsh in particular was the name of a definite prayer spoken as thanks for the Sabbath just beginning. Here again, the thanks was really more than a mere thanks; it was a consecration, i.e. the consecration of the new day just beginning as a holy day, as a Sabbath. The word Qiddūsh expressed that clearly, for it really meant not prayer of thanks but means of consecration; it was that which made a thing qadosh [holy]. The day just beginning was to be removed from the secular character of ordinary days by means of consecration, and made a holy day. The Qiddush prayer was associated with the blessing and dispensing of a cup and the blessing and dispensing of bread. If no wine was at hand, the blessing of bread sufficed. Wine and bread are then enjoyed, and to that extent formed part of the meal; nevertheless, their blessing and distribution constituted a ritual act as such. It preceded the meal according to present usage. But if for special reasons the meal was taken a considerable time before the beginning of the Sabbath, then, as I have experienced in a Jewish home, it could be carried out separately after the meal, and then simply as a rite. And according to Oesterley (*The Jewish Background of the Christian Liturgy*, Oxford, 1925, p. 171) this actually was originally the rule, i.e. the meal was taken first, and the Qiddush came later with a special blessing of cup and bread. Matthew's record correspondingly says Christ undertook his action 'as they were eating.' Now Christ's action cannot have been the formal

Qiddush, since such was only observed on the eve of the Sabbath or of the feast day itself. But the ritualistic blessing of cup and bread did not arise from the Qiddush. The Qiddush presupposed that one knew and practised similar rites before and independently of it.

5. Accordingly, Christ's Last Supper was not an altogether out-of-the-ordinary, spontaneous, new creation. It was not a sudden idea of the moment, nor an entirely exceptional action, nor even a fundamentally new institution. In the intimate circle of the chaberim of a meal already of a consecrated character, he repeated rites which had long been known and familiar at certain meals. These rites were rites of consecration and blessing. And, in accordance with ideas that were not too remote, but in circumstances that were unique, he used certain words to explain the special meaning which he put into the rite. This meaning clung to them henceforth as a new connotation and was carried further by the rite which continued to be practised in the church.

CHAPTER IV

THE ESCHATOLOGICAL CUP OF BLESSING

1. SHAMMAI opposed Hillel and placed the blessing of the wine first. In the question about marriage Christ was on Shammai's side against Hillel. Is it an accident that in the ritual question as to the placing of the cup he also follows Shammai's practice? In any case, according to Lk. xxii. 17, he put the cup first.

This circumstance alone speaks for the authenticity of the early pericope, for it contradicts, and so cannot have derived from the practice to which the other three accounts bear witness. We can easily understand why a cup that originally preceded should be transferred to a place after the breaking of the bread, but no reasons can be discerned for possibly transferring a cup that originally followed to a point before the distribution of the bread. In later practice the cup was occasionally not used at all. Its earliest significance was, in fact, only that of an introductory and subsidiary element to the real action. In the practice of the orthodox churches it was placed after the distribution of the bread. But in addition to the early pericope, there are several witnesses that it once came first.

Pre-eminent among the other witnesses is the account of the eucharist in the Didache. This venerable survival from the earliest period of church history probably originated in Palestinian Jewish-Christian circles; it introduces the eucharist with the blessing of the cup before the blessing of the 'klasma,' i.e. before the breaking of the bread. But traces and memories of an older practice, which likewise still had the cup before the distribution of the bread, seem to me to be present even in Paul. In 1 Cor. x. 16 he says:

> The cup, which we bless . . . the bread, which we break . . .

This sequence, which is the opposite of his own practice in
1 Cor. xi. 23, is very noteworthy; it is not motivated by
anything in the context, nor is it a solitary and fortuitous,
but a formal expression of Paul's. For in v. 21 he again
docs the same thing. Words with the sequence cup . . .
bread, appear to me to point to an older practice in which
the cup still preceded the bread. It still shows its effects
in the expression when it has already yielded to a later
practice.

2. Christ takes the cup. David in Ps. cvi. 13 lifts the
cup. Lifting is the technical expression for lifting aloft
the offering, and, as the parallel in Ps. xvi. 5 shows, the
association of the drink offering is still present in such
elevations of the cup. (Even in the Jewish rite 'the one
who offers the prayer pours a little wine upon the earth,'
cp. von der Goltz, p. 13; i.e. he first offers a libation, and
then distributes the remainder.) We have no means of
knowing whether these ideas were associated with, and
whether these practices were alive among, the people
round about Jesus. But that it was a cup of salvation, a
cup meant to signify and bring blessing, is certain.

3. He gave thanks. This means that he spoke the
berakah over the cup; the formula is well known:

> Blessed be thou, Eternal One, our God, King of the
> world, who hast created the fruit of the vine:

thereby he *consecrated* the cup.

4. He caused the wine that had been blessed to be distributed among the disciples. This ancient feature also
attests the authenticity of the pericope, for it too contradicts the later practice to which Paul bears witness when
he writes that Christ said: 'All ye drink of it.' These words
do not presuppose distribution, but a single cup common
for all (under the influence of motives of which we shall
speak later).

5. Christ accompanied the act of distribution with the
words:

> For I say unto you, I shall not drink from henceforth of the fruit of the vine, until the kingdom of God shall come.

He repeated here words from the ancient wine-berakah, for instead of 'wine' we have the solemn, ritualistic, periphrastic expression: 'the fruit of the vine' (in Hebrew peri haggefen; peri means fruit and product).

6. His words accompanying the cup are also preserved in Matthew and Mark and, indeed, in the fuller form:

> until that day when I drink it new with you in the kingdom of God.

This fuller form seems to me also to be the original, not because it is the more beautiful, but because that smoother and more schematic form might arise from this fuller and more appropriate form, but not vice versa; further, because the latter form lay in the line of Jesus' eschatology, and this again was determined by Enoch's apocalyptic. Enoch, however, had not only promised the coming of the kingdom in a general and conventional way, but also that some day the righteous would share the Messianic meal together with the Son of Man.

But on the other side, Luke gives these words with their eschatological standpoint in the correct place, while they are plainly displaced in Mark and Matthew. When the cup was put second, as in Mark and Matthew, the accompanying words were transposed at the same time, and placed at the end of the entire section. They now followed on the word about the covenant blood, and are quite awkward in that position. After the wine had just been explained as the covenant blood, Jesus could not possibly have gone on to speak of it as a mere festive drink at the future meal.[1]

7. The words about the cup in the early pericope therefore do not refer to blood or to establishing a covenant. Rather, in one respect it is a word of farewell,

---

[1] That was strange to me even as a candidate for confirmation.

and in another, a prediction of fellowship to be renewed in the future. Even as such, however, it was of significance for understanding the later table fellowship of the disciples and their adherents. Whenever they drank in fellowship the kos shel berakah, it was to them an anamnesis (remembrance) of their master's farewell, and also an act of looking forward to their reunion with him at the future meal. It was a rite of memorial and hope, and was to be celebrated with agalliasis, with joy and exultation.

But perhaps the blessing of the cup had a deeper significance than a mere farewell. Did not Christ himself intend it to be understood with a future reference? The cup that was blessed was indeed a kos hajeshuoth, a cup of salvation by which one drank in salvation. The very distribution of the cup of blessing, with its prospect of the meal in the Kingdom of God, was surely intended to give to those who drank an effective guarantee of participation in the future meal and of reunion with the departing Master. There is food for thought in the connection between the use of the word 'for' and the command to divide the cup of salvation.

We can only conjecture the actual expressions used to explain the action to which the blessing of the cup as such was only the introduction.

CHAPTER V

THE DIATHĒKĒ OF A LOOKING FORWARD
TO THE KINGDOM OF GOD

1. AFTER the introduction, which consisted of blessing
and distributing the kos shel berakah, accompanied by
a reference to the future Messianic meal, there followed,
in harmony with ancient ritual, Christ's eulogia, or blessing, pronounced on the bread. This again was immediately
followed by the breaking and distribution of the bread
as a single act, with an accompanying explanatory word.
But the goal of this action, which became obscured in
all later accounts, was in fact logical eschatology. This
point was given in the diathēkē, i.e. in the covenant promise looking forward to the kingdom, in v. 29. For we
read in the immediate context:

> This is my body (i.e. this is I myself as broken) and
> I appoint the kingdom unto you by covenant, as my
> Father has appointed it to me, that ye . . .

2. These words which accompany the single act consisting of breaking, distributing, and eating, and the act
itself, were by no means accidental. They lay in line with
Jesus' whole conception of himself and his mission, a
conception which now came to its logical finale. On the
one hand, we find here all perfect and complete, the
eschatology of Enoch which Christ followed. He was the
Son of Man, of whom Enoch had predicted that some day,
in the new age and at the meal of the new age, his own, i.e.
those bound together with him in close fellowship, should
'eat, recline, rise up, and sit with him upon thrones.' Here
the meaning of the akoluthia or discipleship reaches its
final form. Jesus required his disciples to cleave to him as
the eschatological redeemer and saviour with a view to a
fellowship which began here and was completed in the

T

final age. On the other hand, we find here the final form of Jesus' specific Messianism, viz. his discovery that the Son of Man was Isaiah's Servant of God, who must suffer and die. He had effected the combination of two essentially different Messianic doctrines, from the days when, after his disciples had come to recognize his Messiahship, he began to teach them that the Son of Man must suffer and die.

3. Christ said more on that evening than is contained in the brief records of the ancient pericope. It was not important that it should go into detail, for its only aim was to supply a short document to authorize the rite which was already observed, and which, with all its associated meanings, was known and practised in the church. In a succinct hieroglyph using only the significant words, it said just what was necessary for the purpose. But compact as it is, when understood as a hieroglyph, it is still decipherable. To this end, we have the help of a circumstance which, when superficially read, seems almost paradoxical, viz. that the words 'this is my body' are closely connected by 'and' with the immediately following words which promise the kingdom. This 'and' is not simply additive—which here would be simply meaningless—but indicates logical connection: 'This I am *and as such* (viz. as broken and shared out for partaking) I bequeath unto you the kingdom.' This means that Christ established for them the inheritance of the kingdom, undertaking to suffer death and to give them a share in the protecting and consecrating power of that suffering. By giving them a share in his mortal passion when he distributed the consecrated bread for them to eat, and effectively representing himself as broken, he performed an act—if we may be allowed to use ancient ritualistic terms 'leqadesh otham' (to sanctify them). It was a qaddish, an act that removed from the secular realm, inasmuch as it was a gift of participation in the lutron, the kopher, i.e. the means of expiation provided in the voluntary and obedient surrender of life by the 'Servant of God.' We must discuss this point more in detail.

4. 'As a result of the travail of his soul he will see himself satisfied.' Thus Is. liii spoke of the Servant of God, who in voluntary humble obedience had taken upon himself the suffering of death. The result of this obedience in suffering applied in the first instance to himself, and was his own glorification. Correspondingly Christ said: 'This is I' (i.e. I am broken), and at once continued: as my Father has appointed to me. Even in his case the first result of his obedient suffering applied to himself. Upon the basis of his obedient suffering he himself first inherits the kingdom of God. 'Ought not the Son of Man to suffer thus in order to enter his glory?' But the result for the Servant of God became the same for those who cleaved to him: 'With many will he divide his spoil'—a result which followed from the fact that they had part in the atoning power of the suffering through which the Servant of God had sanctified himself. And this became the real point of Is. liii. Thus also in Jesus' words, the real point was not that he himself inherited—of this only the inserted subordinate statement speaks—but that the disciples inherited as mentioned in the main clause, and it is this main idea rather than that of the subordinate clause, which is closely connected with the words that accompany the distribution and eating of the bread. This again meant that Christ could bequeath to his disciples the kingdom obtained on the ground of his own sanctification, because through the broken bread, which in their eating of it effectively represented the fact that he was broken, he as the Servant of God caused them to participate in the holiness, in the atoning power of his suffering. As thus expiated, as thus consecrated for the kingdom, they were qualified for the testamentum. That is the logical meaning of the connecting word 'and' in v. 29.

5. Diatithemai humīn (I appoint unto you), he says. Diatithesthai is the same as diathēkēn poieisthai (make a covenant). Diathēkē is berith; berith is covenant; and diatithesthai means in Hebrew kārath berith (make a covenant).' At the same time, our English concept of

covenant is somewhat too narrow in comparison with berith. For by covenant we mean something analogous to agreement, namely, a mutual binding, a pledge equally binding on the two parties. But this idea of mutuality is not a necessary part of the meaning of berith. Berith can also be a one-sided, binding pledge of X to Y. We suggest the same idea when we speak of a binding declaration, a binding promise. Such a covenant, a promise binding the promiser himself, is meant in our pericope, when God appoints (stipulates) the kingdom for His Son by a diathēkē; and when Christ in turn appoints unto his disciples the kingdom appointed unto him, i.e. in a binding manner gives them the reversion of it. Berith may therefore be the equivalent of testamentum. This connotation is quite clearly present here in the immediate context of the words: this am I (viz. the one about to die), and I establish (= appoint) unto you. . . . As one who is going to die, he makes arrangements. Consequently the action he performs is in fact his testament to his disciples. This meaning is quite consonant with the situation, and is that in which the word diathēkē is to be understood in the present context. The meaning was still operative when at a later date it was transformed into a diathēkē in his blood, for, in so doing, the close connection with his death was clearly indicated. On the other hand, however, this meaning, which is confined to the historical situation, was obscured by the ancient connotation of a covenant of blood, which the original report neither contained nor implied; the diathēkē as testamentum in the strict sense was distorted to the idea of a covenant as such.

6. Because he voluntarily suffered death the kingdom belonged first to himself as his own inheritance. Only through him and with him would the disciples become the immediate heirs of the kingdom. In other words, he was the mediator of the covenant for them; he was a 'covenant mediator.'

This conception, again, was quite in line with Enoch's apocalyptic and its eschatology of the Son of Man. Even in Enoch, the Son of Man was not merely the judge but, as already shown, an explicitly eschatological mediator. With him and through him the righteous who belong to him inherit the salvation of the new age. On the other hand, the conception is explicitly in harmony with the eschatology of Isaiah's Servant of God. We are therefore brought face to face once more with the fact that Jesus combined in himself two eschatologies of different origin, those of the Son of Man and the Servant of God. The Servant of Yahweh was 'the covenant' for the people of Israel, and was expressly so called:

> I will make you into a berith (a diatheke, a covenant) with the people of Israel (Is. xlii. 6),

i.e. into a mediator of the covenant between me and the people. And likewise in Is. xlix. 8:

> I will preserve thee and give thee for a covenant of the people.

Other passages from Deutero-Isaiah are also instructive, for the idea in our pericope that a diathēkē is a binding pledge of eschatological salvation generally, and for the associations of that pledge with Deutero-Isaiah, e.g. Is. liv. 10:

> My loving kindness shall not depart from thee, neither shall my covenant of peace be removed.

In the immediately following verses, Is. liv. 11 ff, this passage clearly has an eschatological echo in the fantastic portrayals of the future glory, in which apocalyptic and eschatological ideas are obviously sprouting forth. The whole section closes like a 'testamentum,' when it says, in v. 17b:

> This is the heritage of the servants of Yahweh.

But particularly significant is the fact that the entire chapter, Is. liv, which, as we have said, clearly treats of an eschatological heritage, joins immediately on to the closing words of ch. liii:

> Therefore will I give him (i.e. the suffering and dying Servant of God) a portion among the many . . . because he gave up his life unto death and was numbered among the transgressors: yet he bare the sins of many.

This means that the conception of mediating eschatological salvation, as a heritage won on the basis of the suffering of the Servant of God, was prefigured as clearly as possible by joining the eschatological promise in Is. liv to the expiatory death of the Servant of God in Is. liii; the words of Christ, that he would mediate the kingdom on the basis of his suffering, are a simple and short epitome of trains of thought and associated ideas which he found already in the book about the Servant of God. One should read Is. liii–liv and our pericope one after the other in order to get the right impression of this fact.[1]

Indeed, the very terms which Christ uses have their analogy in Isaiah's manner of speaking. If one desired to render the diatithemai humin in Hebrew it would run: ekerethah lakem berith; the object, basileian-mamelakah, would then have to be expressed as an accusative in apposition to berith. We find the corresponding idiom in Is. liii. 3, with an accusative of apposition.

> ekerethah lakem berith—chasede David.
> (I appoint unto you a covenant—namely, the mercies of David = I give you a binding promise of the mercies of David.)

This utterance also agrees in content with Christ's, for the 'mercies of David' are simply the regal glory, the kingdom of the new age. The words, chasede David, refer to 2 Sam. vii. 16. But it is noteworthy that the gifts

---

[1] Consider also that in Jesus' day there were no divisions of chapter and verse, and thus the first verse of Is. liv was actually the immediate continuation of Is. liii.

which are graciously promised to David and his house are the very ones that Christ promised his own: mamelakah and kisse, kingdom and throne.

The formula: ekeroth lahem berith = diathithemai occurs once more in Isaiah in ch. lxi. 8.

THE WORD OF INSTITUTION AT THE DISTRIBUTION OF THE BREAD. CHRIST NOT THE FOOD OF THE SOUL, BUT BROKEN IN DEATH

1. JESUS broke the bread and gave it to his disciples to eat. As he did so, he applied the words: this is my body (as we shall see later, the connotation was: this is myself). He does not liken himself to bread in a general way, in the sense that as bread is food for the body, so am I food for the soul. He compared himself rather to the broken bread. Since he was broken in death he was like this broken bread, and, by the symbolic act of eating, the disciples were meant to participate in the fact of his being broken, in his surrender of life for the many.

2. Breaking of bread occurs indeed at every meal, but in the rite it has specially significant meaning. That was the firm conviction of the oldest tradition of the church, and explains the otherwise unintelligible fact that, in the first church, the rite bore the utterly unusual name for a meal 'klasis tou artou.' It was so called because the act of fractio panis, of breaking of bread, was of crucial significance for the entire action.[1] That was only possible because the breaking itself was a signum, or sign. It signified, objectively and directly, one who was broken in death, the death of Christ and its results, and it kept that reference alive. But this reference, again, was unmistakably meant by the pericope, as we can see when we notice the close union of the diathēkē with the institutionary words: this is I. Christ is not typified as food for the soul, but as one making his last will and testament

[1] On this very important point, see the more detailed discussion in R. Otto, *Religious Essays*, p. 47.

when about to die. Nor does he qualify them to receive his testament by feeding their souls, but by lifting them out of the secular sphere by the atoning power of his death, and consecrating them for the kingdom of God. The special eschatological point of the action is greatly obscured in the other records, but they all preserve this reference as well as the idea of special participation in Christ's suffering unto death.

3. Under the influence of later ideas and motives, the primary significance grew faint in certain circles. Other ideas became associated and changed the meaning as well as the mode of the ancient rite. On this point the attitude of the Fourth Gospel is instructive. This writing is late; it deals with the sacrament of the church and speaks of it and its indispensability in lofty words, in Jn. vi. 53 ff. But two facts at once strike us. On the one hand, it is striking that this gospel says nothing about the supper on the last night, although in other respects it gives a very detailed account of that night. And on the other hand, ch. vi is plainly meant to be the document authorizing the church's sacrament; yet the determinative element in the record is not the idea of Christ's suffering unto death, but that the logos gives himself to be eaten as food for the soul. These two facts must be seen in their necessary connection. No longer do we find anything about the fractio panis. The old symbolic act, its original meaning, and even its original and appropriate contour, have all disappeared. As a consequence, and at the same time, the act has lost the position in the narrative which corresponded to its meaning and the historical circumstances. It has been pushed out of the passion story. There is no longer any mention of the breaking of the bread, because there is no mention of the broken body, nor, indeed, any mention of the body at all. Instead of a body, we now hear of flesh, for flesh, but not body, is food. The result was that it was no longer necessary to give the passage dealing with the sacrament in the context of Christ's passion and death; rather, its right place was now of necessity in the

midst and at the climax of the earthly appearance of the incarnate logos. Of course, by his words and teaching, he was continually offering himself as food for the soul and as the bread that had come from heaven. Therefore the record about it was not in place as a supplement at the end, but in the centre of his teaching activity. And the transposition and displacement were not difficult for the fourth evangelist; it was his style to deal rather freely with the historical materials of tradition, e.g. he transferred the cleansing of the temple from the end to the beginning of Christ's active ministry.

In other words, the later Christology, i.e. the Christology of the Son of Man who was the logos, displaced the Christology of Christ himself, i.e. that of the Son of Man who was identical with the Suffering Servant in Isaiah. Similarly it took the genuine and ancient procedure reflected in the narrative of the Last Supper, which is, by its nature, a witness to the Christology based on the servant of God, displaced it from its natural position, and put the equivalent for it in a place agreeable to the new theology. In so doing, it completely obscured any connection with the death of Christ. The lack of such reference, however, was the final result, not the beginning, of a long theological development.

CHAPTER VII

THE SPECIAL CATEGORY OF CHRIST'S ACTION WITH THE BREAD

ADOLF JÜLICHER saw that Christ's action was not something altogether unique and exceptional, but something that belonged to a class, viz. that of parable. In sharing out the bread the master of parabolic discourse, says Jülicher, was speaking and acting in a parable. That is certainly correct. We shall go further along this line and attempt to define the category of this action more closely in order to understand its meaning more exactly. We express it: What Christ did with the bread in breaking, distributing, and explaining, was really to be taken as a whole, a single act with a twofold reference or category:

(a) that of the prophetic oth, i.e. an acted prediction, and

(b) that of effective representation by an analogous drōmenon (anticipative, representative act).

CHAPTER VIII

THE ACTED PREDICTION, TYPIFIED BY THE PROPHETIC OTH

1. AFTER Christ had broken the bread and while he was distributing it for eating he said: This is my body. In Aramaic, according to Dalmann, the words were: den hu gufi, and the word gufi, 'my body,' in Aramaic has the connotation of 'I myself.' He began by comparing his body, and at the same time himself, as broken, to the broken bread. That was an undoubted parabolic utterance and act. But it is plainly more than parabolic, and is predictive in character, for Christ's being broken was still future and was now being anticipated in the symbolism.

2. Being a prediction and an anticipation, what Christ did and said belongs to a well-known class of prophetic prediction, viz. that of the oth, the acted prediction —which likewise signified anticipation. This type of prediction with the simultaneous use of a symbolic drōmenon is frequently used in Ezekiel, e.g. ch. iv, also in Isaiah, e.g. xxx. 3. In Jer. xix. 10, the prophet is instructed to take a jar, to go outside the gate in the presence of the people of Jerusalem, to break the jar before their eyes, and thereby to predict their lot. He could also have said at the breaking of the jar, in a way similar to Christ: 'This is you.' That is an oth, an acted prediction by means of an analogous drōmenon given as a sign, i.e. an act that portrays, represents, and likewise anticipates, the thing predicted.

Jesus was a prophet. As we shall argue later, ancient prophecy was renewed in him in its typical features. He took bread, as Jeremiah took a jar, broke it, and said of it: den hu gufi: This is myself. Everyone who knew the ancient prophets was aware that that signified: 'What has happened to this bread, will happen to me.'

He at once continued: and I appoint unto you. . . .
The meaning of this connection is evident. As the one
who is broken, i.e. takes upon himself the Messianic
obligation to suffer, he could be, and indeed was, the
mediator of the diathēkē (testament). Even when the
strict eschatological sense of this diathēkē was obscured
in the later accounts, and when it came to be specially
connected with the shedding of blood, the logic of the
link 'and I' ('kai egō') is still preserved. The later accounts
still confirm our interpretation of this kai egō, viz. as
showing the close connection between inheriting the kingdom and suffering unto death as the basis of the inheriting,
'I am broken, and I (as broken) appoint unto you.'

CHAPTER IX

EFFECTIVE REPRESENTATION WITH THE AIM OF GIVING PARTICIPATION IN THE THING REPRESENTED

1. CHRIST's action with the bread is manifestly more than an oth. The bread 'is'—repraesentando—Christ as broken. But the bread, with this fullness of meaning, was immediately distributed for eating. The action was an acted anticipation of something future (namely, the breaking of Christ's body), and also it gave participation in the thing anticipated, and that by effective representation. This corresponds to an ancient view which was found in many places, and still exists to-day. Never strictly defined, but for that reason only the more vivid, the view is that one can transfer or appropriate the essence, the power, the effect, the peculiar nature, the curse, or the blessing which belongs to a thing or process X by the use of a representative of X. Such a representation becomes effective through the will of him who has control over X. The effective representation may be coarsely realistic; then it is the basis of magical machinations. On the religious level it furnishes the basis of the sacrament. As in the case of Christ's action it may be completely spiritualized; then it furnishes the basis of the significant or symbolic act.

2. The idea of effective representation, moreover, corresponds in particular to religious conceptions such as were found even in Israel.

In Is. vi, Isaiah stands before God. He feels himself to be unworthy and unfitted for prophecy, because he is worldly, a man of unclean lips. To become God's messenger he must first be lifted out of the secular sphere and undergo an expiation which will consecrate or sanctify him for his vocation. This was accomplished by a consecrating contact with the holy realm itself; an angel took

302

a coal from the altar and touched his lips. The consecrating contact with the holy was established by an act of effective representation.

The altar, and everything connected with it, was a representative of the numen itself. We ordinarily conceive it as a mere table for offerings, but that is not true to ancient religious feeling. The altar represented the numen, and represented it efficaciously. What happened in connection with it had to do with the numen itself, therefore the blood of the offering must be poured on the altar. He who touches the altar himself becomes qadosh (holy —a condition dangerous in some circumstances for the laity). Hence even Christ said: 'The altar sanctifies the gift.' The representation of the numen by the altar went so far that later on 'altar' actually became a paraphrastic name of the deity. One said altar but meant God. Thus among the rabbis altar, like heaven, became a circumlocution for Yahweh. One swore by the altar, for the altar represented God. The altar and what was upon it could sanctify and expiate. It could do so by effective representation.

3. Things or processes, wherever found, which in themselves have a similarity or analogy to the thing or process to be represented, are particularly adapted as effective representatives. Just because they are analogous, they may spontaneously 'attract' the idea of an effective representation to themselves. In Jesus' action we are faced with the special case of representation by real analogy, and also by spontaneous attraction of the idea. That becomes still more obvious when one considers that Christ could expect his death only in the form of stoning, i.e. an actual breaking of himself and his body, and he undoubtedly always did expect it in this form. (On this point cp. R. Otto, *Religious Essays*, p. 48.) The breaking of the bread was factually analogous to the breaking of a body as in stoning. This unique analogy was already existent and at once available as an effective representation; indeed, it spontaneously attracts the idea of such a representation.

303

Likewise the receiving of food and its strength is in itself analogous to the appropriation of a power or operation of the thing represented, and thus of itself it attracts the idea of effective representation.

4. Christ's action was, therefore, more than mere prediction; it was an acted, anticipatory prediction by representation; even more was it the gift of a share in the power of the thing represented, viz. in the atoning power of the broken Christ. That the bread was changed into Christ's body, that his body or his flesh or he himself was eaten—such ideas were completely absent from this act of sharing out and participating in. Rather their clear analogue is in those undefined ideas in Ps. xvi. 5–8, xi. 6, which we discussed above. The drinking of Yahweh's cup gave Yahweh as one's portion, and gave a portion in Him in the sense that it mediated His jeshuōth, His blessings, and salvation. And the consecrated bread also can do what the blessed cup can do. The ideas of such participation, which are emotional associations rather than ideas, emerge clearly with Paul; in this connection he invented nothing, nor did he import anything from Hellenism. He only took the groups of fluid and undefined ideas which hovered round familiar Jewish rites, and half-shaped them into concepts. With their help he commented, and commented pointedly, on the meaning of Christ's distribution of the bread:

> Behold Israel (i.e. take an example from the usage in Israel's cult). Have not they that eat the sacrifices communion with the altar? (1 Cor. x. 18).

They did not eat the altar, but the offering. But, because the offering belonged to the altar, then by virtue of effective representation one shared in the altar. That again did not mean that one now obtained a part or a stone of the altar, but the power, viz. the sanctifying power of the altar, as a menath, or portion, or that one obtained a portion in the sanctifying power.

Similarly with Paul's conception of sharing in the body

of Christ. Undoubtedly he gave a mystical turn to this conception. But even with his mystical ideas of the sōma Christou (body of Christ) he knew nothing of an eating and drinking of heavenly substances; his prime conception, as the parallel of participating in the altar shows, was purely that of participation through effective representation. 1 Cor. x. 16:

> The bread which we break is it not a communion of the body of Christ (as broken)?

Naturally what was eaten was even now only bread and not the body of Christ, just as in the preceding example the altar itself was not eaten. But, by virtue of effective representation, the one who ate the bread obtained fellowship with the represented body, and this again not in the sense that he now possessed this body or a part of it, but again as with the altar, viz. he partook of the sanctifying power of this broken body.

Moreover, it is instructive that Paul presents all this not as a peculiar, or unusual theory, but with almost reproachful questions, as though he would say: All of this you know, all of this is indeed a matter of course and everyone knows it; yet you do not trouble about it but regard the ceremony too lightly. He was right. For to ancient religious feeling all this was in fact so immediately obvious that Paul only needed to appeal to the conscience of the Corinthians.

CHAPTER X

THE ASSOCIATIONS OF SACRAMENTAL EATING

To us moderns it may seem strange that any atonement could be appropriated by the distribution of bread for eating. The sense of strangeness was doubtless an influence which led to explaining Christ's action as a cult-myth which had been subsequently invented. The theology of the church, it is thought, must have invented the idea, for of course, no one would believe that Jesus himself could have hit upon such an eccentric notion. But such an objection would answer itself, for it presupposes that it was possible at that time to hit upon such eccentric notions. The church possessed it. Was Christ less eccentric than the church, and why? The same consideration holds with respect to the idea of vicariousness. Was Isaiah less familiar to Jesus than to the theologizing disciples? Was the Church able to invent the idea that the Messianic king acted vicariously for the Messianic Church, but Jesus himself not able to conceive it? That a prince or king could, indeed should, act vicariously for his people was not an idea current only outside Israel. David likewise had it, cf. 2 Sam. xxiv. 17.

But with respect to the ideas specially associated with consecrated food and particularly with consecrated bread, we would add the following to what has already been mentioned.

'Eating before Yahweh' was a primordial ceremony, and the term itself was just as ancient in Israel's sacramental observance. It was a sacramental act. It expressed the attachment of this special group to Yahweh, and fellowship with Him was celebrated and renewed by this act. It was both the expression and also a medium of the sacramental union among each other of those who ate together. Both aspects are expressed in the narrative of Ex. xviii. 12. Jethro, Moses' father-in-law, himself a non-Israelite, went to meet his son-in-law. He brought with him animals to slay for a burnt-offering and a sacrificial meal before God. Aaron and all the leading men of Israel came near 'to eat bread with him before God.' On the one hand, the meal was a typical act instituting sacramental brotherhood with one another; on the other hand, it signified that Jethro was accepted as belonging to the God of Israel's cult; both elements are present in the eating of holy food. When the worship in the synagogue, the rites of home fellowship and of pious brotherhoods developed, supplemented or, in distant regions, replaced the temple and its sacrificial cult, the old ideas passed over, as O. Holtzmann noted, to the new rites. That men were still conscious of eating 'before Yahweh,' or 'at the table of God,' has already been noted above.

The bread in particular was universally of special significance and the eating of a person's bread was an act which united one closely with him. 'He who eats his bread' is synonymous with close union and attachment of the one who eats to the one who gives the bread.

How concrete these conceptions were is borne out by a story in the Testament of Job, ch. vii (*Texts and Studies*, v. 1, p. 107), to which D. Frankenberg has called my attention. Here Satan draws near to Job to destroy him. He would like Job to enter into fellowship with him. He asks the girl at his gate for a 'loaf from the hands of Job.' But Job perceives the trick, and sends out a loaf to him, but a *burnt* one. This does not establish the fellowship which would otherwise have been established by 'the loaf from his hands,' but because it is a burnt one, plainly the opposite was to be effected, viz. the most complete separation from Satan. Thus on the one hand we have the idea (in inverted form) that whoever receives bread from someone's hands comes into closest fellowship with that person; and on the other hand a drōmenon with the idea of effective representation. Since the bread which really would establish fellowship was burnt, all fellowship was meant to be destroyed. 'You shall not eat of my bread, because I am redeemed from you.' Job sent this message out to Satan. The state of redemption from him was represented, and also effected, by sending out a burnt loaf.

In particular, the sacrificial bread was a 'most holy thing' (Lev. xxiv. 9). And still more important for our purpose is it to note that to eat of it served to expiate, to lift out of the secular sphere, and to consecrate, cp. Ex. xxix. 33. In v. 32 we read of sacrificial flesh and of the lechem (bread); v. 33 continues:

we akelu otham, asher kuppar bahem, leqaddesh otham.

That is: 'And they eat these things (i.e. the flesh and the bread) whereby the expiation is accomplished for them, to sanctify them (i.e. those who eat).' The bread which was brought as an offering and which is, therefore, consecrated bread sanctifies by being eaten.

He who participated in the sacrificial cult or in the eating of food consecrated by the berakah or blessing, shared in these feelings and experiences. Hence we may say, on the one hand, that to use the breaking of bread to symbolize the breaking of himself was not out of the way in Jesus, for he knew the othoth (symbolic acts) of the ancient prophets, and also was himself a prophet; on the other hand, it was still less strange to make the eating of the bread, which had been consecrated by thanksgiving, the effective representative of participation in the sanctifying power of his Messianic suffering. On the contrary, such a procedure lay near at hand through ancient sacramental associations.

Let us further ask whether such conceptions were specially prepared for also in the apocalyptic circles. At the close of the Slavonic Enoch we read how the saint is together with his own for the last time before his departure. Farewell speeches are uttered. Then it says Sl. En., p. 97):

308

> Methusalem answered his father Enoch and said: 'If it is well-pleasing in your eyes, father, we will prepare food before your face, that you may bless our houses and all your servants and that you may glorify your people and then depart.

In other words, the departing saint was being petitioned to have a farewell meal with his own, and it would also transfer his personal power of blessing (his berakah) to his circle and his people. Hence, in the fellowship meal, and especially in the farewell meal with the saint, there lay a consecrating power blessing those left behind.

On p. 101 they say to him:

> Blessed art thou of the Lord, the eternal king. And now (as one going to God) bless your people and glorify us before the face of the Lord, because the Lord has chosen you and has ordained you as one who takes away our sins.

The one chosen by God, who has consecrated and sanctified himself to Him, upon his departure takes away the sins of those who belong to him. It is further noteworthy in this connection that these ideas appear in these circles quite incidentally and without particular emphasis or further circumstances. As we have said previously, they were simply taken for granted and had no need of being specially taught. They corresponded exactly to the words of the Aged One, which we have already discussed (En. lxxi. 15 f.):

> Thus will it happen to you: all that walk in your ways —you whom righteousness never forsakes—their dwelling and inheritance will be with you.

And that again simply means: For the sake of your righteousness, they also shall be justified and receive their inheritance.

CHAPTER XI

SUMMARY OF RESULTS

1. IN this way a clear light is thrown on the historical context and the meaning of the action and words in all the events of the Last Supper. Ancient and quite familiar rites were carried out. They were filled with a new and distinctive meaning from the special circumstances. After Christ in accordance with ancient custom had first blessed and distributed a kos shel berakah (cup of blessing), which he had already accompanied with a reference to the future Messianic meal, he followed up this introduction with the act upon which depended the real meaning of the action and which constituted its essence. As mediator of the covenant he bequeathed his own inheritance of the kingdom to the circle of disciples, after he had consecrated and fitted them to receive it by giving them a share in the expiatory power of his suffering as Servant of God. By his obedient suffering he sanctified himself for inheriting the kingdom, and he sanctified them by the same means for receiving his testament. This logic of salvation is still echoed by the Fourth Gospel in the words (xvii. 19):

> I sanctify myself for them, that they also may be truly sanctified.

The whole meaning is that he brought to a climax his teaching that the Son of Man must suffer, i.e. that he himself was Isaiah's Servant of God; he deepened the meaning of the sole rite which Jesus' chaburah (association of disciples) already possessed, viz. the consecrated meal of fellowship. He did this in a way made intelligible and clear by ideas which Jews would associate with it.

The ancient rite of the meal was continued in his church. The new meaning which Christ had given it was accompanied and extended by the rite until it had a depth of meaning such as no other religious community can show.

The first and immediate point of Christ's action, however, was the strictly eschatological reference to inheriting the kingdom of God. That was important also for the practice of the rite as we observe it to-day, and for a critical understanding of it. Our practice points to forgiveness of sins as the essence of the significance of the rite. That is not wrong, for forgiveness of sins is implicit in the act of participating in the consecration and atonement effected by the suffering of the Servant of God. Nevertheless it is not correct, for the means is unduly emphasized to the detriment of the purpose. In Christ's teaching, which was meant to be logical eschatology, forgiveness and expiation of sins were not the purpose itself, but only the means to the eschatological final goal. They were means whereby men might enter into God's kingdom, whereby sinners, when redeemed, might be able to see God.

Luther preserved this strictly eschatological element of expiation of sins purely and clearly, not indeed in his doctrine of the Lord's Supper, but in explaining the second article of the creed:

> I believe that Jesus Christ has redeemed me from all sins by his innocent suffering and death, *that* I might live under him in his kingdom and serve him.

The word 'that' corresponds logically to the word 'and' which connects the clause 'this is myself' and the clause 'I appoint unto you' in the earliest pericope recording the Last Supper.

CHAPTER XII

THE LATER DEVELOPMENTS, ALTERATIONS, AND DISLOCATIONS OF MEANING

1. THE Christology of the church at Jerusalem was not Paul's Kyrios (Lord) Christology, nor John's Logos Christology, but Christ's own Servant of God Christology. Its sacred meal was not the kyriakon deipnon (Lord's Supper), but the klasis tou artou, the fractio panis, the breaking of bread. The church took part in the temple worship and undoubtedly also in that of the synagogue. But at home, the church observed in common the consecrated meal of a fellowship of religious brethren or chaberim.

Some argue that, originally, in the primitive church this meal was simply the customary meal accompanied by the usual table rites. The phrase, 'breaking of bread,' simply meant 'take a meal.' The learned reason is added that the name for a meal was of course everywhere the term perusah, and perusah meant the breaking of bread. I do not know who started the latter assertion. It is a learned invention that is passed on from commentary to commentary, and is wrong. Perusah never means meal; wherever it occurs it means a thing broken off, pars fracta; it does not designate the act of breaking bread, but the fragment of bread broken off. Nowhere is it the name for a meal. Breaking of bread as a *name* is a singular name invented for this special ceremonial action; it is only applicable to this particular ceremony of this particular fellowship, and points to a singular, new meaning occurring only here.

The translation of perusah by breaking of bread goes back perhaps to G. Klein, 'Die Gebete in der Didachē, in *Zeitschrift für neutestamentliche Wissenschaft*, 1908, p. 139. He says: 'The benediction (i.e. over the bread) was also

named paras, perusah, breaking of bread.' He refers to
J. Levy, *Neuhebräisches Wörterbuch*, s.v. paras, No. II, and to
the passage from Roshhashanah 29*b*, which he translates:

> One may not speak the blessing at the cutting of the
> loaf for guests, except when one eats with them.

Löschke refers back to Klein, and others appear to be
dependent on both. But the sentence by Klein contains
four errors. J. Levy nowhere says that perusah meant
breaking of bread, he cannot say that, because it would
be foolish. Perusah is a passive participle and means not
breaking but that which is broken. It can be used in a
broadened sense, but neither for breaking bread nor for
blessing, but for bread. Perusah in the sense of bread is
found occasionally, as is intelligible, since the loaf on the
table was always a broken one. The term is used in the
passage cited from Roshhashanah, where it means neither
cutting, nor speaking a blessing, but klasma, i.e. the
table bread. In the Didache the holy act itself is not
called perusah, but eucharistia; here again perusah, i.e.
klasma, means bread, and nothing further.

Paras may—a fact, however, which does not interest
us for the meaning of perusah—actually be connected
with 'to utter benedictions.' This paras, however, has
nothing to do with breaking of bread, but, according
to J. Levy, *Wörterbuch ueber Talmudim und Midraschim*,
signifies 'divide the benedictions of the Shema,' i.e. so
divide them that two come before and one after the
Shema itself. It has, therefore, not the least connection
with breaking of bread.

The passage from Roshhashanah, however, runs ver-
batim:

> One may not break the bread for guests, except
> when oneself eats with them. But one may break it for
> one's children and household (even without oneself
> eating with them).

(Cp. Goldschmidt in the most recent translation of the
Babylonian Talmud, III, 611.) The breaking of bread
was naturally accompanied by the customary berakah;
it was not, however, called benediction, but simply
breaking of bread. Nor was it called perusah. And least
of all was the meal itself called breaking of bread here

or elsewhere. The issue in this passage is simply as follows. The Rabbis distinguished between a meal of those who were not members of one household (e.g. the meal of a chaburah) and a household meal. In the former case, no one who did not himself take part in the meal should break the bread. But in the latter case, he should do so, even if he did not partake, probably in order at all events to preserve the table custom.

That the breaking of the bread was a Jewish ceremony, as Löschke says, is so obvious and well known that we need not cite passages for it. The thing that would have mattered would have been to show a single passage where breaking of bread was a name for holding meals. There are no such passages, and those which Billerbeck cites to prove it, all provide proof directly to the contrary. In short, the facts are that the first Christian community assembled in their homes in order to break bread; that this phrase unquestionably signifies this meal; that at meals generally and as a regular thing bread was broken; that at no time and in no place before or elsewhere was a meal called breaking of bread. Accordingly this meal had its particular meaning precisely as breaking of bread, which must now have had a particular meaning not otherwise connected with it. Q.E.D.

Undoubtedly, the entire assumption that breaking of bread was the name for Jewish meals and was called perusah was only manufactured out of the fact that it is so called in Acts. The first person ventured the opinion, the second took it as proved, the third said as a matter of course: Perusah means breaking of bread and is of course the name for a Jewish meal.[1]

That the eating of the bread followed the breaking of the bread was a matter of course. That a real meal followed —at least as a rule—was probably the case for a long

[1] Moreover, the passage from Roshhashanah is interesting in another respect. In the case of a chaburah meal, it commands that he who does not eat shall not break the bread. It therefore presupposes that sometimes the opposite occurred. Thus it is actually possible, as has sometimes been contended, that Jesus blessed and then distributed the wine and bread without himself partaking of them.

time.[1] But when such a celebration is called the breaking of bread, and thus a name is chosen according to a circumstance wholly trivial in itself, the breaking is proved in this case to be by no means trivial, but is the significant element of the celebration. A particular *ritual* feature was meant and this was so charged with meaning that it gave its name to the entire celebration. The central feature consisted in the being broken. That could only be so when the being broken was significant. But it could only be significant when it was a signum, viz. of Christ's being broken in death. In other words, the rite of a religious fellowship meal was itself ancient, but it was now filled with the meaning of celebrating, and ritually participating in, Christ as broken. To this extent, therefore, the ceremonial of the primitive church corresponded completely to the meaning of Christ's original action.

It also corresponded to it in that the name was not derived, for example, from the distribution of the cup. As we have seen, this was not the central point of Christ's own action. In what Christ himself did, the cup was not accorded a significance equal with the fractio panis. The meaning of what he did was, in fact, made to turn on the act of the fractio panis alone, and if we desired to give to his action a short and pithy title, presumably even we would begin to speak of 'Christ's breaking of bread.'

The rite was celebrated en agalliasei, with rejoicing, in ecstatic joy, characteristic of a Messianic and 'enthusiastic' association, whose members knew themselves to be the heirs of the Son of Man.

2. Now let us examine the further evolution of this rite. For comparison we now give the account from Mt. xxvi. 26 ff. side by side with the original account, corrected according to p. 265 ff.:

---

[1] But that it could also occur as a separate rite is suggested by the scene at Troas (Acts xx. 11), for after midnight it is scarcely likely to have been a real meal, but, even at that hour, a short sacred rite of fellowship could have been observed in connection with religious discourses.

THE PRIMITIVE ACCOUNT	THE ACCOUNT IN MATTHEW
And when the hour was come, he sat down, and the apostles with him.	But as they were eating.
And he took a cup, gave thanks and said: Take this and divide it among yourselves.	(lacking in Matthew.)
For I say unto you: no more will I henceforth drink of the fruit of the vine, until the day when I drink it new with you in the kingdom of my Father.	(displaced to the end in Matthew.)
And he took the bread, gave thanks, broke it, and gave it to them, saying: this is my body,	Jesus took bread, and blessed, and brake it; and he gave to the disciples, and said, Take, eat, this is my body.
and I appoint you in covenant,	And he took a cup, and gave thanks, and gave to them, saying, Drink ye all of it; for this is my blood of the covenant, which is poured out for many unto remission of sins.
	But I say unto you, I shall not drink henceforth of this fruit of the vine, until that day when I drink it new with you in my Father's kingdom.
as my Father has appointed the kingdom unto me in covenant, that ye may eat and drink at my table in my kingdom; and ye shall sit on thrones judging the twelve tribes of Israel.	The words of promise to the Eleven. (They are lacking in Matthew.)

In its similarity to ancient table rites, but also in its combination of a merely introductory cup with the real main action, the primitive account plainly tells of a symbolic action of Christ. The record is completely in accord with the historical situation, but is also strictly bound to the historical circumstances and therefore beyond invention by a later age. Hence it is possible almost to see how this ancient record, and the practice pictured by it, began to be affected by contemporary influences, to be changed feature by feature, and to absorb new elements.

3. The most striking difference in the later account is not the change of the introductory cup into a cup of blood, for this is simply a case of doubling the symbolism by assimilation; nor is it the change of order in giving the cup. The outstanding thing is rather the omission of the words of promise to the eleven. That change must certainly have occurred first.

Automatically and necessarily it followed from the fact that the old chaburah meal did not continue to be confined to the narrow circle of the eleven disciples, but lived on in an ever-growing community of such as had not themselves participated in Christ's last supper. The diathēkē, appropriate in earnest for the eleven, now necessarily and of itself lost the narrow and strictly temporary outline. It became a diathēkē in general, and drew to itself a meaning which was not reproduced in the early pericope, viz. that of a new covenant in contrast to the old covenant of Sinai. This was not wrong in itself, since in contrast with the ancient dispensation, Christ began something absolutely new, and abrogated 'the law and the prophets;' he himself expressed the change sharply enough and it corresponded to the content of his message. Nevertheless, it widened his own original saying to the eleven about the special diathēkē of the kingdom and the heavenly meal. With this unavoidable alteration of meaning, the next result was the obscuring of the strict and narrow eschatological reference of the rite in general.

4. Thus we can explain the circumstance that foreign insertions were quickly able to force a way into the early pericope. The words: 'and I appoint unto you . . .' were no longer recognized as being closely connected in meaning with the words used about the bread; indeed, they could no longer be so recognized. The connection became loose. 'I appoint unto you . . .' necessarily appeared as isolated words which had nothing specially to do with

the klasis tou artou, as soon as the latter was understood as the sacrament of the church. Thus they could drift away by themselves as does an ice-floe from its continent. Reminiscences from the Old Testament meant that first Judas' saying, and later other sayings, could find a way in. The words of promise to the eleven became isolated and were actually placed after the incident of the dispute among the disciples; they now required their own motivation, and this was attempted—awkwardly, as we have seen—in Lk. xxii. 28.

Indeed, the words of promise to the eleven not only might be separated, but had to be separated, and loosed as much as possible from their original context. The meaning of the rite had naturally been enlarged in the meantime, and was actually threatened by those words. Their connection with its action, with the verba institutionis, was no longer tolerable.

Thus, those words stand alone and isolated in Lk. xxii. 29 f. Mt. xix still retains them, but he has removed them far from his account of Christ's last night. He also omitted the significant word concerning the diathēkē of the kingdom of God:

as my Father appointed me, so appoint I you,

for the diathēkē had long since received a wider meaning. He inserted the mutilated remainder awkwardly into a wholly different logion spoken in another situation. In connection with a wholly different occasion, he tells us (Mt. xix. 27 ff.):

> 27. Peter said unto him, Lo, we have left all, and followed thee; what then shall we have? 28. And Jesus said unto them, Verily I say unto you, that ye who have followed me, in the regeneration when the Son of man shall sit on the throne of his glory, ye also shall sit upon twelve thrones, judging the twelve tribes of Israel. 29. And every one that hath left houses or brethren, etc. . . . shall receive much more, and shall inherit eternal life.

That v. 28 here originated from our ancient text is clear. But every trace of the historical circumstances is lost; the word about the diatithesthai has gone; a phrase which Jesus never used, viz. rebirth as an expression for the future kingdom was inserted; and the disciples are assumed to be twelve, an assumption which was not found in the ancient text. There is also lacking the original reference to eating and drinking as in the ancient text. One sees again how an ancient saying original to Jesus is in process of submersion. At the same time, the saying was artificially embedded, as we have said, in another saying belonging to another set of circumstances. This can still be detected in the sequence of words in Matthew. Peter says: 'We have left all.' Verse 29 corresponds exactly, 'every one that hath left . . .' and this was naturally the beginning of the original answer to Peter's question. Verse 28 was artificially added. That this is a true account is fortunately capable of direct proof, for the ancient logion in which Matthew here artificially embeds our words in order to give a foothold to a loose fragment of tradition is still preserved in pure form and by itself in Mk. x. 28 ff. Here Jesus' answer corresponds exactly to Peter's question. And here the bed is found in which Matthew has inserted the saying, and which he had made into a procrustean bed for our early saying. But the early words of promise to the eleven, of which Matthew still desired to preserve at least a memory, were completely suppressed by Mark as no longer in keeping with the setting.[1]

5. The bread was indispensable for the meal; it was doubly indispensable if one wished to repeat Christ's celebration, for it carried the symbolic meaning of the act. Wine was drunk when one had it, otherwise nothing was drunk. Even for the rite of fractio panis the cup was not required unconditionally, for in Christ's last supper,

[1] We may here call to mind also that in the Beelzebub incident Mark suppressed Jesus' original saying, which was no longer in keeping with the setting: 'The kingdom of God has come unto you.'

it was not an essential. In this way we may explain the fact that, in certain Christian communities, the rite was practised as breaking of bread and nothing else. In the poor primitive church in Jerusalem it must have occurred often enough in this more simple form.

6. In Christ's Last Supper, the cup had only been an introduction; it had an eschatological reference which in itself had to do purely with the historical circumstances. From the viewpoint of the fractio panis, it must either have seemed purely an accident and thus become super-fluous, as actually happened in many circles; or else it would have to be interpreted from the viewpoint of the central action with the bread. The meaning of the bread would then be extended to the accident, and the cup was necessarily assimilated to the bread. Moreover, the process of assimilation was faciliated by an almost unavoidable analogical influence. The broken bread was the broken body of Christ. What assumption lay nearer, than that the wine (originally poured from the mixing cup into the individual cups) was the shed blood of Christ? The original equation, bread = body, attracted by association the later equation, wine = blood. Such a construction by analogy was then expressed in the words Paul found in the account which he used: 'In like manner.'

When the body and the blood were being put side by side and yet were distinguished in this way, a linguistic cir-cumstance perhaps co-operated. In Aramaic, Christ had said: den hu gufi, and this had also the connotation, 'this is I myself.' If in Greek-speaking communities, 'to soma mou [my body]' was then put for gufi, the specific Aramaic connotation 'I myself' was obscured. It became now only the body of Christ. The broken bread now meant body in a narrow and one-sided sense, and it was almost inevitably associated with the wine regarded as blood.

But as soon as this happened, then with equal necessity the cup before the distribution of the bread (understood as body) was placed after it, for the blood could not be shed before the breaking of the body.

The desire to regularize the transposition probably explains the origin of the explicit words:

He took the cup also *after the supper*.

The words are striking. In a rite whose sequence was quite fixed there was no need expressly to mention that *b* followed *a*. Indeed, in its exact sense the saying is really contrary to fact. For if Christ distributed the cup in analogy to the bread, of necessity he did so after the distribution of the bread, but in that case it would have been immediately thereafter and not at a time far removed from it, when the meal was over. The addition, superfluous in itself, and not very skilful, looks very much as though the intention was expressly to guarantee a practice which was known to conflict with another and earlier practice, viz. where the cup had preceded. The transposition of the cup, however, was made easy by the circumstance that in ritual meals there were actually several cups, and freedom existed in arranging them. Thus Rabbi Cohn of Marburg informs me 'that it was a frequent custom to take the kos shel berakah also after a completed meal, and indeed twice if the meal was a fellowship meal.' It is, therefore, possible that at the Last Supper cups actually did circulate even after the supper. Even when Qiddush is observed, this happens in connection with the special cup preceding the meal and also preceding the blessing and distribution of the bread; but at the meal itself more wine is poured into the cups and drunk.

7. Since the distribution of the cup was assimilated to the distribution of the bread, and the wine was transformed into an analogue of the blood; since at the same time the testamentum of the kingdom of God became a kainē diathēkē (new covenant) and as such was contrasted with the old covenant which had been established with the blood of sacrificial animals, the ancient ideas of sacrificial blood and of a blood covenant became associated. This circumstance was one of the causes why Christ's Last Supper was later conceived as belonging to

the class of a passover meal. For the blood of the passover lamb had been used as an apotropaion [agent to avert evil] against the wrath of Yahweh.

8. From what Christ did, strictly in keeping with a unique historical situation, there has evolved in Matthew's account the church's sacrament. Instead of looking forward to the kingdom, the heavenly meal, and the thrones for the eleven as a result of the sacrament, there has appeared the forgiveness of sins, a blessing which was sought and bestowed in the church. That again is not, indeed, wrong. For, according to the New Testament conception itself, the forgiveness of sins is conceived eschatologically as a gift of and a part of salvation in the Messianic age. Forgiveness of sins was, of course, one of the circle of associated ideas which, in Is. liii, also surrounds the redemptive work effected by the suffering of the Servant of God. But on the one hand, as we have already said, in Matthew the means for attaining the kingdom has stepped into the foreground at the expense of the end itself; on the other hand, the ideas associated with the suffering of the Servant of God, and accordingly also with the necessity of Christ's Messianic suffering, are (more vague, indeed, but also) more manifold than mere forgiveness of sins, as Is. liii shows. Into the place of the emotional, undefined, yet richer group of ideas, steps the narrower concept which was already assuming a dogmatic character.

9. Ancient sacramental meals, as we have said, were celebrated with the idea that there was a close connection and, indeed, unity of the participants among themselves and with the officiant (the hēgoumenos). The unity of the bread eaten in the eucharist came to expression in the prayer given in the early writing, the Didache. The associated ideas are shown in the words that as this bread has become one from many grains, so also may the many scattered believers on earth be brought together into the unity of the kingdom of God. Paul says that those who eat the one loaf are themselves one. Paul's eucharist and that

of the Didache or 'Teaching of the Apostles' are independent of one another. That such closely related ideas are, nevertheless, found in both suggests that these ideas have a common ground in conceptions which must have germinated very early and were, perhaps, expressed in so many words when Christ observed the Last Supper. In our section there can be no doubt that we only possess an account which has been compressed into the smallest possible compass.

10. In Jn. xvii. 22–23 these ideas are clearly expressed in words used by Christ when he was about to depart. We must briefly discuss these remarkable verses.

We have examined above the reasons why in the Fourth Gospel the aition or explanation of the church's sacrament had to be transferred from the passion story and placed at the height of the earthly activity of the Logos-Christ as described in the sixth chapter. In spite of its late Logos Christology, it is nevertheless this very gospel which contains many surprising individual traits pointing to distinctive and good historical traditions. Thus, we read in Jn. xvii. 22 :

> The glory which thou hast given me I have given unto them.

We grant that these words are not set in close connection with the phrase 'this is I,' i.e. with the propitiative breaking of Christ, and we have found the reason for that. But on the other hand, it would be difficult to find in any of the other gospels such an echo of the promise of the kingdom as is preserved in our primitive pericope. Even if presented in Johannine terminology, it could not be more exactly nor more clearly expressed than in these words. John says doxan [glory] instead of basileian [kingdom]. But that Christ gives as it has been given to him is the same as 'I appoint unto you, as was appointed unto me.'

We read further:

> that they may be one, I in them and thou in me, that they may be perfected into one.

323

Instead of the eschatological fellowship meant in our primitive pericope, Lk. xxii. 30 (that you may eat at my table in my kingdom), we now find a mystical fellowship, corresponding to other Johannine mystical transfigurations. But fellowship is the content of the testament in both cases. Indeed, in our primitive pericope, the idea of mystical fellowship is already present as a small and invisible germ in the feeling of the communion which is represented and carried out in a sacramental meal.

> That such ideas of sacramental unity are not specifically and exclusively Pauline ideas is proved by the example of the Didache. They are ancient emotional ideas associated with consecrated table fellowship, indeed with fraternal meals generally. As such yet another element is drawn in, suggesting the idea of sharing in Christ's own fate and its results by eating the common loaf.

11. The eating of the bread assimilated to itself the drinking of the cup and imbued it with its own meaning; so also the idea of communion passes over to the cup, and thus, instead of the original instruction: '*divide* this among yourselves' (which presupposes a number of individual cups), we now find the injunction: 'all ye drink of it,' i.e. from a single cup no longer divided.

12. Christ had established his testamentum for the eleven. In Matthew's section the eleven have become 'many.' We have recognized the reason for this. But the appearance of the striking phrase 'for many' has the same ground as 'the Son of Man is come to give his life for many.' It is the same expression as we find thrice repeated in Is. liii, to indicate those who obtain part in the atoning power of the Servant of God.

13. Jesus did not establish a new rite, but he took old rites, well known, self existent, and self perpetuating in Israel and in Jesus' chaburah, and gave them a meaning which was in closest harmony with the circumstances of the time. Therefore he did not say: 'so and so shall be your procedure henceforth, this and this you shall do.'

So and so had they long acted and done, and so they would certainly have continued to do apart from the Last Supper; if they continued together at all as a chaburah, they would celebrate the accustomed common meal.

All became different as soon as the rite passed over into circles where previously such rites were neither practised nor known. The whole proceeding necessarily appeared now as a new and distinctive institution. Supplementary words were now necessary and had to be inserted; they required the rite to be carried out, and that in a certain manner and with a certain purpose: 'This do in remembrance of me.'

Later words like these are explained simply enough from the fact that what was at stake for Gentile Christians was not that new ideas were being brought to bear on a long familiar rite, long practised as such. Rather a rite was being instituted, and naturally it needed a distinct and express command for its introduction and celebration.

14. In cases calling for special decisions when Paul wanted to speak with authority, he appealed to a precept of the Lord, e.g. 1 Cor. vii. 10, ix. 17. These prescriptive words of the Lord came not from himself, but from the Lord. They came not through a special private revelation, but, of course, mediated by the tradition of the church into which he had entered and through whose paradosis [tradition] he had received the paradosis from the Lord. That is also the obvious meaning of the opening words of his section on the Lord's Supper in 1 Cor. xi. 23:

For I received from the Lord . . .

He delivered that which was received from the Lord in the form of a narrative, and this had evidently long possessed a fixed stylistic form. This fact presupposes that the rite itself had long been observed in a fixed form. It is a narrative account whose form is simply impossible as a direct revelation on the part of the exalted Christ. Christ himself cannot have revealed to him that

The Lord Jesus in the night in which he was betrayed.

Rather, we have here a human manner of narration; it is a church tradition becoming canonical. In Damascus, Paul was accepted into the church; since he received baptism in the church he was obviously received at the same time into the sacramental table fellowship of Jesus' Messianic community. Perhaps at first he participated in the rite in the ancient form which still had the cup in the first place; this would explain Paul's occasional placing of the cup before the bread, which we have considered, above. Perhaps he then took over, possibly in Antioch, the more developed tradition and recognized this as the one willed by Christ. He did not artificially invent his account, nor even individual features of it. What he records is clearly traditional material long since rounded off, a piece of tradition which had long possessed a firm ritual, and which he simply had received, as he himself says. This account which he had received was already further developed than those in Mark and Matthew, but the line of development is the same. Moreover, as regards the eschatological meaning of what Christ did, Paul preserves the ancient heritage better than either Matthew or Mark. For although Christ's promise of the kingdom is omitted, it still shines through in the supplementary words of v. 26:

> For as often as ye eat this bread, and drink the cup, ye proclaim the Lord's death till he come.

Moreover, it is impossible to assume that a simple church meal, as observed in Jerusalem, had been given a quite different meaning by Paul. He spent fourteen days in Jerusalem, to visit Peter (historein = visit, with the secondary meaning of, to make the acquaintance of and to question). He was aware of and became acquainted with the fact and the method of the breaking of bread as practised there. That does not exclude divergences in the details of the practice of the rite, but it absolutely excludes any possibility that the fundamental meaning of his own rite diverged completely from that in Jerusalem.

Only if the fractio panis in Jerusalem itself had the meaning of an atoning celebration of Christ's death could Paul hold his own account of the meal as one coming from the Lord.

15. We have discussed the treatment of the church's sacrament in the Fourth Gospel. The odd formula cited above from the high priestly prayer is an echo of the fact that Christ, voluntarily suffering death, sanctified himself in order thereby to sanctify his own also. But the Logos Christology has long since stepped into the place of the primitive Messianism of the pais theou [Servant of God] type. As light, life, knowledge, truth, Christ himself constituted the blessings of salvation which the logos imparted. Hence, the anamnēsis [commemoration] of his death was not now the important thing, but the impartation of his life as vital power. Therefore, as we have seen above, the normative sacramental words were not in place at the end, but at the height, of the earthly activity of the logos in his earthly appearance. The body, i.e. Christ as broken, did not matter, but rather his 'flesh' as food of the soul. The flesh represented (as body could never do) the spiritual feeding through the vital powers of the logos. If we now conceive the influence of such conceptions as active in shaping the meaning and practice of a liturgy which was still fluid and, moreover, was shaped by Spirit-led enthusiasts and their unformulated, freely-inspired prayers, then we can guess, *a priori*, what form the eucharistic prayers and the like must have taken in such circles. They must have been similar to the sequence of thought in the 'high priestly prayer' and the farewell discourses in the Fourth Gospel: prayers of petition and thanks, e.g. for the bread of life, for light, knowledge, truth, for the immortality, which Christ is and has and which he gives in that he gives himself with the bread and wine to be eaten as spiritual food. Meanwhile, the ideas associated with suffering death receded and perhaps vanished completely. As if by chance, certain eucharistic prayers of this kind, partially determined by Johannine ideas, have been preserved for us in the Didache.

16. In the impressive eucharist of the Didache, both the ancient heritage and a transforming influence are clearly discernible. In the form preserved to us, it seems to come from Egypt. But the materials gathered together in it must in part be from Palestine itself, for only in Palestine, certainly not in Egypt, can one gain the idea that grain grows on mountain tops. This eucharist also shows the clearest parallels to Palestinian-Jewish and Jewish-Christian table rites and table prayers, and especially to the rite of the Qiddush. On the other hand, it shows in its terms a close relationship to Johannine and Gnostic conceptions. Thus it has connection with most ancient elements and also with influences that, at a later date, distorted certain ideas.

The elements significant for us are these:

(a) The cup comes first. Further, the wine is called the ampelos (vine), obviously retaining Christ's original words accompanying the cup as in Luke. This ampelos is at the same time the ampelos of David. We recognize the kos jeshuoth, the 'cup of deliverance' which David raises (and which he shares out at the Messianic meal). Jesus had 'revealed' the vine of David, which, as such, is the eschatological cup of deliverance. In other words, he has bestowed it in truth, whereas David could only prophesy it. At the same time, it is clear that all the words accompanying the cup are a Christianized version of the ancient Jewish berakah.

(b) In like manner, the saying accompanying the bread shows both Jewish and Christian features. The blessings of salvation which the consecrated bread bestows are, as in John, life and knowledge (and later in the great prayer of thanksgiving: name, knowledge, faith, immortality, spiritual food and drink). It follows that 'Johannine' influences have worked with transforming effect, e.g. the broken Christ is replaced by the Logos-Christ. Nevertheless, the eucharist of the Didache stands closer to ancient tradition than does John, for the bread is still expressly called klasma. The breaking of bread as such is still

328

emphasized, and it continues to be an important feature in the entire ceremony. Moreover, Jesus is thrice called the servant, showing that ideas associated with the genuine Christology of the Servant of God are still operative. In regard to this older Christology, it is further to be noted that Is. liii. 11 expressly states of the Servant of God:

> through his knowledge will he, the righteous one, my servant, procure righteousness for the many and take upon himself their iniquities.

(c) Christ's original eschatological diathēkē and the eschatological objective of his original action are all echoed by this venerable writing in the words of the petition:

> let thy church be brought together into thy kingdom from the ends of the earth.
> Redeem it from all evil, complete it in love, and gather it, a sanctified church, into thy kingdom, which thou hast prepared for it. Let grace come, let this world pass away.

In spite of adventitious influences, this eucharist is still a completely eschatological sacrament. It has preserved *this* original trait of Christ's action more faithfully than is done even in the account which Paul had received, and it also points back to its source in our original pericope with its strict eschatological logic.

CHAPTER XIII

CONCLUSION

THUS the influence of motives operating at that time is recognizable in the later accounts. These may be explained as derived from our ancient pericope, but this cannot be explained from any of the later accounts or practices. Nor is there the slightest reason for regarding it as, e.g., the product of the very ancient theology of the church instead of as an original account of what Jesus really did. For our pericope only continues in a straight line what Jesus himself expressed when he said that the Son of Man must suffer; here the implication was that the Son of Man was the Servant of God; it also confirms the statement that Jesus really taught this concerning himself.

Jesus did this in an original, symbolic action such as was done by the ancient prophets to whose category he belonged, but not an action such as the fantasy of disciples subsequently fabricated.

And the point of this action: 'I will to you, as my Father willed to me,' is partly that it involved a content and application conditioned purely by the historical circumstances, and partly that it was so original, so like Jesus, that at a later time the theology of the church might indeed obscure but could not invent it.

In my book, *Religious Essays* (Oxford Press, 1931), pp. 45 ff. in the essay: 'The Lord's Supper as a Numinous Fact,' I have discussed the value and meaning of the church's anamnesis or remembrance of what Christ originally did, the celebration of the Lord's Supper in a church of to-day, and the manner in which it should be ordered. I have given a sketch of its form for ceremonial use in the same book, p. 59, in the essay: 'A Form for Celebrating the Lord's Supper.

BOOK FOUR

THE KINGDOM OF GOD
AND THE CHARISMA

CHAPTER I

THE CHARISMATIC TYPE

1. AT the beginning of this book we examined the background on which the figure of Jesus was to be placed from the point of view of the history of religion. Instead of background we could have said category as exemplified by Jesus. The 'obēr,' or itinerant preacher, belonged to the same category. Under this head, however, there is still more to be said about Jesus, especially that which I have already sketched on page 162 of my book, *The Idea of the Holy*. Our records about Jesus are typical of the religio-historical genus in being of a hagiological character; the figure which they describe is a holy man, and, as such, belonging to a certain class. A typical saint is conceived within the limits prescribed by the charisma, a charismatic character and endowment.

Our accounts speak of this in various ways. The problem is: are they genuine, do they narrate what really took place, or are they pure legend, a crown of miracle narratives woven at a later time and placed upon the head of a mere preacher? They are without doubt often genuinely hagiological in certain respects, viz. naïve faith in miracle, heightening of the unusual and marvellous, heightening of natural actions and effects into the miraculous, delight in miracle, borrowing and importation of conventional miracle narratives and motifs. That is characteristic of all hagiological records, and is repeated in all kinds of hagiology. But from the point of view of the history of religion it would be a mistake to pass over the entire class of charismatic phenomena in a modern spirit of scepticism, or to neglect seriously testing the accounts in order to determine what is really historical, simply because the matters do not appeal to our taste. Moreover, the point at issue is not only to assign these matters to their literary

species, to classify one as fable, another as legend of the
itinerant type, a third as cult myth, but to make an earnest
attempt at a very different kind of investigation into the
species. Our task is to ask what kinds of actual occurrences
are typically found in a charismatic milieu, in order in
this way to gain a criterion for what actually happens;
to make this criterion as certain as possible, in order then
to apply it together with criteria drawn from literary and
historical criticism, to early records.

2. Among the last mentioned, we find in particular
the criterion of self-consistency of personality. For our
purpose, we ask: Is the reported charismatic equipment
a merely accidental element in the otherwise comprehensible figure and message of Christ, or does it plainly
belong here by its essential inner nature? The latter is
to be affirmed, and the title chosen for this part, 'The
Kingdom of God and the Charisma,' is intended to
express the essential connection between the self-consistent
person and the message of Christ.

The kingdom of God, as already at hand, is dynamis,
the inbreaking miraculous power of the transcendent. As
such, it is operative in the exorcistic dynamis of its messenger, and equally in the exousia and the charis of his
preaching. He himself is charisma. The messenger is not
only preacher and announcer of this kingdom, but is an
integral part of the inbreaking miracle of the eschatological
order itself. Thus it was not by a strange coincidence, but
of essential necessity that he should possess the gift of
healing. He was a charismatic in accordance with the
self-consistent meaning of the whole. The fact that he
was a charismatic integrates and confirms in turn our
belief that we have rightly grasped the meaning of
his person and message. The whole confirms the impression of the parts of the picture; the parts confirm
the whole.

3. It is perfectly plain and historically certain that Paul
belonged to the class of charismatics. The milieu of the
primitive church in general was charismatic. Paul did

not appeal to the spiritual charisma as a novelty peculiar to himself and his churches, but said:

we also have received the Spirit;

he legitimates himself in the face of the early church by appealing to a common possession. Now in a charismatic milieu the charisma passes over from the master to the disciples. Our accounts tell that the disciples received from their master the charismas of exorcism, of healing, and of preaching. These facts and these records harmonize with the record and the fact that at the beginning there was a master who was not a mere rabbi and teacher, but a remarkable charismatic person, who worked in a charismatic manner.

4. The class of the great writing prophets of ancient Israel rose from that of the ancient nebiim; these were primitive seers, men of hearing and sight, of the gifts of healing, of blessing and cursing, of far-sightedness and of pre-vision, and so were 'men of God,' i.e. saints of God and charismatics of a primitive type. In more profound form, the charisma remains in the higher prophets as the gifts of higher vision, of seeing and hearing, of momentarily inspired experience; and not least it is the gift of the poetic capacity by virtue of which the manteis [seers] receive the oracles of their God in finished artistic form, shaping them and transmitting them in poems which belong to the immortal artistic creations of mankind. The type of the momentarily inspired prophet then changes in Deutero-Isaiah into that of the—almost lyrical —preacher. He experiences the burden and the word of Yahweh not in single sudden rushes, but (Is. lxi. 1–2) is 'anointed' with the Spirit as with a permanent gift, an endowment which is at his disposal as the poetic endowment is at the disposal of the poet. Nor does Christ belong to the class of momentarily inspired prophets; his category corresponds to that of Enoch who does not proclaim individual oracles which come upon him intermittently, but who preaches and in preaching approximates to the

335

type of the teacher of wisdom. But at the same time we find explicitly repeated in Jesus the ancient traits of the ish Elohim, the man of God, the 'saint of God'; indeed in their mutual relationships they are traits characteristic of a holy man of this kind. This very circumstance is important, viz. that with Christ we have to do not with a mere congeries of traits but with a coherent group which belong together elsewhere in a typical manner in the charismatic man of God. It confirms the genuineness of the picture, and at the same time his category may serve as a criterion of what has been added or enhanced by legend. Moreover, with Christ these traits are not the qualities of a mere charismatic, not the powers of a mere miracle-working rabbi, nor again the equipment of a mere prophet; in Jesus they are the operations of the power of the dawning kingdom of God itself:

> If I by the finger of God cast out demons, then is the kingdom of God come upon you.

5. Further, the consciousness or the awakened feeling of the operative and present kingdom of God as the dynamis of the transcendent provides an atmosphere not only in which miracle stories are invented and sub-sequently added, but in which charismatic experience and activity find suitable conditions. Also, it is only a milieu thus prepared that can provide the soil later on for a spirit-filled, enthusiastic church with its spirit-inspired experiences. Only in this milieu are the visions and transcendent experiences possible which will found the church, i.e. visions of one risen from the dead and experience of the spirit itself.

6. The charismatic type is repeated later in the figures of Christian hagiology. It appears spontaneously again with surprising similarity in the Islamic Sufis, who, as travelling and itinerant holy men, offer on the whole and in general the most noteworthy analogies to the Synoptic milieu. The charismatic can be studied as a type in these and other, even recent examples. If we have come to

recognize it here as a definite type and have grasped its nature quite definitely, we can recognize it wherever it appears. We can see that it is not the product of a socio-logical and collective phantasy, but a type of experience and existence which—no matter how much phantasy-pro-ducing legend may constantly enhance and expand it— actually occurs in real men. This type is like a forma substantialis [substantial shape] which is realized in its representatives at different times. It may be studied in documents of great antiquity, and it may appear to-day equally well. Persons like Blumhardt and Cyprien Vignes, who are near to us in time, have embodied it; a closer study of such persons would put criteria into our hands for reaching more definite conclusions, and would free us from personal prejudices as to what once could and did happen in Palestine.

7. In the New Testament the charismatic type is plainest in Paul, who comes next to Jesus in this respect. Here we are dependent not on subsequent testimonies of Paul's admirers and disciples, but on his own indubitable words.

Suppose no personal, written remains and words of Paul's had survived, nothing that contemporaries said about him as in the We-narrative of Acts, but perhaps only an aretalogy or a 'saint's life' from a later time, originating within the orbit of the post-Pauline churches where he himself had long been recognized as a saint and martyr (and that always means also the hero of a develop-ing cult). How would it all look? What should we find?

Presumably we should find: logia, short summaries of his message; these would be fragmentary and probably oft-times impoverished, flattened, harmonized, polished, and overlaid with explanations of a later time. Perhaps they would be assembled by naïve and unschooled authors, who had included traditional material long handed down only in oral form by a memory which gradually became indistinct. Then again, this material would be embedded in a saint's legend which included historical data, poorly

Y   337

arranged in a 'saint's life,' and everything overlaid with the glitter of the saint. This 'saint's life' would then contain things which the student of species[1] would at once classify as typical fable motifs, as legendary travel motifs, as Hellenistic myths of gods and heroes; he would discover scenes which had been manifestly idealized, and would point out that accounts of the circumstances and the background had obviously been spun out of originally unconnected logia. Within the limits of what was manifestly a purely phantastic travel narrative describing the oddest zig-zag movements, he would discover maxims and apothegms, controversies with all sorts of adversaries, rudimentary discourses and teaching, fragments with the strangest changes of style, sober doctrinal sayings, and almost ecstatic outbreaks which would with difficulty be ascribed to one and the same author, descriptions of conventional situations, equally conventional types of opponents, purely Palestinian, plainly Hellenistic, and undoubtedly Gnostic material.

And all this would be found embedded in miracle narratives described as obviously fanciful. Let us make it more concrete: we begin with a scene describing a 'call' by the personal appearance of the heavenly king—obviously an ideal scene, which clearly shows the characteristics of Hellenistic theophanies. Study of the history of the species shows it to be one of, and naturally just as unhistorical as, these theophanies. Revelation continues to come from the side of the heavenly king; alleged speaking with spiritual tongues—plainly a motif deriving from the most primitive of popular mythology; dreams and visions; healings and at least one raising from the dead, namely, that of the so-called Eutychus—Eutychus means the fortunate, even the name proves that we have to do here with an ideal scene; an appearance in a vision of a Macedonian from afar who brings a heavenly message; a

[1] By 'student of species' is meant the modern critic who seeks to classify the material in ancient documents according to the literary species or 'forms' found in the ancient material.

visit of angels who announce a miraculous deliverance; probably also a miraculous blessing of bread, through which all persons on the ship receive a satisfying meal; a transport into Paradise, probably by now definitely in bodily form; a long-range operation over the sea from Ephesus to Corinth: indeed, an actual visit over the sea in the spirit to the Corinthians: a visit which is perhaps already recounted as a personal extorisatio and apparitio of one who was really far distant; powers of blessing and cursing, through which he delivers a sinner to the power of the devil; the gift of imparting the Holy Spirit by laying on of hands; in addition at least a dozen miraculous deliverances from all sorts of dangers which have befallen him, especially a deliverance from a storm at sea—a typical free-moving legend with known parallels in the rabbinic literature; especially also the prophetic gift of foreseeing his own future suffering. It would then be clear and indubitable to the sceptic that the well-known myth motifs of Hellenistic aretalogy have been transferred to an impressive preacher who had presumably once existed.

But unfortunately for the sceptic we now have authentic writings of this Paul and a largely trustworthy travel narrative from eye-witnesses of this man. These prove that free-moving Hellenistic fairy stories have not been transferred here but that the things mentioned really occurred, at least as subjective happenings. They are not the literary production of a posthumous church, but go back to events in an actually existent charismatic milieu and to the life and labour of a typical charismatic. Nor is Eutychus a fiction, in spite of his name. He really did fall out of the window upon his head, and Paul really awakened him out of his insensibility. Paul really did see the Macedonian in the dream, and in the danger at sea he thought he heard the voice of an angel. He really experienced the storm at sea, and, in spite of the most beautiful free-moving fairy tales of Orpheus, Arion, and other mythical heroes, he was a charismatic who really knew that the storm would do him no harm. He really was the man who, fourteen years before, believed he was transported into Paradise, not knowing whether he was in the body or out of the body at the time. He really did foresee his sufferings as other charismatics have done. He not only believed in but possessed charismas. We should study him as a charismatic type, so that we can recognize it again when we meet it elsewhere and in a figure greater than Paul's.

8. Both the nature and the inner connection of the charismatic gifts may be recognized in Paul. The points to consider are:

The gifts do not in any way involve omnipotence or omniscience.

They are not magic powers such as a goētēs [sorcerer] thought he possessed.

They are mysterious heightenings of talents and capacities, which have at least their analogues in the general life of the soul.

They are not magic invasions into the life of nature; they do no violence to natural power nor are they magically increased natural powers. They work no nature miracles as portenta, miracula, prodigia, such as the standing still of the sun or the collapse of the walls of Jericho.

But they are:

Capacity for spiritual and psychic experiences of a distinctive kind.

Heightened talents such as kubernēsis [guidance] and diakrisis [discernment].

Operations of the soul and of psychic powers upon other souls, phenomena which indeed far surpass the limits of normal psychic operation, but are nevertheless rooted in the general mystery of the psychic processes of the will.

They form an approximately closed circle of possibilities which have a perceptible relationship of kind among themselves. They are regarded as of a miraculous character, and yet the charismatic knows himself to be different from the real miracle-worker and rejects miracle in the sense of a miracle of display, i.e. a nature miracle as portentum or prodigium.

9. Finally, an important note on this very point: Paul knew the powers of the spirit to be operative in himself and yet he censured the Jews in asking for miracles (1 Cor. i. 22):

> The Jews require miracles; the Greeks ask for wisdom; but we preach Christ, the crucified.

Instead of adducing worldly wisdom and working miracles, he appealed to the preaching that was his duty. He did not appeal to any miracles which he worked.

Christ was a greater charismatic, and he also typically refused when the Pharisees demanded of him a real miracle in the technical sense. In the same way, also, he appealed instead to his preaching as the real sign (Lk. xi. 29). He censured the desire for miracles as the mental attitude of 'an evil and adulterous generation.' No more than in Paul's case does that mean that as a matter of fact he worked no miracles, and in another connection indeed he did actually refer to them. But he knew that his charismatic activity, miraculous as it was, could not be called miracle in the technical sense; it was not portentum or prodigium; not a nature miracle or a miracle of display, but the spiritual dynamis of the indwelling charis of the kingdom of God. In *Die Predigt Jesu vom Reich Gottes*, p. 142, Johannes Weiss says: 'No mighty deeds succeed in being heavenly attestation.'

So also with Muhammed. He was a charismatic in so far as he and he alone possessed the spiritual capacity to perceive the revelation of Allah, to hear the voice of the angel; in so far as he read the eternal Quran of Allah, and believed he had transcendent experiences and adventures. But just like Jesus he denied being a real miracle worker, and he likewise pointed to the spiritual miracle of the Quran instead of to portents. The same is also true of the later charismatics of Islam. Here the charismatic gifts are called karamath. But Macdonald, in his work:

The Religious Attitude and Life in Islam, rightly says that these karamath are distinguished from the real miracles. The latter are called mu'ǧiza, the 'obvious' miracles, which are strictly distinguished from the karāmāth.

This distinction of charismatic activity from magical activity or from technical miracle working belongs to the very category of the real charismatic. The difference between charismatic working and the real miracle is never strictly defined, but it is felt and asserted so much the more definitely.

Another aspect of Jesus' charismatic works, as the Synoptics still imply, is that their effectiveness is largely dependent upon the faith of the recipient. In Mt. ix. 28 Jesus first asks the blind men:

Believe ye that I am able to do this?

In ix. 29 he says:

According to your faith be it done unto you.

In Mt. xiii. 58 we read:

He did not many mighty works there because of their unbelief.

Particularly noteworthy is the passage Lk. v. 17:

And it came to pass on one of those days, that he was teaching . . . and the power of the Lord was with him to heal.

In other words, the charismatic power had its particular hours when it was present for healing, and manifestly also those when it was not present. It is therefore stronger or weaker. It comes and goes.

10. In 1 Cor. xii. 4 ff. Paul mentions a whole catalogue of charismatic gifts. The gifts of grace are synonymous with ministrations and mighty work (charismata, diakonia, energēmata); here he classifies the word of wisdom, logos sofias, and of knowledge, gnōseōs; pistis, faith as mightily working (mountain-removing) faith; healing;

energēmata dynameōn, i.e. miraculous mighty works of a kind not closely determined; prophecy; glossolalia as ecstatic speech; the strange diakrisis pneumatōn, the distinguishing of spirits. In addition ch. xiii describes the religious functions in the narrower sense, such as charismatic love, and manifestly also faith and hope. Furthermore, we find in Paul: horasis, the gift of seeing in dreams and visions; experiences of rapture such as his own transport into the third heaven; and the gift of exorcism, which Paul himself also exercises. Plainly he does not include everything possible among the charismatic gifts. Rather, he obviously restricts them to a definitely limited group of heightened psychic powers similar in character and flowing from a single pneuma. Their working is not unlimited. The gift of prophecy is not omniscience; the gift of healings is not omnipotence and not every sick person is healed; the exousia of the proclamation is not infallibility. The charismatic himself is not a completely exceptional, marvellous, and miraculous being, but has gifts which can really appear in all believers who have received the spirit. Taken together, however, they yield a definite spiritual type recognizable as a unity.

11. Paul traces the gifts of grace back to the pneuma. At the same time he knows that this pneuma working in charismatic gifts is not, as it were, a speciality of his Hellenistic churches. Comparing himself with those in Palestine, he boasts, as we have said previously, that his church has *also* received what the churches in Palestine have previously received. But naturally the latter had it rightly and in the first place, The charismatic gifts and the pneuma were therefore not peculiarly Hellenistic, but originally and first of all Palestinian, a prime possession of the original church.

CHAPTER II

CHRIST HIMSELF PRIMARILY CHARISMATIC

IF one has grasped the type of the charismatic as seen in Paul, one can recognize it again in the Synoptic Jesus, in spite of the fragmentary character of the tradition.

1. The original tradition describes Christ as a charismatic. We submit that this description is genuine, for in this way and only in this way can we explain the historical consequence, viz. the production of a spirit-led, enthusiastic church. It is genuine, again, because its individual traits harmonize into a unity of the charismatic type. Yet, again, it is genuine because this whole charismatic type harmonizes with, and has the same meaning as, the message of the kingdom of God which is already breaking in, and which has been experienced as dynamis.

2. Paul traced the charismatic gifts back to the pneuma. Jesus himself equated the secret power of the divine kingdom with the pneuma, by applying Isaiah's prophecy to himself:

> The Spirit of the Lord is upon me, because he anointed me to preach good tidings to the poor: He hath sent me to proclaim release to the captives, and recovering of sight to the blind, to set at liberty them that are bruised, to proclaim the acceptable year of the Lord (Lk. iv. 18).

We note that here again we have a typical little catalogue of charismatic gifts, and indeed the very gifts characteristic of Jesus himself:

> the gift of besorah, the exousia of preaching (and indeed of preaching the acceptable year of the Lord, which is exactly the same as preaching the final dawning of the hoped-for time of salvation);
> the gift of exorcism: proclaiming release to the captives

344

(which on Jesus' lips and in Jesus' time could only mean release from the captivity of demons);

the gift of healing generally: giving sight to the blind.

While in the Beelzebub incident the gift is the dynamis of the present kingdom, here it is explained as being anointed with the divine spirit. Correspondingly another passage says that Christ uttered warnings about blasphemy against the spirit which is working in him. The dynamis of the kingdom was the same as the spirit even for Christ. Already the operative eschatological order was pneuma, and the later pneuma remained, even in Paul's case, the gift of the final age, i.e. the very fact of the eschatological order at work in advance.

3. The passage Christ quoted from Isaiah was only a compact summary. But partly in manifest traits, partly in traits scarcely noted or suggested by the tradition, as soon as our sight has become keen, we can see ever more clearly that Christ embodied comprehensively the characteristics of a charismatic, and they round out into a coherent picture which by its very consistency bears the stamp of genuineness.

In ancient Israel one would have recognized and classified him as the typical ish Elohim, as a 'man of God.' Such a man of God was a holy one of God: I presume that in Christ's time the name of the typical holy man was 'the holy one of God,' and that as such it meant not the Messiah but simply an acknowledged holy man.

We find this title in the mouth of sick persons whom Christ healed. It is almost a matter of course that such a title, which in itself perhaps only meant the ish Elohim, was afterwards heightened to Messianic significance, and then regarded as a testimony to Jesus' Messianic rank on the part of the demons possessing the sick person (which testimony he naturally had to reject as coming from the devil).

The individual traits of such an ish Elohim we must examine briefly in the following paragraphs.

THE GIFT OF HEALING AND EXORCISM

1. In 1 Cor. xii. 4 ff. Paul names the energēmata as charismatic gifts and explains them in v. 10 as energēmata dynameōn [workings of powers]. The Synoptists apply the same concept of dynamis to Jesus' own activity, and they say of him that he bestowed upon his disciples the dynamis [power] in addition to the exousia [authority].

Paul connects the iamata closely with them. The iamata are the gift of healings, the spiritual gift so characteristic of Jesus.[1] In Mt. iv. 24 the character of these healings is clear. No case is related, e.g., of the cure of bodily injuries, broken limbs, and the like, the healing of which would be a real miracle. Rather the verse refers to manifold sicknesses and painful ailments, with specific mention of demoniacs, lunatics, and paralytics. In other words, they were ailments which go back to essentially nervous and psychic causes, disturbances, and inhibitions, i.e. just the paralytic manifestations which to-day are often traced back to nervous disturbances and specifically to psychic complexes, and which often vanish when such complexes are resolved. We must also mention women suffering from haemorrhage, a phenomenon which is hysterically conditioned. Even blindness, deafness, and dumbness are often hysterically and nervously conditioned. With regard to healings of this sort, there is much to be learned from the authentic autobiographical record written by Blumhardt shortly after the healing of a blind and dumb child.[2]

---

[1] Cp. Fr. Fenner, *Die Krankheit im Neuen Testament*, Untersuchungen Zum Neuen Testament, vol. 18, 1930, for a thorough and methodical investigation, making use especially of modern psychotherapy.

[2] *Briefliche Aeusserungen aus Bad Boll*, p. 7.

That such healings can also happen outside the charismatic sphere, by simple psychic influence, has long been known. A physician related to me healed a blinded woman in this way. F. von Edelsheim wrote in *Das Evangelion nach Markos*, 1931, p. 249:

> Last year Professor Stock, director of the University Clinic at Tübingen, by a few minutes of suggestive command restored the sight of a man blinded by a powder explosion, and healed him.

More difficult to believe are the healings of lepers. But as D. Frankenburg informs me, leprosy in South Arabia is actually called the 'royal sickness.'[1] 'Royal sickness' means the sickness which only a king can heal by the charismatic gift of his particular position. The name points at least to a general widespread belief that there were such healings. F. von Edelsheim says on p. 57:

> Leprosy is called saraat in Aramaic. There were two kinds, the ordinary saraat and the naga saraat. It is not lepra, but a sickness known to-day under the name vitiligo. A nervously occasioned form of the same disease is known. It is characteristic of this sickness that the skin appears snow-white at a certain stage.

Of all healings perhaps the healing of 'possession,' of demoniac control, appears to us most intelligible to-day. It was compounded of elements of schizophrenia and domination by fixed ideas, was rooted in religious ideas, and, for the latter reason, was particularly and most easily accessible to the spiritual power of a 'holy one of God.'

To the charismatic gift of healing one must add the charismatic's power to bless a little food, in itself too little to satisfy hungry people, and make it sufficient to satisfy the hunger of many who receive a portion from his hands. Similar tales occur even in the narratives from

---

[1] According to ancient conception, kings are of a numinous character and possess particular charismatic gifts. Vespasian healed blind people, according to Tacitus' narrative. In like manner the French and English kings used to heal.

Bad Boll, and they are also found in the life of St. Francis. In Christ's life the 'miraculous feeding' is in place here. The miracle-loving phantasy of those who handed down the tradition developed out of it a miraculous increase of the bread. However, a record in the apocryphal Acta Johannis helps us to conjecture what it was originally. (*Texts and Studies*, p. 9.) In ch. viii we read:

> When Christ was invited and went to a meal, we went with him. Before each of us a loaf was then laid, and Christ also received a loaf. He then blessed his loaf and divided it among us. And from the little (which each received as part of the bread blessed by Christ) each one of us was satisfied. But our own loaves remained whole (and uneaten).

This story may show us what was meant originally in the gospel narratives, viz. the power of the charismatic to satisfy the hunger of the recipients by a small gift which he had blessed. The manner of the working is analogous to that of healing.

2. In later tradition, these mighty deeds of Christ's are conceived in the special sense of proofs of Messiahship. Hence, later tradition was influenced by the later Christology, according to which Jesus had come as the full Messiah, and from the outset had appeared and revealed himself as Messiah. His charismatic acts are now fused with the pragmatism of the epiphany of the Messiah. They were certainly not so conceived in the mind of Christ and our narratives still show it. His charismatic acts were not done by him in order to supply proofs of his Messianic rank or the like. They were not carried out in accordance with some plan; rather they flowed spontaneously from the love-filled disposition of him who knew that he was sent to seek and to save that which was lost. In the fact that they took place, they confirmed what Jesus had taught, viz. that the kingdom was in the act of dawning as God's power, but they were not done in order to afford that proof.

3. Some of the traits used in performing an exorcism may seem strange, but to test their historicity the thing needed is not to look for some floating fairy tale as the basis, but to study how exorcists really proceed and what sort of phenomena occur, whether hallucinatory or genuine, as applied to the case of the sick person or that of the onlookers. In this respect Blumhardt's own account of the healing of Miss Gottliebin Dittus is instructive.

The lady was said to be possessed, and the process of healing took two years. An eye-witness, whose veracity is undoubted, describes features which reduce almost to insignificance those in the gospel narratives which are said to be incredible. The problem still remains, however, as to what extent they took place objectively. The important point is to establish the nature of that which people in a charismatic milieu are subjectively convinced they have heard or seen. One feature of Christ's practice in exorcising is significantly illuminated when Blumhardt writes expressly: 'I never permit the demons to speak. I command them to be silent.' That is how a typical charismatic actually proceeds. If Wrede had taken the charismatic milieu and the typical charismatic procedure into account, he would hardly have made the assertions that he did.

Among the healings which Jesus performed are those which took place at a distance, e.g. the case of the centurion of Capernaum. The sceptic's comment is: Surely no one can believe in an operation at a distance like this. We reply: Quite so if it were not better, instead of passing facile judgment, to study for once the matter itself and its actual setting, i.e. in actual and attested experiences. Blumhardt's narratives provide material enough. How the phenomena may be explained is another matter, but that they occur as actual phenomena is to-day no longer in question. A more thorough examination of the whole subject of charismatic phenomena might lead to circumspection. Macdonald was a thorough expert in the charismatic milieu of Islam, and as early as 1908, in his

349

introduction to *The Religious Attitude and Life in Islam* (Chicago, 1908), he expressed his view that:

> I am driven to regard telepathy as proved.

Moreover, it is not in accordance with sound method to ask first: Did the word of the charismatic, who promised a healing at a distance, produce objective results? The results might have been fortuitous or interpolated by the narrator. The first question is: What was the charismatic confident that he could do in certain circumstances? Is it credible that Christ dared to say and actually uttered a word of power in such and such a form? Can that be confirmed by analogies? It can be confirmed, and the analogy is again offered us by the charismatic Paul. In all reality and without hesitation he belived that he was capable of operating spiritually at a distance. He wrote from Ephesus about the case of incest in Corinth:

> For I verily, being absent in body (i.e. remaining in Ephesus) but present in spirit (i.e. in Corinth), have already as though I were present judged him that hath so wrought this thing; in the name of our Lord Jesus, ye being gathered together, and my spirit, with the power of the Lord Jesus, to deliver (the incestuous person) unto Satan for the destruction of the flesh.

Acting together with that of the Corinthians while far away across the sea, Paul's spiritual power was to exercise a physical effect—in this case not a healing, but a disturbing effect—on the wrongdoer. Of the result we know nothing; there is no doubt that it would have been described in a 'saint's life' of Paul. The sceptic may stick to his scepticism but he has no historical justification for raising a doubt that Christ intended to act in this way.

CHAPTER IV

CHARISMATIC PREACHING AND THE
DISTINGUISHING OF SPIRITS

1. IN close connection with the other charismatic gifts, Paul mentions that of the logos, i.e. preaching. He regards it as a spiritual gift. It is the fundamental charisma of Christ and is explicitly conceived in the Synoptists as a charismatic gift. Thus Lk. iv. 18 gives the quotation from Isaiah as used by Jesus himself:

> The spirit of the Lord is upon me, because he anointed me to preach to the poor.

The gift of preaching, as we have said already, is here regarded as an effect of being anointed with the spirit, and Jesus as a preacher is the charismatic bearer of the spirit. In his preaching the charismatic gift is operative. As a consequence, the hearers exclaim:

> What is this? A new teaching with exousia.

Exousia is at times translated by 'full authority.' But that is too limited a meaning. Exousia is a late Greek word, which Delitzsch reproduces by geburah, mighty power. Thus Lk. xii. 5 uses it of God Himself: exousian echonta [having power], and similarly, therefore, in Mk. i. 27:

> he commandeth even the unclean spirits.

Preaching and power over the demons are regarded here as on the same level, i.e. the level of supernatural charismatic power. Compare also Mt. xiii. 54:

> Whence the wisdom and the dynameis?

We have already discussed the term charis = charisma in Lk. iv. 22. Charis means grace, and hence blessing as a gift of grace. In this way, it becomes a synonym of dynamis. Compare Acts vi. 8:

> Stefanos pleres charitos kai dynameos [Stephen, full of grace and power].

Stephen does 'signs and great wonders' as a charismatic; his gift is characterized by charis and dynamis.

2. Probably the strangest of all the charismatic gifts is the distinguishing of spirits, the diakrisis pneumatōn, the discriminatio spirituum. As the very name indicates, the conception and the thing itself come from the sphere of second sight and necromancy, and are related to the gift of exorcism. No wonder therefore that this gift was found in Jesus. In it, again, we find the typical interrelation of characteristics, and hence a unity which is itself a criterion of genuineness.

The gift is primarily that of being able to distinguish spirits, i.e. evil spirits from good ones, in order to lay the former and call forth the latter. Secondly it is, in particular, the gift of discerning whether an evil or a good spirit impels a man who is possessed. From this point the meaning widens; it now becomes the capacity of being able to look into another person, to read his inner state, to read his evil or good thoughts. In Arabic, diakrisis is called firasa, from farasa = to distinguish. The gift of firasa plays the same role in legends of Arabian saints as diakrisis in Christian legends. The expression firasa may finally lose its original charismatic and supernatural meaning; it then signifies in general the gift of intuitive knowledge of men, and particularly the gift of reading a man's conduct and features so as to understand his inner being, his good or bad character, his nature generally. Thus firasa finally becomes a name for physiognomy and the study of character.

But in a charismatic milieu, the gift of discrimination and firasa always retain their original meaning of a gift of grace peculiar to the charismatic. Among the walis and the sufis of Islam, this gift is particularly characteristic.

It is reported of nearly every great master among them. It was likewise characteristic of the charismatic circles of early Christian monasticism, where it received the special name of charisma dioratikon, the power of penetrating vision, a favourite subject in the lives of the great monks. (Cp. Holl, *Enthusiasmus und Bussgewalt*, for which a better title would be: *Charisma und Bussgewalt*.) This gift of discrimination as gift of 'penetrating vision,' of dioratikon, is a capacity which has its analogies in peculiar occurrences which are beginning to be seriously investigated to-day in so-called mediums. French psychologists call it *lucidité*.

3. With such a gift of penetration is connected at times a capacity of second sight, that is, the ability to scent, have a foreboding of, become aware of, at times actually to see, things or events at a distance. In Arabic this also is reckoned as firasa. This gift of second sight is one of the oldest of all charismatic gifts, and is the thoroughgoing characteristic of the primitive charismatic. The name of such a person in Israel was choseh, seer or visionary, like Samuel. A quite primitive form of this gift appears as the capacity of seeing and finding stray animals at a distance. Such persons are still found among primitive tribes. In Sanskrit there was the particular name govinda, cow-finder, for those thus endowed. It was an important gift for nomadic cattle-breeders. In the Old Testament the gift retains this form in the great early seer of Israel, Samuel, who finds Saul's stray asses for him.

4. Jesus' charismatic gift of diakrisis is recorded only as it were in hidden corners of our tradition. The narratives about it might in themselves seem to have no importance, but the very fact of their incidental character is historically important because it enables us to recognize the type, to perceive how coherent it is, and how one trait supplements, furthers, and confirms another.

Hence, the narratives abound in such statements as:

But he knew what was in men.

Or again:

But when he perceived their thoughts.

A particularly typical firasa narrative (as penetration and likewise as second sight) is Jn. i. 47. Nathanael comes to Christ, and Christ says to him without sounding or questioning him:

Behold an Israelite indeed, in whom is no guile!

That is the capacity of dioratikon, of firasa, which is in process of becoming an intuitive knowledge of the inner man. He proceeds:

Before Philip called thee, when thou wast under the fig tree, I saw thee.

At first the words seem to constitute an isolated, enigmatic hieroglyph, the story of a miracle that just happens to have been preserved. But to be content with that impression and to write the matter off in this way would be perverse. To deal with it methodically and historically, we must first determine quite definitely the class of the event which is itself at least alleged to have occurred, and we must find in the event the typical characteristics of the class. In the above case, we have to do with the well-known firasa which can be studied as a category. We have to do with a trait which is almost regularly repeated, e.g. in the biography of the Islamic saints. We may read how a worldly person mocks him or comes to him with doubt. He reveals to that man his innermost thoughts, reads his soul, or even relates an incident from his life. The mocker is overcome and recognizes his master, just as in Nathanael's case. Later, these features become conventional elements in the record, and as such are almost naturally and automatically applied to the saints as a class. But that does not raise doubts about their historicity generally nor that these stories originated in some historical event.

5. A trait characteristic of the primitive firasa is also

354

reported of Jesus when he saw by second sight the water-carrier who was to lead the disciples to the house of the Last Supper. Compare on this point the story of Samuel in 1 Sam. x. 3 which belongs to the same classs. If Samuel had not really been able to find distant asses, Saul would not have gone to him and would not have paid him a quarter of a silver shekel. But if Samuel had this gift of second sight, one cannot perceive why a greater charismatic should not have had it. Even if the story that he saw the distant water-carrier be a legend, we must nevertheless recognize the importance of understanding the kind of notions which formed the original environment of Jesus' miracles. These notions reveal the elements typical of charismatic endowment and behaviour.

6. One further trait, preserved by pure accident and scarcely observable, is that of charismatic metonymy, i.e. the descriptive renaming of disciples on the basis of firasa. Simon becomes Peter; the sons of Zebedee become Boanerges, sons of thunder.

Taken by itself and in isolation, metonymy looks like another curiosity, a personal idiosyncrasy. It loses this aspect when one sees it in the context of charismatic firasa. When I was a young man, and visited the east for the first time, I was invited to a notable ceremony in the house of the Sheikh el Bakri. The venerable old man sat on an elevated seat. Men of different ages were brought to him. He whispered something into their ears, whereupon they retired and were congratulated by those standing around. They had received a new name which they henceforth bore. The sheikh was the head of the descendants of the Caliph Abu Bakr, and also of the dervish orders. The hereditary charisma of the Bakrids united in him with that of the sufis. The whole ceremony was a crystallized form of what was originally a firasa in the form of a metonymy and had a charismatic purpose.

7. One further remark may be made in regard to the charismas generally, and especially to that of healing. Here, as in the case of other charismas, is an unusual gift,

without doubt. But this gift is not an absolutely new faculty
of the soul and its exercise is not *absolutely* distinguished
and separated from ordinary activities and capacities. So
it is also with the gift of firasa; it surpasses while it includes
the natural gift of feeling what is going on in the soul of
another. So it is with prophecy; it surpasses ordinary foresight, deliberation, and mere conjecture, but it undoubtedly
takes these into its service. And so it was with Christ's healing; it went beyond the exercise of mere skill in healing; he
was a miraculous physician. But at the same time he really
was a physician, and on occasion he used the remedies of
folk medicine. This is indicated by small, individual, and
inconspicuous traits, which were naturally brushed entirely
aside in the course of later Christological thought. E.g. he
bestowed the gift of healing upon his disciples, but he also
permitted them to apply a remedy used in folk medicine,
anointing with oil. He healed charismatically the man
born blind, but he used the healing remedy, moistening
the fingers with spittle; he did not accomplish the healing
with one stroke like the magicians, but as a healing process,
gradually, and in stages. When, by virtue of his healing
gift, he healed Jairus's little daughter of a condition of
severe catalepsy, he gave orders like a physician's that the
child was to have something to eat, an order which was
natural if the Saviour was a miraculous physician, yet not
simply a miracle-man but a healer. Thus we can quite
understand if on occasion his healing word is described
by the technical expression for medical activity, i.e.
therapeuein: Mk. i. 34, iii. 10; Mt. xiv. 14. In fact, his
charismatic healing was not divided from, but united to,
a work of natural healing. Jesus as a miraculous physician
was really a therapeutēs, i.e. a physician, and therefore
gave advice natural in a doctor.

CHAPTER V

THE CHARISMA OF PROPHECY. OTHER CHARISMATIC TRAITS

1. PAUL reckons the gift of prophecy among the obvious charismatic gifts. Prophets formed one of the natural constituent elements in the early churches. Paul himself possessed the gift. After an angelic vision, he prophesied the certain deliverance of himself and the ship's crew from peril at sea. The prophet Agabus used an oth given in a symbolic action, after the style of the Old Testament prophets, and showed Paul what he would meet in Jerusalem. Both predictions were fulfilled.

2. The character of such prophecy, whether in the New Testament or among the ancient prophets of Israel, was not simple prediction out of the void. It was not made without knowledge or consideration of the situation and the circumstances, from which perhaps even natural intelligence could draw reasonable conclusions as to a possible event in the future. Nay, all this is definitely presupposed. An Isaiah or a Jeremiah knew the circumstances of his own time exactly and did not 'speak oracles in the dark.' Knowledge of historical conditions and circumstances was presupposed in, but was not a sufficient basis for, their prophecies; nor did they speak out on the basis of deduction and inference. It was divination, not ratiocination; it was presentiment and anticipation; it was therefore never infallible. Karl Hase said sarcastically that genuine prophecy was characterized by occasionally failing of fulfilment. His words are true to the extent that genuine prophecy proceeds from a mysterious talent not explicable by reasoning and is not omniscience; as to its certainty it may be subject to waverings both in the believers and in the prophets themselves. Jesus saw his death with prophetic gaze; nevertheless Gethsemane remained

possible. His disciples had received his prophecies; nevertheless they succumbed to despondency and to doubt when the catastrophe fell on them.

3. The gift of prophetic divination known in ancient Israel emerged anew in Christ. He did not take over a dogma that the kingdom of God was at hand, but he knew it was coming as the prophets knew that the day of Yahweh would come. Like them, he prophesied the fall of Jerusalem and the destruction of the temple. His prophecy, like theirs, rested on knowledge of and insight into the politically ominous situation of Jerusalem and a menacing and aggressive world power, and yet it was not based on considerations of probability, nor did it arise from a rational calculation. His prophecy, like that of old, was occasionally vague; the original form of the prophecy in Mk. xiii. 2 lacked the concrete individual traits of the catastrophe which took place later. And just as was the case occasionally in early prophecy, so he overdrew the picture. Thus, he prophesied:

There shall not be left here one stone upon another,

but the mighty hewn stones of the Herodian temple building remain even to-day.[1] And as with the prophecy of the ancient prophets, so his own prophecy became the instigation and starting point of later additions; later prophecies were put forth under his name as had been the case with theirs.

4. The prophecies of the early prophets dealt with the fate of people and city. But ocasionally the power of the ancient choseh was found in them, enabling them to sense individual destiny in advance; e.g. Is. xxii. 15. Jesus possessed this capacity. He prophesied to the sons of Zebedee that they should be baptized with his baptism, and drink his cup. (Half this prediction was fulfilled, as it seems, but only half.) He

[1] Dr. Otto would doubtless have revised this sentence had he lived.—B. L. W.

foresaw that Judas would betray him, and that Peter would deny him—perhaps this was a typical firasa rather than real prophecy.

He predicted his death. It was almost a constant feature among the later charismatics that they foreknew their own death. Paul's case, however, offers a closer parallel. He says of himself in Acts xx. 23:

> I go . . . unto Jerusalem, not knowing (by human calculation) the things that shall befall me there: save that the Holy Spirit testifieth unto me in every city, saying that bonds and afflictions abide me. But I hold not my life of any account as dear unto myself . . . I know that ye . . . shall see my face no more. . . . I know that after my departing grievous wolves shall enter in among you.

As man, 'he does not know,' he is uncertain, he wavers between the prospect of his end and hope that it will be averted; as inspired by the Spirit, he *knows*. Words describing a conflict within the charismatic himself between two kinds of knowing are very characteristic; on the one hand a natural knowing, accompanied by a natural striving against a fate which may possibly still be averted; on the other hand and on a higher plane, the knowing by the spirit. Christ knew that his fate would be fulfilled in Jerusalem; nevertheless, Gethsemane remained possible with its final uprush of natural hope, which was soon quieted. Some scholars have regarded such a conflict as impossible, but it showed its normal features again in the charismatic Paul.

5. Moreover, Jesus' prediction of his death was not the oracle of a soothsayer, nor did it come out of the blue. It was conditioned by insight into the circumstances, into the opposition which he would necessarily encounter if he expressed any premonition he might have of the fall of city and people; if he saw the approach of the kingdom of God which would destroy all world powers, even that of the Romans; if he attacked the authority of the magis-

trates in a revolutionary way by the cleansing of the temple; if he aroused the masses by his eschatology; if Zealots were among his disciples and if he tolerated them; if he let the excited masses pay homage to the coming kingdom of David and made no objection; if he knew the fate of the prophets and their persecutions, and if he had read Is. liii and referred it to himself. All these were the *conditions* of his prophecies just as the genuine predictions of the early prophets had their conditions.

6. According to the later accounts Jesus was like a soothsayer, and foresaw all the details of his end, including scourging, spitting, and mocking. That would be omniscience and not prophetic divination. But it is plain that these traits are interpolated, and it is still possible to follow the different stages in the gradual increase of this interpolation into Jesus' simple original words which had the character of divination.

The simplest form, which is quite vague, and indicates nothing but a premonition, is preserved in isolation in Lk. xii. 50:

I have a baptism to be baptized with; and how am I straitened till it be accomplished!

This was no oracle, nor was it finished dogma which he had taken over. It is a piece of genuine prophetic anticipation. But at the same time one can feel how he shakes with the same inner shuddering as that which later broke forth once more in Gethsemane. No later person would have invented a vaticinium ex eventu in such a form. In particular, the words: 'how am I straitened till it be accomplished,' were beyond the invention of any later person equally with those spoken by Jesus in Gethsemane itself. Likewise the context is instructive. Jesus foresaw that his work would cause a terrible division, a contest among the people. It seems to have been his opinion at first that he himself would fall in such a struggle.

Clearer phraseology is used in Mk. ix. 12:

> How is it written of the Son of man, that he should suffer many things and be set at nought?

Here again the prediction is purely suggestive, without any concrete conception in detail; it simply repeats ancient words of Isaiah. Jesus has in mind first of all that his people will set him at nought and reject him. He was certainly thinking of his death, since he quoted Isaiah, but of the manner of his death and the identity of his executioners there is no word. We find similar phraseology in Lk. xvii. 25:

> First must he suffer many things and be rejected of this generation.

The phraseology is clearer in Mk. ix. 31:

> The Son of man is delivered up into the hands of men, and they shall kill him.

So far this phraseology is identical with the original. It mentions nothing of being delivered to the judgment of the Romans, gives no details, says nothing of crucifixion. The perfectly general expression, 'be delivered up into the hands of men,' is all there is to say. Certainly Jesus had not yet begun to think of a trial in official form. The expression is much too vague for that. He thinks that he will fall into the hands of excited fanatics. And it is just as indubitable that he was not thinking of crucifixion, but of stoning by a popular mob. That is what actually happened to Stephen. He fell literally 'into the hands of men.' They took him and dragged him out and stoned him. And that is what almost happened to Paul (Acts xiv. 5 and xiv. 19):

> But there came Jews thither from Antioch and Iconium: and having persuaded the multitudes, they stoned Paul, and dragged him out of the city, supposing that he was dead.

James the Just also died by stoning. That Jesus actually had this conception is proved by the passage, Mt. xxiii. 37:

361

O Jerusalem, Jerusalem, that killeth the prophets, and stoneth them that are sent unto her!

The same conception is found in his last prediction of his death, where he says at the Last Supper: This is my body. We repeat that he compared his body, i.e. himself about to die, to the *broken* bread.

The question has been raised as to how he could compare his being killed with the breaking of the bread. This question has a certain justification, since in crucifixion, which means hanging on a stake, the body is not broken. But the comparison is of course apt and immediately illuminating, if and when it refers to stoning. This very circumstance proves the genuineness of the saying. Had the Last Supper been invented later, when it was known that Jesus had been crucified, the accompanying words would not have been cast in a form which was not fulfilled literally. (Cp. R. Otto, *Religious Essays*, pp. 48 f.)

Let us return to Mk. ix. 31. Being delivered into the hands of men and being put to death correspond entirely with the original formula. But at this point we find the first interpolation plainly due to a later standpoint:

and when he is killed, after three days he shall rise again.

Here the theology of the church is beginning to press in. The words used in the first half, however, remain untouched in their original form; there is nothing of mocking, nothing of delivery to the Gentile authorities, indeed nothing at all as yet of a delivery to any authority whatever, but only a simple falling into the hands of men.

The interpolation then goes a step further in Mk. viii. 31. Here also we have first the simple original form:

The Son of man must suffer many things, and be rejected . . .

But now comes a much fuller addition:

by the elders, and the chief priests, and the scribes.

And the insertion is still further developed in Mk. x. 33:

362

and they shall condemn him to death (this is a concrete prophecy of a detailed judicial process, of which the previous formula had said nothing), and shall deliver him unto the Gentiles (i.e. the delivery to Pilate, which Jesus simply could not anticipate); and they shall mock him, and shall spit upon him, and shall scourge him, and shall kill him (this is to anticipate almost the entire passion in detail).

Finally, Mt. xx. 19 gives the fullest form, identical with the preceding, except that it expressly adds:

and they shall crucify him,

and thus presents anticipation of the last detail as vaticinium ex eventu. In fact, that is how we can recognize a real vaticinium ex eventu. In a crude way it makes the prophet predict that which has come to pass, and gives all the concrete details. This very fact, however, shows up the real nature of the original records. No one would have invented them later, for they were too indefinite, and actually contained elements which did not come to pass. The general inference is that Jesus really did foresee his suffering. He possessed the charisma of prophecy and exercised it with reference to himself.

7. This type of prophecy has yet another quality. The prophet at times ventures a particularly bold prediction which is not fulfilled and which embarrasses those who come after. These then try to find a way out either by suppressing the unfulfilled prophecy or by attempting to correct or reinterpret it. That is what has happened in the case of the prophecy made to Peter after the response of Jesus to Peter's confession. This has been preserved in the highly disputed phrases contained in the words of Mt. xvi. 18:

Thou art Peter, and upon this rock I will build my church; and the gates of Hades shall not prevail against it.

In Mark the whole of Christ's answer is lacking. R. Bultmann has rightly seen that Mark knew of it, but struck it out. That a response of some kind must have followed Peter's confession is indubitable. Jesus must have acknowledged Peter's confession in some way. Matthew records it, whereas Mark strikes it out. R. Bultmann supposes that Mark did this because of a general tendency to reject the authority and person of Peter. That seems to me an unnecessary assumption, and Mark could not have deleted a primitive saying of Jesus solely from such a motive. The reason is different and more cogent, viz. Jesus' answer in its original form contained a prophecy which had not been fulfilled. Mark therefore suppressed it, but Matthew attempted to correct it.

Harnack set forth the true state of affairs in his article, 'The Sayings about Peter, Mt. xvi. 17 ff.,' in *Sitzungsberichte der Preussischen Akademie*, 1918. The words, 'The gates of Hades shall have no power over . . .' refer in our present text to the church, the ecclesia. But the expression ecclesia was not used by Jesus; he desired to renew Israel, not to create a separate community. Furthermore, the expression: 'death shall have no power over . . .' means unambiguously that 'the person concerned shall not see death.' Jesus said in another prophecy, v. 28:

> There are some of them that stand here, who shall in
> no wise taste of death, till they see the Son of man coming
> in his kingdom.

He prophesied similarly before the Sanhedrin that the judges themselves should see the Son of Man come. Hence, the one concerned is promised that he will not die, but, while still living, see the parousia of the Son of Man. Now one cannot say of a community, 'it will not die,' but only of a person. The church was not meant, but a person, and the person was Peter.

According to the twofold testimony of Ephraem Syrus, Tatian read 'te.' His text therefore was: 'Death shall have no power over thee, Peter.' And as late as Origen, Jerome, and Ambrosius, the exegetical note was: Peter is promised that he shall not see death. Jerome and the others then exert themselves to give an allegorical interpretation.

Our discussion shows that the original form of the text said:

Thou, Cephas, shall not see death.

These words could not be brooked by those of a later time. Mark and Luke simply struck them out and thus mutilated the original text. Matthew alone preserved the answer, but he corrected it by an interpolation. He deleted the word 'thou' and inserted 'the church.' This insertion into the ancient text gave rise to the surprising expression that the church would not die, an expression which even yet proves that something has been disturbed in this passage.

All this shows us Matthew's style as we have met it many times. He is conservative, and, here as elsewhere, preserves ancient sayings of Jesus, but he treats them in the present instance in the manner which we have discussed. He deals with them as in the parables of the growing seed and of the net, by introducing his idea of the church.

Then come the words:

I will give unto thee the keys of the kingdom of heaven.

Possibly these words too are only an insertion. Yet that is not so certain as it was with the preceding words. Jesus says of the Pharisees in another passage (Mt. xxiii. 13):

Woe unto you . . . because ye shut the kingdom of heaven against men; for ye enter not in yourselves, neither suffer ye them that are entering in to enter.

If Christ could speak of shutting, he could also speak of keys. The opening and shutting of the kingdom of heaven, however, had a very simple sense, which had nothing to do with the heavenly keys of Peter in the dogmatic sense. It referred to the function of teaching and instructing. If this was wrongly done, one shut the kingdom of

365

THE KINGDOM OF GOD AND THE CHARISMA

heaven against hearers; if done rightly, one opened to
them the door of the kingdom of heaven. In this sense
Jesus might very well have prophesied of Peter that,
above and beyond the other apostles, he, by right
preaching, would give men access to the kingdom of
heaven. In this simple form, then, we may well assume
that Jesus now destined Peter to be his Caliph [authorita-
tive successor] for the time when he himself would be
taken away from his followers and when Peter would
have the leading place in preaching.

This latter prophecy actually came to pass in part.
For undoubtedly in the beginning Peter had a position
comparable to that of a Caliph in the first church. He
was the first to see and proclaim the living Lord; the
apostles reassembled around him; he was the centre
round which arose the first church; he actually did at
first rule in it like a Caliph of the Risen Lord.

On the other hand, it would appear that also in this
case the gift of prophecy nevertheless had its limits even
with Jesus. For very soon a change took place in the Caliphate in Jerusalem. As in the Caliphate of Muhammed,
blood relationship won the upper hand. The Caliphate
passed over to James, the brother of the Lord. Peter was
pushed out of his authoritative position. He became the
most significant *apostle* among the Jewish circles, but he
was no longer a Caliph. With James the Caliphate as
such expired.

8. When we come to deal with the influence of later
Christology, we shall have to consider how a simple
prophecy as originally uttered was transformed and enlarged until it was made to exhibit the foresight of an
omniscience extending even to the concrete details of the
future passion. We have often mentioned this Christology;
its influence served gradually to exalt Jesus into the super-
human sphere. As this took place, the charismatic, who
preached a gospel and who knew himself destined to be the
Son of Man, gradually developed into an incarnate deity.
It is equally plain that a type of prophecy which sensed,
and anticipated, and left things indefinite, would undergo
a parallel change and become omniscience; and that a

dim and groping comprehension of some divine ordinance would become clear knowledge of all its details. The true state of affairs can still be glimpsed behind the traditional record, and is best explained on the basis of the nature of one belonging to the charismatic category. This we can see in Paul and in those cases where it is historically certain that Jesus offers analogies to the prophets.

9. We have already discussed the charismatic gift of forgiveness of sins. In the charismatics of early monasticism, it was typically connected with charisma dioratikon and charisma iaseōs. This typical connection is just what we find in Christ.

10. The charismatic sometimes possesses a further and very peculiar trait, that of being charmed against injuries, e.g. by poisons, and particularly by poisonous creatures such as serpents, vipers, and scorpions with their injurious sting. As if to exhibit the charismatic type to the last detail, even this trait is not lacking in the picture of Christ. It is preserved, again as if by chance, in an unsuspected piece of tradition (Lk. x. 19):

> Behold, I have given you authority (baraka) to tread upon serpents and scorpions, and over all the power of the enemy (demon): and nothing shall in any wise hurt you.

Moreover, in the spurious conclusion of Mark, which here repeats quite primitive ideas, we read (Mk. xvi. 17):

> And these signs shall accompany them that believe;

and then follow signs, which, just because they are linked together, are characteristic of the charismatic type:

> In my name shall they cast out demons; they shall speak with new tongues; they shall take up serpents, and if they drink any deadly thing it shall in no wise hurt them; they shall lay hands on the sick, and they shall recover.

This also is a typical catalogue of charismatic gifts.

CHAPTER VI

CHARISMATIC APPARITIO:
CHRIST'S WALKING ON THE SEA

IN conclusion, a word may be added concerning Christ's walking on the sea, which seems particularly interesting as an illustration in a systematic discussion of miracle stories. From the point of view of classification, we must first ask, not to what literary category the narrative belongs, but what type of alleged experiences does the subject of the narrative represent. After that we may ask the general question: Are experiences of this sort only alleged, or is there any such thing? Literary criticism must here be united with criticism of content.

According to the ordinary view, the issue has to do with a real walking on the water. Such would have to be classified specifically among Yoga phenomena. These are capable of description and classification quite apart from the question as to their reality, whether subjectively real (as alleged experiences) or objectively real (as actual events). The narratives seem to confirm my view that the issue is as to a quite different phenomenon, that of a typical apparitio, and this in turn requires a purely charismatic milieu.

1. The narrative is found in Mark and Matthew. In Matthew it is shorn of a few significant elements. He leaves out the significant words of Mk. vi. 48:

> And Christ, seeing them distressed in rowing . . .

and also the words in Mk. vi. 48b:

> he would have passed by them.

The latter words are striking. They disturb the context, for the words in v. 48:

> He saw that they were distressed,

prove that he came with the desire to comfort and help them in danger, but not to pass them by. This fact alone suggests that an alteration has been made, and that an originally different and simpler narrative has been re-moulded. A fortunate circumstance confirms this supposi-tion, for a similar but much simpler record of the pheno-menon is remarkably enough preserved in Jn. vi. 16 ff. :

> And when evening came, his disciples went down unto the sea; and they entered into a boat, and were going over the sea unto Capernaum. And it was now dark, and Jesus had not yet come to them. And the sea was rising by reason of a great wind that blew. When therefore they had rowed about five and twenty or thirty furlongs, they beheld Jesus walking on the sea, and drawing nigh unto the boat: and they were afraid. But he saith unto them, It is I; be not afraid. They were willing therefore to receive him into the boat: and straightway the boat was at the land whither they were going.

The gospel of John has elsewhere a tendency to heighten the miracles of Jesus and to recount them with the greatest possible breadth and detail. The style of the gospel is not to lessen the miraculous aspect of a narrative in its sources nor to shorten a detailed narrative. If therefore it now reproduces a less miraculous and shorter narrative, this was in its source. John's narrative brings us nearer to the original alleged phenomenon; presumably the original narrative was even more simple than the form in John. Thus we are in the position to follow step by step the tendency of a legend to heighten the miraculous: an original narrative, which at first, perhaps, told simply the strange phenomenon of an apparitio, well known in the charismatic milieu; then came in John the addition that after the apparitio the ship was quickly and suddenly saved and brought to land; in Mark the further addition that when Jesus appeared the disciples received him bodily into the boat; in Matthew the further heightening that Peter actually descended from the boat to go and meet Jesus who, in bodily form, was walking on the water. If we reverse this process and call in the aid of parallel phenomena, otherwise known from the area of charismatic occurrences, we may be able to determine with approximate certainty what was originally recounted, and fit the alleged phenomenon into a definite and well-known class.

2. We have to do then not with a mere miracle as such, but with the quite definite category of an apparitio, and especially with that of the charismatic who in hours of need and of mortal danger appears from afar in phantom form and gives help. The charismatic 'appears,' although he himself is in a distant place. By hallucination he appears to be visibly present. The gospel of John never says that Christ in bodily form entered the ship to the disciples. The words, 'they were willing to receive him into the ship,' definitely exclude this. Unintentionally, the passage plainly testifies to an 'appearance,' comforting and helping in great need. The strange words in Mark, 'he would have passed by them,' also show that the original view was not that Christ was taken into the ship. He had appeared and given reassurance, but had not entered bodily into the ship. After giving reassurance, he had 'passed them by' and vanished again. And this is surely what was reported at one time.

3. Presumably, therefore, a phantom-like apparitio was originally meant, which tradition materialized into a bodily walking on the water. The latter phenomenon is often the subject of miracle narratives. A Yogin in particular possesses the art, and he obtains or thinks he obtains it by developing magic powers in the training of the Yoga. But the magic siddhis of the Yogin must be placed in a different category from charismatic phenomena. The arts of the Yogin are: to make himself light or heavy; by levitation to keep himself physically suspended in the air; to fly through the air; to pass through fire; to stride bodily over streams and seas; to pass through solid walls and bodies; to make himself invulnerable; to make his body as hard as stone; to fall voluntarily into a cateleptic state and so to continue possibly for days and

weeks; to let himself be buried as a seeming corpse and be reawakened; to touch the moon or the sun with his finger; to assume various bodies: to be here with the one body, there with the other; to exercise the maya arts of evoking hallucinations and mass hallucinations, etc. Siddhis and charismatic gifts may resemble one another in certain achievements; nevertheless their combination of features, their essential structure, and particularly their meaning, are different. The siddhis deal in magic arts, attained by training in magic; they use magic formulas and manipulations by a refined method. But the charismata and the karamath, when genuine, are gifts of grace, free gifts of the spirit which blows where it wills. They are not destined for exhibition, but are preferably kept hidden. They are bestowed to promote salvation and love, and conditioned by a God-consecrated and sanctified life.

Charismatic apparitio must be understood in this sense. It is not intended to exhibit supernatural powers, but to grant a presence that will reassure and help. This is indicated by the phraseology preserved in Mark:

seeing them distressed in rowing.

It is connected on the side of the charismatic with an act of firasa, of charismatic second sight, of recognizing the need in which the disciples find themselves.

4. With respect to the genuineness of the original narrative, logically the first question is how far it fits into the thought-forms proper to the charismatic milieu of the New Testament generally, and into the modes and experience which are at least alleged to be at home there. This brings us at once to a conception of which Mt. x. 12 f. still bears witness quite naïvely. The verse deals with the power of the 'greeting of peace'; the one giving the greeting can send it out from himself, and it returns to him like a personal messenger who has found no lodging. Paul's conception is even clearer; he can be present in spirit among the Corinthians across the sea, in order to work with them and to exercise influence along with them. According

to the ideas of the time, that did not mean that he would only be with them in his wishes and thoughts or prayers, in the figurative sense we employ.

5. Even when we moderns say of an absent person: 'I felt his nearness, I knew he was near me,' our immediate feeling still goes beyond a mere metaphor. Particularly in difficult situations where we must make some decision, or are in distress, we may gain the full intensity of feeling that the other person is actually present, and we find reassurance. One might be tempted at first to interpret the experience of the disciples on the basis of mental reactions of this kind such as are accessible to us moderns, and such as may possibly be heightened in those qualified for them to visual and auditory impressions. The disciples were alone in the storm. They had already had one experience of Christ's saving power in a storm. His protecting figure must have stood before their eyes. If Paul in a similar situation received a reassuring vision of angels, it is no cause for wonder that they in their situation felt their master near them, as on the former occasion, to comfort and help. And if the feeling of nearness is heightened to a visual apparitio, there is no ground for surprise or for doubt about the record when we remember we are dealing with men of a milieu in which visions and auditions, operation at a distance, and possibly even the real nearness of a distant person offered no difficulty.

But from the point of view of method, a historical analogy from a related milieu is better than these attempts to find a psychological explanation. Such is the charismatic milieu, and in it the apparitio of a distant saint is so persistent and typical a feature that it was undoubtedly a real subjective experience among believers. It recurs in the milieu of the awliat in Islam. It is also found in the charismatic milieu of Christian hagiology. At least one example may be given. In the life of Symeon Stylites, who was a typical charismatic, we read:

> Often the blessed one appeared plainly on the sea to many sailors in distress in the time of trouble when bad

weather and storms arose. They came and related to him how they had plainly seen him at the time when they were in danger.

An interesting point here is that the persons having the experience themselves first, as it seems, reported to Symeon that they had seen him. This naïveté enables us to see that what we have to do with is not something that Symeon himself had performed, but a purely subjective experience of the believers.[1]

6. But perhaps the time is long since past when men believed that they must trace strange phenomena such as these back to purely subjective impressions, while they persistently passed over phenomena testified by the history of religion, and by analogous phenomena in general psychic experience. In view of the investigations and scientific collections of materials by Myers and Podmore[2] it is no longer permissible for a serious investigator to pass over these things with the remark 'of course we cannot believe it.' Real spiritual operatio in distans is now a subject for serious research. It is especially true of the kind of operatio where one person intends to affect another; this is perceived by the latter, possibly in a hallucinative visual way as a vision of the distant person. Circumstances, such as the moment of death or times of great affliction, are most prominent in this respect.

7. For the occurrence of such an event, better conditions could not be conceived than those of the disciples in the storm. Christ had left the multitude, and had sent his disciples ahead, in order that he might observe his custom— again a feature closely associated with the charismatic as a type—and be alone to spend the night in prayer. That is typical of the situations in which the higher powers of a charismatic are concentrated and braced. The storm breaks out and his solicitous thoughts are naturally projected

---

[1] *Texte und Untersuchungen*, 32; Lietzmann, *Leben des Symeon Stylites*, p. 151. Further accounts of such apparitions, crudely raised to the miraculous, are given on pp. 152 and 153.

[2] *Phantasms of the Living*, London, 1918.

to the disciples. Here too the charismatic phenomenon does not appear without warning, nor without general and natural psychic data as its antecedents; rather it is excited along with as well as by them, though it also surpasses them. The spiritual eye of the firasa opens. The master now *sees* the disciples in their straits. His will to reassure and help stretches across to them. This natural and psychic datum prepares the way for the irrational charismatic contact of his soul with theirs, a contact which is to them a comforting experience of nearness and presence. This experience, moreover, was prepared for 'naturally' by the psychic tensions of the disciples which impelled them to seek their master and helper in the time of their distress.

> May we suppose that the apparitions of the Risen Lord are also to be interpreted in this way—as real self-attestations, which became visual appearances to those who received them?

CHAPTER VII

CONCLUSION

THE whole of the charismatic sphere may well appear strange and surprising to a modern man. If he studies history in order to relate it to his own (modern) nature, he will ignore the subject of charisma. But he cannot avoid this subject if he is willing, as he should be, to begin by making an objective, scientific investigation, and on that basis to report what actually took place formerly. If our object is to discuss the person of Jesus, we must deal seriously with the exorcistic and charismatic elements in him. His charismatic gift was not an accidens in him, but was of the essence of his person, and helps to reveal its significance. And only when we understand his person and its meaning is the meaning of his message of the kingdom disclosed. The kingdom for him was the in-breaking power of God into salvation, and he was not a rabbi but an eschatological redeemer, who was an integral part of the eschatological order itself. Charisma and kingdom of God belong together by their very nature and they illuminate one another.

Thus much has to be said from the standpoint of the history of religion.[1] For the theologian the standpoint of the history of religion falls away like a dry leaf as soon as it has done its preparatory work. But the fact of charisma becomes so much the more important to him. For the historian of religion it is a significant phenomenon, a psychic factum which he must include among his historical causes and explanatory factors, if he wants to avoid a false reconstruction. For the theologian the charisma, together with the pneuma, as an anticipation of the escha-

[1] Concerning the difference between the religio-historical and the theological aspect, cp. R. Otto, 'Gefühl des Ueberweltlichen,' *Religionskunde und Theologie*, p. 58.

tological order is an essential element of a community which is intended to be a church of the Nazarene. That this church has lost its charisma, that men look back to it as to a thing of past times, that men make it and the inbreaking kingdom belonging to it trivial by allegories, does not show that this church is now on a higher level, but is a sign of its decay.

BOOK FIVE

APPENDICES

I

WINDISCH ON THE PNEUMATIC CHARACTER OF CHRIST

For the charismatic character of Christ, compare the study by H. Windisch on 'Jesus und der Geist,' in *Studies in Early Christianity*, edited by S. J. Case (New York, 1923). Windisch says on pp. 225 ff.:

> Upon closer observation we see that the description of Jesus as a pneumatic is not limited to the few incidents and words where the word pneuma explicitly occurs. The evangelists make it clear in other ways that Jesus was a pneumatic like any other of the prophets.

In support of this statement, Windisch rightly points to the pneumatic, or better, charismatic terms such as exousia and dynamis, and to the antithesis between Mk. i. 22 and parallels, and the function of the rabbis who only expound and hand on tradition:

> He who possesses exousia has a mission from God; his words have the same validity as those spoken by the spirit.

He further says on p. 226:

> In Mk. ii. 10 a simple comparison with Jn. xx. 22 teaches that the subject is some sort of pneumatic right. Without a full supernatural authorization and supernatural capacity for discerning the inmost soul of men, such a right should not be exercised. Both qualifications were bestowed by the spirit.
>
> The expression 'man with full authority' is accordingly a pre-dogmatic interpretation of Jesus, and it reproduces the impression made by his appearance (i.e. the numinous impression).[1]

---

[1] The parentheses are my own insertions.

Thus the numerous cases where Jesus says elthon [I came] are also proofs of a prophetic and pneumatic consciousness of power (better, of a consciousness of mission on the part of an eschatological redeemer).

All exorcistic and medical (better, therapeutic) works of Jesus are thereby shown to be deeds of power willed by the spirit (as karamath by baraka).

According to the tradition Jesus transferred the prophetic (more correctly, charismatic) power and exousia to his disciples (they pass over in a charismatic milieu from the master to the successor, as from Elijah to Elisha, and, in such a milieu, to attain and receive them by transference is part of the meaning and aim of the akolouthia, which is first and essentially always something quite different from a mere relationship between pupil and teacher).

But not only is his exorcistic activity demonstrated as pneumatic, but also the independence and certainty with which he makes his decisions in questions of religion (accordingly the charisma of preaching).

When the disciples ascribed an exousia to him, they meant that he had a spirit (p. 229).

But in that case, we cannot avoid the conclusion that Jesus himself traced the powers, abilities, and authorities in him back to the spirit working in him. (To be sure; and if that is true, it is entirely arbitrary to assume that the interpretation of Is. lxi. 1 as referring to the charismatic activity of Christ was due to the later theology of the church. Jesus could not avoid seeing himself described in this verse.)

That Jesus ascribed his deeds to a numinous power, and that this power, the Holy Spirit, was present in his person, can be regarded as good tradition.

Even in the pre-literary tradition there was a tendency to suppress the traces and testimonies of pneumatic endowment. . . . I would postulate an older pre-literary form of the story of Jesus, in which the pneumatic element, the impulse of the spirit and the stimulation by the spirit, appeared more frequently and more powerfully. The present condition of the tradition is thus the result of two opposing processes: suppression (of the pneumatic traits of Jesus), reintroduction of the pneumatic element (in the community).

Only one step is required to pass from the pneumatic Jesus to the Messiah. Among the people Jesus was hardly held to be the Messiah during his lifetime. That individuals among his disciples held him to be so seems certain to me, but they expected the revelation of his Messianic power only in the future. Probably Jesus shared this faith, or better, he suggested it to his disciples.

I hope that in the present volume we have gone beyond a mere probability, and even beyond making a suggestion. What I still miss in the expositions of this esteemed author is that we are not concerned merely with gathering together a few details, but preparing in a scientific way to obtain a view of a type of charismatic person in its *entirety*. I miss also a view of the unity between this person and his conception of a kingdom dawning as dynamis (which is also the dynamis, the exousia, the pneuma in this very person). H. Windisch concludes:

> But then the result is a greater continuity between Jesus and the (later) church. The church was filled with the spirit in the same way as the historic Jesus, its founder, had been a pneumatic. Apostolic Christology is (therefore) an interpretation—influenced by speculation and myth —which received its first impulse from Jesus' own consciousness.

That is the thesis which I have championed for thirty years in opposition to those who would tear Jesus away from his church. I rejoice to see it put forward by a New Testament scholar. The continuity, however, is ultimately this, that the spirit is identical with the eschatological order itself as dynamis working in advance; and this is the very mystērion which Jesus proclaimed, felt, and knew to be working in himself, viz. the kingdom.

LITERARY COMPARISON BETWEEN THE PREACHING OF JESUS AND THE BOOK OF ENOCH

THE close connection of the preaching of Jesus with the tradition of Enoch is confirmed by a literary comparison of their style. The agreement is so great that they must be regarded as belonging to the same definite class. As contrasted with the ancient prophetic, and also the characteristic wisdom literature, the apocalyptic strain of thought had developed a characteristic kind of exhortation and preaching, and this was in process of creating its own style and its own method. Both recur so definitely in Jesus that one cannot mistake either the tradition with its stamp like that of a school, or the close connection in which he stands with it. The connection is so definite that one must regard his own way of preaching as belonging to the same genus. As we have said, he combines this common tradition with the finished artistry of his parables, and these are not foreshadowed in that class of literature. But the relationship is all the more marked in the case of his maxims, where there is the clearest connection. Particularly noteworthy in point of literary style is the method of casting exhortation and admonition in the form of a beatitude or a woe. This method had already become fixed, as also the tendency on occasion to combine the exclamations and to arrange them in series. Cp. En. xciv. 6 ff. :

> Woe to those who raise up unrighteousness and violence and make deception the foundation stone, for suddenly will they be uprooted and have no peace.
> Woe to those who build their houses by sin, for they shall be torn loose from their foundation and fall by the sword.

Woe to you rich, for you have trusted in your riches and you shall have to depart from your treasures, for in the days of your riches you have not thought of the Most High.

Woe to you who utter your maledictions; on account of your sin healing shall be far from you.

Woe to you who cause evil to your neighbour, for according to your work it will be recompensed to you.

Woe to you sinners for your persecution of the righteous, for you shall be handed over and persecuted.

Or En. lviii. 2 :

Blessed are ye the righteous and elect, for glorious will be your lot.

Or Sl. En., p. 39 :

Blessed is he who fears the name of the Lord. . . .

Blessed is he who executes a righteous judgment, not for the sake of reward, but for the sake of righteousness, not hoping for anything at all (in return).

Blessed is he who clothes the naked with a garment and gives bread to the hungry.

Blessed is he who judges a righteous judgment, and helps the orphans, widows, and every wronged person.

Blessed is he who turns from the crooked way of this vain world and walks upon the straight way which leads to the life without end.

Blessed is he who sows righteous seed, for he will reap sevenfold.

Blessed is he in whom is truth, so that he speaks truth to his neighbour.

Blessed is he in whose mouth is mercy and in whose heart is gentleness.

Blessed are those who recognize every work of the Lord. For the works of the Lord are righteous. But the works of men are in part good and in part evil. And by their works are the artificers known.

Cp. also Sl. En. p. 46, where this literary form is consciously used as an artistic form, and where exclama-

tions of blessedness or cursing are interwoven in a series
with parallel members.

Moreover, the inner structure of the maxims of Jesus
is to be found already complete in Enoch: the construction
with one, two, or three strophes; the way in which occasionally the confirmatory strophe develops into a longer
sequence of sentences. Compare first the simplest form
in two parts, where we have an exclamation of blessedness or woe followed by an explanatory clause beginning
with 'for,' and giving the good or evil result:

> En. lviii. 2: Blessed are ye, the righteous and elect,
> for glorious will be your lot.
> Mt. v. 4: Blessed are they that mourn, for they will
> be comforted.
> En. xciv. 8: Woe to you rich, for . . . your usury
> will completely destroy you.
> Lk. vi. 24: Woe to you rich, for ye have your consolation.

Compare next the simple exclamation of woe without
the evil result, instead of which the offence is explicitly
characterized:

> En. xcvi. 4: Woe to you sinners, in that your riches
> show you (seemingly) to be righteous, but your heart
> convicts you as sinners.
> En. xcvi. 5: Woe to you who consume the best of
> the grain, drink the power of the roots of the spring,
> and tread down the lowly by your power.
> Mt. xxiii. 27: Woe to you, scribes and Pharisees,
> hypocrites, for ye are like unto whited sepulchres, . . .
> but inwardly are full of dead men's bones.

Observe next the transition and the enlargement of the
mere woe into a long peroration enlarged by associated
ideas, occasionally with the introduction of the excuses
of the people blamed:

> En. xcvii. 8: Woe to you who acquire silver and gold
> for yourselves by unrighteous means, while ye *say*: We
> have become very rich . . . now will we carry out what
> we purpose, for . . . our granaries are filled. Like water

shall your lie flow away. For ye have acquired everything by injustice and ye shall be delivered up to the great condemnation.

Mt. xxiii. 29: Woe unto you, scribes and Pharisees, hypocrites! for ye build the sepulchres of the prophets . . . and *say*, If we had been in the days of our fathers . . . Wherefore ye witness to yourselves, that ye are sons of them that slew the prophets . . . how shall ye escape the judgement of hell?

At the same time the relationship in ideas becomes visible. Not only formally but also in content, most of the quotations just cited from Enoch could be shown to have parallels in Christ's words alike as to form and content. Both exhibit an ethic drawn, not from a specifically Jewish, but a simple humanitarian sphere. Both reveal a specifically Jewish feature in the milieu of the 'anawim, as seen in the conventional figures of the oppressed, of those afflicted by the rich, and of the persecuted, the weary, and the heavy-laden. The idea of reward in eternal life belongs to the ethics of both, and both show the utmost urgency as to fulfilling the divine will just because it is the divine will. And Jesus' parable of the labourers in the vineyard, which destroys the old idea of reward, was prepared for in the statement quoted above from Enoch: 'not for the sake of reward, but for the sake of righteousness, not hoping for anything at all (in return).' Moreover, the afflicted and persecuted in Christ's beatitudes are not martyrs of the period after Jesus, introduced by the theology of the church, but are part and parcel of Enoch's tradition which Jesus followed. Thus the peacemakers of his beatitudes are found among the beatitudes of Sl. En., p. 47:

Blessed is he who plants peace and love; accursed is he who disturbs those who are peaceful through love.

And (the Slavonic) Enoch had already arranged his beatitudes on a sevenfold plan. Jesus' double form of the Golden Rule, the foundation principle of all humanitarian ethic, has its analogue in Slavonic Enoch, p. 41, and his praise of the pure heart in Slavonic Enoch, p. 42. Jesus' position in regard to swearing and to oaths seems to have been a specific doctrine of this school and is given in Sl. En., p. 45:

> I swear to you, my children, but I do not swear to you with an oath (that means: I assure you, but I avoid the real oath) either by heaven or by the earth, or by any other creature which the Lord has made. For the Lord says, There is with me no oath nor unrighteousness but only truth. If there is no truth (trust?) among men, they may swear with the (mere) word: Yea, yea; nay, nay.

The virtues of the Sermon on the Mount that are distinctive of Jesus are found in Sl. En., p. 45:

> In patience and gentleness pass the number of your days. Every blow and every injury and passion and every evil word, when trial and injury come upon you for the sake of the Lord, suffer it all for the sake of the Lord, and recompense neither the distant nor the near, for the Lord is the one who recompenses.

For Jesus' treasure in heaven compare Sl. En., p. 46:

> Let every one of you corrupt (lose?) his gold and silver for the sake of his brother, in order that he may receive a full treasure in that age. Hide not your silver in the earth.

Jesus' condemnation of anger against one's brother stands in Sl. En., p. 41:

> He who manifests anger to any man (even) without (doing him) injury, the great wrath of the Lord will reap him.

His story of the rich fool is prepared for in En. xcvii. 3:

> Woe to you . . . because ye say: We have become rich, have treasures and possess everything that we desire;

now will we carry out what we purpose, for we have gathered silver and filled our granaries. For your riches will not remain unto you, but will suddenly depart from you . . . and ye shall be delivered to the great condemnation.

His promise to his disciples that they will sit upon thrones stands in En. cviii. 12:

I will set every one upon the throne of his honour.

If we made a detailed comparison of the ethic of Jesus with that of Enoch, we should naturally have to show the contrast between Jesus and this tradition. That contrast is obvious. Instead of exhortations in a fluid mass with indefinite outline as found in Enoch, the ethos of Jesus shows a definite trend towards greater fixity and concentration; one is almost tempted to say, a trend toward the systematic. Above all, it is notable that Enoch, in spite of all the exhortation, nevertheless preserves the standpoint of the 'anawim. As distinct from the rich, the godless, the unrighteous, they know themselves very definitely to be the community of the righteous and elect, who are fundamentally on the right way. But Jesus is an innovator, and he opposes the ethical tradition he has entered into when he says that even the 'anawin, indeed they in particular, must turn, that the call to repentance holds good universally, that all presumption of one's own righteousness falls to pieces as hypocrisy, and that the thing to do is to see the beam in one's own eye and not to judge. But this difference does not alter the fact that he presupposed, and was affected by, this tradition. He knew it, and therefore knew also the figure of the Son of Man as found in Enoch. He regarded that figure as a prophecy and conceived himself after that pattern.

III

THE ENOCH TRADITION IN THE FORMATION OF LEGEND IN THE PRIMITIVE CHURCH

THE account of the supernatural conception of Christ arose in the later days of the primitive church. Where did its roots lie? It seems to me indubitable, and also of great significance for the historical connections which we have attempted to sketch, that even these ideas had been previously formed in the circles where Enoch's tradition was current. N. Bonwetsch adds to his translation of the Slavonic Enoch an appendix (pp. 107 ff.) 'Concerning the Priesthood of Methusalem, Nir, and Melchisedek.' Here the miraculous birth of Melchisedek—in whom it was soon believed that a type of Christ was to be recognized—is recounted in a manner that almost compels us to assume the existence of literary connections. The priest Nir has lived with his wife Sopanima without intercourse. In her old age she becomes aware that she is pregnant. When Nir perceives her pregnancy, he censures her and is minded to divorce her. She assures him of her innocence: 'I do not know how the innocency and faithfulness of my body have conceived.' When he still does not believe her, she dies and is concealed from the eyes of the people. Thereupon the boy is born from her dead body, and the signet-ring of the priesthood is upon his finger. 'And Noah and Nir said: "Behold, God renews the blood of the priesthood after us in accordance with his will," and they called his name Melchisedek.' During the deluge, the boy was preserved in the garden of Eden, that he might eventually be 'Melchisedek the consecrated priest for ever.'

The motive here is plain: The bearer of the renewed priesthood is too holy a figure to issue from man's act. He must have his origin in an immediate miracle of God.

SON OF MAN AND PRIMORDIAL MAN

1. THE transcendent figure of the Son of Man in the book of Enoch is compared in appearance to a man, and the statements about him are of such a kind that the book prepares the way for giving him a title in the form of 'the Son of Man.' Moreover, there is probably no longer any doubt about the fact that this expression—whether used in a solemn and emphatic manner, or in accordance with the simple linguistic usage in Aramaic—was intended to mean 'man.' Nothing in the book of Enoch itself indicates that this designation, which is at first thought so surprising when applied to a transcendent being, has been taken over from some other source or found ready at hand. But if it is true that the title Anthrōpos occurs in Iranian speculation for a divine figure, in the sense of primordial man, then one may assume that some such a mythical figure is behind that of the Son of Man in the book of Enoch. If that were true, the pagan origin of this title would have been obscured intentionally; the title would have been retained, but have been allowed to come forward anew as if from nothing. But if this theory is correct, all essential traits of a primordial man have also been assiduously suppressed, for the figure of the Son of Man in Enoch has not a single trait specific to primordial humanity. From Enoch alone no one would dream that the Son of Man was once meant to be the archetype, the prototype of the species man. The figure of the primordial man would have survived here only as the general conception of a transcendent being dwelling with the highest deity. The name would also have survived, but for very different reasons now than in the myth of primordial man. Yet the origin of this enigmatic divine or semi-divine being, subject to the highest deity, conceived as a

mediating being between deity and mankind, might perhaps be explained in some such a way.

But if we hold to the ideas given in Enoch itself, we are
led rather to other conceptions, which I should like to
express, at least by way of conjecture: The Son of Man
is not a primordial man. He is simply the fravashi of
a righteous man taken as exemplar, viz. Enoch. In harmony with general Iranian conceptions, he is finally
united with his fravashi.

2. In *The Theological Journal*, III, 12, on p. 514, J. H.
Moulton discusses the words of the maid Rhoda: 'It
is his angel,' and also Christ's view of the 'angels of the
children.' He proves convincingly, as it seems to me, the
influence of Zoroastrian ideas of the fravashi. These angels
are not guardian angels in the ordinary sense but, as we
have suggested, the heavenly spiritual counterparts of
Peter and the children respectively. On p. 521 he adds
that only the pious really possess such a fravashi, which
would mean that the fravashis themselves, in the language
of Enoch, are 'righteous and holy.' He goes on to say that
these conceptions go back to an original belief, as we also
have conjectured, in the ancient manes:

> It would seem that the concept of the fravashi includes
> elements from different sources. Many of their features
> are those of the manes, who from the tenth to the
> twentieth of March revisit the earth and are feasted by
> the living.

He adds that:

> It is easy to recognize here the pitaras, the 'fathers' of
> the Rig Veda.

And:

> They belong not only to the dead but to the living
> who are *not yet born*.

The latter circumstance would explain the fact that on
the one hand the 'righteous and holy ones' in Enoch will

some day live in the heavenly places, but, on the other hand, it is quite clear that they already live with the Lord of Spirits and are actually conceived as near Him, and active even now in intercession and in sending down the dew of righteousness. He says further on p. 522:

> The later teachers in later Parseeism define man as made of body, life, soul, form, and fravashi,

and the fravashi is

> the part of man which is in the presence of Ahura. It is an inseparable part of man, the part which is hidden with God.

We recall that the Son of Man 'was hidden' with God. The expression is strange, for a mere general tarrying in the heavenly world does not mean being hidden with God. Moulton now adds that:

> The soul at death becomes immortal by union with the fravashi.

This conception that the fravashi of the pious is hidden with God, and that the pious man himself will one day be united with it, seems to me to be glimpsed in other traits in Enoch, and throws a noteworthy light on the Son of Man and on Enoch's relation to him. Is not the Son of Man simply the fravashi of the exemplary and uniquely righteous man, i.e. Enoch? He would not be the pre-existent Enoch, for human pre-existence is simply not part of the teaching. But, like all fravashis, he would be the spiritual counterpart previously created in the spiritual world, or, as Darmesteter suggests in his footnote, the spiritual element of the human person, in the present instance, the person of Enoch. We should then comprehend the noteworthy oscillation between ideal and real existence which we have remarked; we should understand what is meant by the exaltation of Enoch to be the Son of Man, and we should understand the bodiless state of Enoch. For this idea teaches that 'The body of the man goes into the earth, his life into the wind, his "form" into the sun; only the completely unclothed soul itself is united with the frohar (= fravashi).' We should also understand why, at Enoch's exaltation, the figure of the Son of Man, which was earlier described so concretely, remains strangely invisible, and why only now is 'the Son of Man born unto righteousness.' For only at the union of the soul with its fravashi does the man enter upon his real complete existence. Such a viewpoint could very easily assume the specially Jewish ideas of a pre-temporal election and predestination. According to Jewish ideas, the unique righteous one had been previously predestined and previously selected and as such 'named with God' before all beginning; according to Zoroastrian ideas that was his fravashi, created by Ahura before all time and 'hidden with him.' And what the fravashi was for a Parsee, that the one who was eternally elect must have been for a Jew.

V

NO ONE KNOWS THE FATHER SAVE ONLY THE SON

WAS Christ conscious of possessing a unique, new, and incomparable knowledge of God? Are words which express such an idea of Gnostic import, or are they from Jesus?

He knew that he would build a new temple, not made with hands, in place of the old. On an earlier page, we were tempted to say that this fact almost includes the idea that he intended to establish a new religion. It certainly includes a completely new and unique understanding of God, which was felt to be in opposition, and superior, to inherited belief, even that cherished by the Pharisees and by followers of the Baptist. Jesus did not offer new speculative items of knowledge, not Gnostic or theosophical mysteries, 'not a new theoretical conception of the relationship between the deity and the world, between the infinite ground of things and its appearances and operations, between the eternal and the temporal, between the beyond and this world.'[1] Rather we read of him: 'This man receiveth sinners and eateth with them,' and this attitude in fact reflected a new, different, and higher God than the Pharisees and the followers of John had known. For their God was a God of 'the righteous,' while Jesus' God was a God of 'sinners.' 'What is the final, the innermost truth in the New Testament conception of God, the conception which most decisively distinguishes it from all mere theism (and likewise from the Pharisaic and Johannine conceptions)? It is that which is revealed in the immortal parables of the gospel which speak of seeking and finding, and of being happy over the lost but now found. The real Christian God, whom neither theism

[1] R. Otto, *Leben und Wirken Jesu*, p. 47.

nor any other religion whatsoever conceives in the same way, is the seeking God, i.e. the God who seeks the lost.'[1] He is the God who does not wait upon righteousness but, with seeking and pardoning love, takes the initiative; who does not thrust the lost one down deeper into his lost state, but seeks him out in his lost state in order to save him; who does not wait for love in order to pardon for its sake, but pardons in order through love to produce love.

This Paulinism before Paul is in fact a new and unique knowledge of God on the part of Christ, and it is rightly formulated in the words:

no one knows the Father save only the Son.

Among modern writers, M. Goguel has pointed to the completely new character of this idea of God in his book: *Au Seuil de l'Évangile*, pp. 264 ff. He rightly contrasts it with John in particular, and he rightly refers back to K. Holl:

Jesus preserves fully in his idea of God the attributes of holiness and righteousness, but he introduces also—and this, as Karl Holl has admirably shown, is what is most original and new in his thought—the ideas of compassion, of pity, and of love . . . he desires their salvation, he desires their forgiveness, not by a kind of placid paternity, of easy indulgence, but under conditions which assure that they will rise again.

This is what sets his thought in quite another direction than that of John the Baptist. Where John had spoken of righteousness, Jesus, without sacrificing righteousness at all, speaks of forgiveness and the gift of God. In the final development of his thought, he goes on to speak even of redemption.

Whence comes this entirely new idea of God?

Goguel shows that it did not come from contemporary Judaism, and then proceeds:

From the Jewish point of view, says Holl, a faith in God such as Jesus preached, according to which God

[1] R. Otto, *Religious Essays*, p. 42.

gave Himself to sinners, was the death of all serious moral effort. It was nothing else than blasphemy. It was for that reason that the Jews sent Jesus to the cross. Jesus' idea of God is therefore something absolutely new.

That is indeed true, and consequently Jesus could say: 'No one knows the Father save only the Son.' Goguel adds:

> The origin of this conception can only be sought in the mystery of the personality of Jesus, in the depths of his consciousness.

This also is true, and therefore the words: 'and no one knows the Son save only the Father' are not necessarily spurious, even if they have a Gnostic colouring, for—as we have said—in an apocalyptic milieu what may be called Gnostic is no criterion of spuriousness.

GNOSTIC ELEMENTS IN ENOCH'S
APOCALYPTIC

1. THE section which we cited above on p. 184, from the Slavonic book of Enoch, contained a perceptibly Gnostic speculation about creation. Out of the illimitable and incomprehensible proceed the limited and comprehensible, out of the originally undivided proceed the great antitheses of light to darkness, of the above to the beneath, of spiritual and pre-temporal creation to material and temporal creation and the first of a series of eons. I should like to refer particularly to one broadly Gnostic trait.

The primeval God who dwells in his illimitableness and incomprehensibility—a primeval divinity more than a primeval god—calls forth Adoel and Archas[1] who are mutually opposed. They stand over against one another like poles. But between these poles there is also a difference. Adoel has a dignity which sets him above Archas. He consists of light, and light breaks forth from him; it is worth noting in regard to this light that we read:

And I (God) was in the midst of the light.

Adoel is more than the mere opposite pole to Archas. The *eternal deity itself* is repeated and begotten in him.

2. This saying stands like a hieroglyph and is manifestly a fragment or a relic of a more comprehensive speculation. As far as I know, the meagre remains of primitive Parsee speculations which have penetrated into the Zoroastrian teaching throw no light on the strange idea of a primordial god who makes himself a creature in this world of opposi-

---

[1] D. Frankenberg tells me that the Chaldean arkā means earth, which fits Archas. As the eon of the earth, of the beneath, the dark, the heavy, he stands in opposition to Adoel, the eon of the above, the light.

tions that has come into being, and enters into it as a second form of himself. It becomes clear, however, as soon as one sees it in connection with ancient Aryan speculation to which India still bears witness. These speculations go back into the Veda itself. I have examined these traces in the Veda in my book, *Gottheit und Gottheiten der alten Arier*. Here I have referred to the song from Atharvaveda ii. 1, and I have offered a translation of the song (p. 133). Out of the eternal, the 'That' which rests in itself above all separation and multiplicity, is born 'This,' viz. this world of plurality. But in it as the lord of 'This' there rules the Father, who is our father, our begetter. Rig-Veda x. 129 tells also of the eternally One, beyond death and life, unknowable because concealed by the transitory. 'But through the power of its fire it effected its own genesis' (in that out of the existence above, it became real in the existence of this world).

Such ideas, still to be glimpsed in Enoch's creation myth, we find delineated in fuller detail in Mandean Gnosis; cp. Reitzenstein, *Vorgeschichte der Christlichen Taufe*, p. 14. The conceptions presented by this Gnosis re-echo conceptions of the Indian Upanishads to such an extent that I conjecture a direct importation from India, especially when I consider the further astounding parallels to Indian ideas that I have already assembled in my book, *West-Oestliche Mystik*, second edition, pp. 440 ff. The Mandeans settled in Maišan, the gate of entry for Indian trade and intercourse in Mesopotamia. Maišan's port had an Indian temple. Indian tribes colonized Maišan, and later colonized it further. Indian caravans passed through Maišan and likewise through Nabataea. Indian merchants, wherever they went, were importers and missionaries of Indian ideas. There need be no surprise therefore if direct Indian imports are found in the syncretistic medley of Mandean Gnosis.

It is not necessary to assume direct Indian influence on the apocalypse of Enoch. Here we have to do with purely Zoroastrian ideas, although we repeat, one must think of the mythology and religion found in Iran before, in the time of, and after Zoroaster as similar in nature to the Indian-Aryan type; and one must also assume that cultural and religious contacts and interchange continued between India and Iran.

The atmosphere of the predicates which describe Enoch's primitive deity is, however, quite Indian: the unlimited and incomprehensible, the anantam and acintyam of Indian primitive deity. Another Indian feature is the restless walking alone in the boundlessness and incomprehensibility which preceded the creation of plurality and the antitheses. We find the same feature in the Indian primordial One. In its aloneness and solitude it 'wishes,' and its wish is: 'I will go forth; I will be many.' Then it creates. And it creates first of all the fire, just as Enoch's primitive God first creates the light.

INDEX OF NAMES

399

REFERENCE INDEX